GALICIAN-ENGLISH
ENGLISH-GALICIAN
(GALEGO)
CONCISE DICTIONARY

GALICIAN-ENGLISH
ENGLISH-GALICIAN
(GALEGO)
CONCISE DICTIONARY

(Northwestern Spain)

JOE VIKIN

HIPPOCRENE BOOKS, INC.
New York

ISBN 0-7818-0776-X

For information, address:
HIPPOCRENE BOOKS, INC.
171 Madison Avenue
New York, NY 10016

Printed in the United States of America.

DEDICATION/DEDICATORIA

To my wife Sonia Gilabert,
without whose steady support
this dictionary would not have been possible.

A miña dona Sonia Gilabert-Vikin,
que Co seu apoio fixo
que este diccionano se rematase a pesar
dos múltiples atráncos que se atoparon
ó compila-lo.

ACKNOWLEDGMENT/AGRADECEMENTOS

The author would like to thank Joachim J. Varga,
ATV Enterprises, for the technical assistance he
provided to make this dictionary a reality.

Ao Sr. Joachim J. Varga, de ATV Enterprise, que
coa sua asistencia técnica permitiu que este
diccionano chegase a ser unha realidade.

CONTENTS

INTRODUCTION

THIS HIPPOCRENE CONCISE DICTIONARY consists of some 8,000 words most frequently used in the present Galician lexicon. Their selection is based upon the "Pequeno Diccionano da Lingua Galega," A Small Dictionary of the Galician Language, published in 1993 by the Real Academia Galega in Corunna, Spain.

Galician, a Romance language, is one of six spoken in the Iberian peninsula, together with Basque (euskara), Spanish (castelán), Catalan (Catalá), English in Gibraltar and Portuguese.

Among the first written expressions of the Galician language are the "Cántigas de Santa Maria," at the time of King Alfonso X the Wise, in the 13th century. Those four hundred poems were composed, to be sung, in honor of the Virgin Mary. Representatives of Galician literature include Rosalia de Castro (1837–1885) who wrote "Cantares Galegos" and was instrumental in the Rexurdimento, (literary renaissance), of the Galician language and culture. Others are Emilia Pardo Bazán (1851–1921), Ramón Maria del Valle Inclán (1869–1936), and the writer and historian Salvador de Madariaga (1886–1978), who was born in Corunna. The beauty of the Galician language moved the Andalusian poet Federico Garcia Lorca (1899–1936) to write poems in it.

The Autonomous Community of Galicia is located in the northwestern corner of Spain, occupying some 11,256 sq. miles (29,434 sq. km), whose population in 1991 was 2,731,669, 94% of who understood Galician and 88% spoke it. The province is bounded on the north by the Cantabrian sea, east by the Principality of León and the Communites of Castile and Asturias, south by Portugal and west by the Atlantic Ocean

Notables whose ancestors hail from Galicia include the Puerto Rican born American actor José Ferrer (1909–1992) and the Cuban ruler Fidel Castro (1927–). Francisco Franco Bahamonde (1892–1975), the late Spainish chief of state, was born in El Ferrol, Galicia.

The city of Santiago de Compostela (in Latin "Campus Stellae," "field of the stars") is the focus of a pilgrimage to visit the tomb of the apostle Saint James in a Cathedral whose construction began in 1078. The tomb was discovered at the end of the 9th century by a hermit who saw bright lights and angels singing upon the place where the apostle was buried. The discovery of the tomb was confirmed by Bishop Theodomir of Iria Flavia.

Thus Galicia became one the bases for the *reconquista* of Spain from the Moslems. The battle cry of the Christians was "Santiago." Eventually the apostle, Saint James became the patron of Spain.

Although Francisco Franco forbade the use of this, and other minority languages after the Spanish Civil War, Galician remains very much alive today and it is thriving. This dictionary is another contribution to the preservation of the Galician language.

INTRODUCCION

Este Diccionano Conciso Hippocrene abrangue preto de 8.000 palabras que se empregan a cotío no léxico galego actual. A selección baseouse no *"Pequeno Diccionano c/a Lingua Galega,"* publicado pola Real Academia Galega na Coruña.

O galego, lingua romance, é unha das seis linguas faladas na Peninsula Iberica, xunto co vasco (éuscaro), castelan (español), catalán, inglés (en Xibraltar) e portugués.

Unha das primeiras manifestacións da literatura galega son as "Cantigas de Santa Maria" do rei Afonso X, O Sabio, no século XIII. Estas catrocentas cantigas foron compostas para seren cantadas en honra a Virxe María. Entre outros representantes da literatura galega destacan Rosalia de Castro (1837–1885) autora de "Cantares Gallegos" e peza dave no Rexurdimento da lingua e da cultura galega. Tamén son escritores senlleiros de Galicia Emilia Pardo Bazan (1851–1921), Ramón Maria del Valle Inclán (1869–1936) e o escritor e historiador Salvador de Madariaga (1886–1978), nado na Coruña. A beleza deste idioma moveu ó poeta andaluz Federico García Lorca (1898–1936) a escribir poemas en galego.

A Comunidade Autónoma de Galicia atópase no noroeste de Espana, ocupando unha superficie de 29.424 quilómetros cadrados (11.256 millas cadradas). A sua poboación en 1991 acadaba os 2.731.669 habitantes, dos cales O 94% entenden o galego e O 88% falano. Limita ao norte co mar Cantábrico, ao leste co Principado de Asturias e a Comunidade de Castela e León, ao sur con Portugal e polo oeste co Océano Atlántico.

Entre os persociros con antepasados galegos, cómpre salientar a José Ferrer (1909–1992), actor norteamericano nado en Puerto Rico, Fidel Castro (1927–) actual gobernante de Cuba.

E coñecido tamén Francisco Franco Bahamonde (1892–1975), anterior xefe do estado espafiol, natural de Ferrol (Galicia).

A cidade de Santiago de Compostela (en latin "Campus *Stellae", é* dicir, *Campo das Estrelas)* é lugar de peregrinaxe para visitar a tumba do Apóstolo Santiago, o evanxelista, nunha catedral que comezou a construirse no ano 1078. Un ermitán descubriu o sartego a finais do seculo IX cando viu luces brillantes e anxos cantando sobre o sitio onde o evanxelista estaba soterrado. O bispo Teodomiro de Iria Flavia confirmou o descubrimento. Deste xeito, Galicia foi unha das bases da reconquista de Espafia. O berro de batalla dos cristiáns foi "¡Santiago!". Máis tarde o Apóstolo Santiago convertiriase en patrón de Espafia.

Ainda que Francisco Franco prohibiu o uso deste e doutros idiomas minoritarios en España despois da guerra civil española (1936–1939), a lingua galega continua moi viva e hoxe segue a florecer. Este diccionano é unha contribución a sua preservación.

ABREVIATIONS — ABREVIATURAS

&	- and	- e
a.	- adjective	- adxetivo
abr.	- abbreviation	- abreviatura
adv.	- adverb	- adverbio
art.	- article	- artigo
bot.	- botany	- botánica
conj.	- conjuction	- conxunción
f.	- feminine	- femenino -a
fam.	- familiar	- familiar
inter.	- interjection	- interxección
m.	- masculine	- masculino -a
mus.	- music	- música
n.	- noun	- substantivo
neu.	- neuter	- neutro -a
p.	- phrase	- frase
pl.	- plural	- plural
pr.	- pronoun	- pronome
prep.	- preposition	- preposición
sing.	- singular	- singular
v.	- verb	- verbo
v.u.	- vulgar use	- uso vulgar
V.	- see	- ver

THE GALICIAN ALPHABET
O ALFABETO GALEGO

Letter Grafia	Name Nome	Pronunciation Pronuncia
a	a	<u>ah</u>
b	be	b<u>e</u>d
c	ce	<u>th</u>ermal
ch	ch	<u>ch</u>eck
d	de	<u>d</u>ent
e	e	n<u>e</u>t, p<u>e</u>t
f	efe	e<u>ff</u>ect
g	gue	g<u>u</u>errila
h	hache	ha<u>tch</u>et (h is silent)
i	i	<u>i</u>diom
l	ele	<u>e</u>lement
ll	elle	<u>ll</u>ano (lyä 'no)
m	eme	<u>eme</u>rald
n	ene	<u>ene</u>my
ñ	eñe	lasa<u>gn</u>a
o	o	<u>oh</u>
p	pe	p<u>e</u>r
q	cu	lo<u>o</u>p
r	erre	e<u>rr</u>or

s	ese	<u>ese</u>nse
t	te	<u>te</u>rminal
u	u	b<u>u</u>sh
v	uve	b<u>e</u>d
x	xe	<u>xe</u>rox
z	zeta	<u>the</u>ta

GALICIAN-ENGLISH DICTIONARY

A

á contraction a & art.f. the

a first letter of the alphabet

a modo a. slow

á n.f wing

a pr.sing.f. the

a prep from the Latin ad- indicates direction or tendency

a prep indicates direction

aba n.f. lateral

abáboro n.m. hornet

abade n.m. abbot

abadesa n.f. abbess

abadexo n.m. codfish

abadía n.f. monastery, convent

abafado a. suffocated

abafante a. asphixiating

abafar v. asphyxiate, suffocate

abafo n.m. asphyxia

abaixar v. incline

abaixo adv. down

abalar v. rock, swing
abalo n. swing, rocking
abanador n.m. fan
abanar v. fan
abandeirar v. raise a flag
abanear v. oscillate
abaneo n.m. oscillation
abano n.m. fan
abarcar v. embrace
abarrotar v. stow cargo, cram, pack
abastecer v. supply
abater v. throw down to, cast down
abázcaro V. abáboro
abdome n.m. abdomen
abecedario n.m. alphabet
abeiro n.m. shelter
abelá n.f. hazel nut
abeleira n.f. hazel nut tree
abella n.f. bee
abellón n.m. bumble bee
abeluría V. croque
abeneiro V. ameneiro
aberto adv. open
abertura n.f. opening
abesullón -ona a. meddler
abeto n.m. shrub

abillar v. install a faucet
abisal a. abysmal
abismal V. abisal
abismo n.m. abyss
ablución n.f. ablution
abnegación n.f. self-denial
abnegado -a a. self-denying
abó V. avó
aboar v. fertilize, credit
abobío n.m. ornament, decoration
abofé adv. truly, certainly
abogado V. avogado
aboiar v. float
aboliar v. abolish
abolición n.f. abolition
abolir v. abolish
abollar V. agromar
abominable a. abominable, horrible
abominar v. hate, despise
abonar v. make partial payment
abondar v. abound, be sufficient
abondo -a a. sufficient, enough
abondoso -a a. abundant, numerous
abono n.m. security, guarantee
abordar v. board a ship or a plane
abordaxe n.f. act of boarding a

aborixe a. aboriginal
aborrecer v. hate, abhor
aborrecibe a. hateful
abortar v. abort
aborto n.m. abortion
abotoar v. button, clasp, buckle
abouxar v. deafen
abovedar v. vault, make vault-shaped
abra n.f. cove, inlet, small bay
abraiar v. astonish, amaze, surprise
abraira n.f. hazel, hazel tree
abrancazado -a a. pale, whitish
abrandar v. soften
abranguer v. contain, include
abrasar v. burn, scorch
abrazadeira n.f. clasp, clamp, brace
abrazar v. hug, embrace
abrazo n.m. hug, embrace
abrelatas n.m. can opener
abrente n.m. dawn, daybreak
abreviar v. abridge, shorten
abreviatura n.f. abbreviation
abriao n.m. surprise, amazement
abridor n.m. opener
abrigadoiro n.m. refuge, shelter
abrigar v. shelter, protect, cover

abrigo n.m. shelter, protection, overcoat
abril n.m. April
abrillantar v. shine
abrir v. open
abrochar v. button up
abrochar v. germinate
abrocho n.m. shoot
abrollar v. germinate
abrupto -a a. sudden, abrupt
abscisa n.f. abscisa
absentismo n.m. absenteeism
absolución n.f. absolution
absurdo -a a. absurd
abulia n.f. lack of appetite
abundancia n.f. abundance
abuñeiro n.m. strawberry bush
abur inter. Good-bye
aburrido -a a. bored
aburrimento n.m. boredom
abusar v. abuse
acá adv. here
acabar v. finish, end, conclude
acacia n.f. acacia
acadar v. get, reach, attain
academia n.f. academy
acaer v. fit, suit

acalar v. silence
acalmar v. soothe, calm down
acalorar v. excite
acampada n.f. camping
acampar v. camp
acanear v. balance
acaneo n.m. balancing
acantilado n.m. cliff; steep, sheer coast line
acantoar v. corner
acaparar v, monopolize, hoard
acaramelar v. caramelize; fig. be tender, affectionate
acaravillar v. lock with a latch
acarear v. confront
acareo n.m. confrontation
acariciar v. caress
acariñar v. caress
acaroar v. bring or move closer
acaso adv. perhaps, maybe
acastañado -a reddish brown
acatamento n.m. obedience & respect
acatar v. obey, respect, revere, revere, pay homage to
acatarrar v. catch a cold
acatarrar v. give or catch a cold
acazapar v. hide

acceder v. accede
acceptar v. accept
accesible a. accessible
accésit n. compensation, reward
acceso n.m. access
accesorlo -a a. accessory
accident n.m. accident
accidental n. accidental
accidentar v. tp meet with an accident or
   sudden illness
acción n.f. action
acea n.f. mill
acedar v. sour or make sour
acedia n.f. acid
acedo -a a. acid
acedume V. acedia
acéfalo -a n. headless
aceiro n.m. steel
aceitar v. oil
aceite n.m. oil
aceiteira n.f. oiler
aceitoso -a a. oily
aceleración n.f. acceleration
acenar v. make faces
acendedor n.m. gas burner, cigarette lighter
acender v. light up

aceno n.m. gesture
acento n.m. accent
acentuar v. accentuate
acepción n.f. acceptance, approval
acerca de pre. in regards to
acercamento n.m. approach
acercar v. move close, grow near
acerto n.m. good aim, hit
aceso -a a. lit, lighted
acevo V. acivro
acevro V. acivro
achacar v. impute, ascribe
achacoso -a a. sickly, ailing, infirm
achado n.m. find, finding
achaiar v. make even, flatten
achandar V. achaiar
achantar v. support
achaque n.m. weekness, infirmity
achar v. find
achatar v. flatten
achega n.f. help
achegado -a a. near, related, allied
achegar v. gather, raise, collect
achegar v. grow near
achicar v. extract
acibeche n.m. anthracite

ácido n.m. acid
acio n.m. cluster of grapes
acivro n.m. holly tree
aclamar v. acclaim, cheer
aclaración n.f. explanation, clarification
aclarar v. clarify, explain
acné n.f. acne
acó adv here
acochar v. hide
acocorar v. crow
acoitelar v. knife
acolá adv. there, yonder, thither
acolchar v. soften
acolledor -a a. welcoming, inviting
acometer v. undertake
acomodar v. accomodate, settle, adapt
acompañamiento n.m. attendance, making
    company
acompañar v. accompany
aconsejar v. advice, counsel
acontecemento n.m. event, incident, occurrence
acontecer v. happen, come about
acorar v. suffocate
acordar v. remember
acordeon n.m. acordion
acordo n.m. pact, agreement

acorrer v. help
acortonar v. make rigid as a cardboard
acostumar v. accustom
acougar v. rest, repose
acougo n.m. rest, repose
acrobacia n.f. acrobatics
acta n.f. record, proceedings of a meeting
actitude n.f. attitude
actividade n.f. activity
activo -a a. active
acto n.m. act, action
actor n.m. actor
actriz n.f. actress
actuación n.f. action, performance
actual a. actual, present
actualidade n.f. present situation or state of
    affairs
actuar v. act
acuarela n.f. watercolor
acuático -a a. aquatic
acudir v. come the rescue
acuerdo s.m. agreement, accord
acugular v. overfill
acumular v. accumulate, hoard
acurtar v. shorten
acusación s.f. accusation, indictment, charge

adaptar v. adapt, fit
adecuado -a a. adequate
adegueiro -a n. keeper of a wine cellar
adelgazar v. lose weight, become thin
ademáis adv. moreover, further
adentar v. nibble at, bite
adeprender V. aprender
aderezar v. dress, prepare
aderezo n.m. dressing, seasoning
adestrado -a a. trained, coached
adestrador -a n. trainer
adestrar v. train, instruct, coach
adeus inter. good-bye
adherir v. adhere
adhesivo -a a. adhesive
adiantar v. advance, move forward
adiante adv. ahead, forward
adianto n.m. advance, progress
adiar v. postpone
adicto -a a. addicted
adiñeirado -a a. rich, wealthy, affluent
adival (pl. adivais) n.m. rope, cord
adiviña n.f. foretelling, prediction
adiviñanza n.f. prophesy, prediction
adiviño -a n. soothsayer, prophet, fortune teller
administración n.f. administration

administrar v. administer, manage
admiración n.f. admiration
admirar v. admire
admitir v. admit
adobar v. season
adobiar v. adorn, bedeck
adobo n.m. dressing for seasoning, condiment
adoecer v. be ill
adoitar v. adapt, acustom
adolescencia n.f, adolescence
adolescente a. & n. adolescent
adondar v. soften
adoptar v. adopt, embrace (an opinion)
adoptivo -a a. adoptive, adopted
adorar v. adore, worship
adormecer v. make or become sleepy or drowsy
adornar v. adorn, decorate, embelish
adorno n.m. decoration, ornament, adornment
adquirir v. acquire, obtain
adro n.m. atrium
aduana n.f custom house
adubar V. adobar
adubo V. adobo
adular v. flatter
adulterar v. adulterate, corrupt, falsify
adulto -a a. adult

adverbio n.m. adverb
adversario-a a. adversary
advertencia n.f. warning, advice
advertir v. warn
adxetivo n.m. adjetive
aereo -a a. aerial
aeroporto n.m. airport
afacer v. acustom
afán s.m. eagerness, urge
afastar v. separate
afección n.f. affection, fondness
afeccionar v. become fond of something or someone
afectar v. affect, influence
afecto n.m. affection
afeitar v. shave
afeito a. used to, accustomed to
aferrar v. grasp, grapple, seize
afialapis n.m. pencil sharpener
afiar v. hone, sharpen
afición V. afección
afillado -a n. godson, goddaughter
afin a. related
afinar v. polish, tune, refine
aflixir v. afflict, cause sorrow to
afluente n.m. tributary (of a river)

afogar v. drown

afondar v. submerge

aforcar v. hang, cause death by hanging

aforrar v. save

aforro n.m. saving(s)

afortunado -a a. fortunate

africano -a a. African

afrouxar v. loosen

afumar v. cure by smoke

afundir v. sink, plunge under; beat, pull down

agachar v. lower, bow down, bend

agaminar v. caress

agardar v. wait for, await

agarimo n.m. affection

agarrada n.f. quarrel

agarrar v. catch, grab, grasp

agás prep. although

agasallar v. receive, treat well; regale, entertain

agasallo n.m. present, gift

agatuñar v. climb, as a cat does it on a tree

agoiro n.m. omen, augury

agomar V. agromar

agonía n.f. agony, extreme sorrow

agora adv. now

agosto n.m. August

agra n.f. collective land used for cultivation

agradable a. plesant, agreeable
agradar v. please
agradecemento n.m. gratitude
agradecer v. be grateful, be thankful for
agrado n.m. pleasure, liking
agravar v. aggravate, make worse
agre a. sour
agredir v. assault, attack
agresión n.f. aggression
agricultura n.f. agriculture
agro n.f. land, countryside
agromar v. sprout
agromo V. xermolo
agrupar v. group, cluster
agua V. auga
aguantar v. support, suffer, endure
aguardente V. augardente
agudo -a a. acute, sharp, keen
aguia n.f. eagle
aguillada n.f. goad with an iron point
aguillón n.m. punch, awl
agulla n.f. needle
aí adv. here
ai inter. ay! , ouch!
aiga V. aguia
aillar V. illar

ainda adv. still

ainda que conj. even though

aira V. eira

aire n.m. air

alucinación n.f. hallucination

aixada n.m ax

alá adv. there

ala V. á

alacrán n.m. scorpion

alameda n.f. poplar grove, public walk, avenue

alancada n.f. long stride

alargar v. elongate, lenghten

alarma n.f. alarm

alarmar v. alert, alarm

alba n.f. dawn

albanel n.m. bricklayer

albañil V. albanel

albarda n.f. saddle bag

albaricoque n.m. apricot

albedro V. erbedeiro

albergar v. lodge, house, accommodate

albergue n.m. lodging, shelter

albóndega n.f. meatball

alborada n.f. dawn

alborotar v. stir up, arouse, excite, agitate

alboroto n.m. disturbance, tumult, turmoil

álbum n.m. album
alcalde n.m. mayor
alcaldesa n.f. mayoress
alcance n.m. pursuit, reach
alcanzar v. reach, attain
alcatrán n.m. tar
alcipreste V. ciprés
alcoba n.f. alcove
alcohol n. alcohol
alcohólico -a a. alcoholic
alcol V. alcohol
alcroque V. croque
alcumar v. give a nickname
alcume n.m. nickname
alcuñar V. alcumar
alcuño V. alcume
aldraxar v. outrage, affront
aldraxe n.f. outrage, affront
aledar v. please, delight
alegrar v. make marry, gladden
alegre a. merry, happy
alegría n.f. joy, mirth
alemám V. alemán
alemán n.m. German
alemana. n.f. German
alentar v. encourage, inspire, cheer

alento n.m. breath, wind, spirit, courage
alerta adv. careful, cautious
alertar v. alert
alerxia n.f. allergy
aleta n.f. fin
alfabeto n.m. alphabet
alfafándega n.f. customs
alfaia n.f. jewel
alfinete n.m. pin
alfombra n.f. rug
alfóndega (peixe) n.m. tern (fish)
alforxa n.f. saddle bag
alga n.f. alga
algo pr. something
algodón n.m. cotton
alguén pr. somebody
algún pr.m. some
algunha pr.f. some
algures adv. anywhere
alí adv. there, in that place; then, at that time
alianza n.f. alliance
alicates n.m.pl. pliers
alimentación n.f. nourishment, nutrition
alimentar v. feed
alimento n.m. food, feed
aliñar v. season

aliviar v. relieve, mitigate, assauge, soothe
alixeirar v. lighten
allo n. garlic
alma n.f. soul, spirit
almacén n.m. warehouse, store
almacenar v. store
almanaque n.m. calendar, almanac
almofada n.f. pillow
almorzar v. have breakfast
almorzo n. breakfast
aló adv. there
aloe (planta) n.m. aloe plant
alongar v. lengthen
aloumiñar v. caress
aloumiño n.m. caress
aloxamento n.f. lodging, accomodation
alpendre n.m. shed, barn
alporizar v. become angry or annoyed
alta n.f. discharge from a hospital
altar n.m. altar
altavoz V. altofalante
alterar v. alter, change
alternar v. alternate
alternativo -a a. alternative
altitude n.f. altitude, height
alto -a a. high

altofalante n.m. loud speaker
altura n.f. height
aludir v. allude, refer
alugar v. rent
alugueiro -a n. renter
aluguer n.m. lease, rent
alumar v. illuminate
aluminio n.m. aluminum
alumno -a n. pupil
alustro n.m. lightning
alzadeiro n.m. cupboard
alzar v. elevate, boost, rise up
amable a. kind, amiable
amainar v. decrease, lower in intensity
amalló n.m. shoe lace
amalloa V. amalló
amañar v. do cleverly; get along with someone
amañecer n.m. dawn
amañecer v. dawn
amaño n.m. cleverness, cunning
amansar v. tame, domesticate
amante a. lover
amar v. love
amarelo -a a. yellow
amargar v. embiter, make bitter
amargo -a a. bitter

amarra n.f. cable, hawser
amarrar v. tie, fasten, lash
amasar v. knead
ambición n.f. ambition
ambicioso -a a. ambitious
ambiente n.m. ambient, surroundings
ambiguo -a a. ambiguous
ámbito n.m. area, sphere, scope
ambos -as pr. both
ambulancia n.f. ambulance
ambulante a. ambulatory
ameixa n.f. clam
ameixeira n.f. plum tree
amenaza n.f. threat, menace
améndoa n.f. almond
amendoeira n.f. almond tree
amendrentar v. frighten, terrify
ameneiro n.m. alder tree
americano -a a. American
amieiro V. ameneiro
amiga n.f. friend
amígdala(s) n.f. tonsil(s)
amigo n.m. friend
amizade n.f. friendship
amnistía n.f. amnisty
amo -a n. master, mistress

amoblar v. furnish a house or a room

amoestación n.f. disturbance, annoyance, inconvenience

amolar v. disturb, annoy, inconvenience

amolecer v. soften

amolentar V. amolecer

amontoar v. pile up, heap

amor n.m. love

amora n.f. blackberry, mulberry

amornar v. make lukewarm

amorodeira n.f. raspberry bush

amorodo n.m. raspberry

amoroso -a a. lovable

amorriñarse v. miss someone, long for, pine

amosar v. show, display

amparo n.m. favor, aid, succour, protection

ampliar v. broaden, enlarge, extend

amplo -a a, ample, sufficient

amputar v. amputate

amuleto n.m. amulet

anaco n.m. bit, piece, fragment

anada s.f. harvest

analfabeto -a a. illiterate

análise n.f. analysis

analizar v. analyse

analoxía n.f. analogy

anano -a. midget
anarquía n.f. anarchy
anarquismo n.f. anarchism
anatomía n.f. anatomy
anca n.f. haunch
ancho -a a. wide
anchoa n.f. anchovy
ancían n.m. old man
anciana n.f. old woman
anciño V. angazo
áncora n.f anchor
andamio n.m scaffold,
andar a ganchas p. walk on all fours
andar v. walk
andazo n.m. epidemic
andel n.m. shelf
andoriña n.f. lark, swallow
anécdota n.f. anecdote
anegar v. flood, inundate, submerge
anel n.m. ring
anemia n.f. anemia
anestesia n.f. anesthesia
anexo -a a. joined, annexed
anfibio -a a. amphibious
angazo n.m. rake
anguía n.f. eel

ángulo n.m. angle
angustía n.f. anguish, anxiety
anicarse v. kneel down
ánima n.f. soul
animado -a a. animated, inspired, excited
animal n.m. animal
animar v. animate, inspire, excite
ánimo n.m. soul, spirit, will, courage
aninñar v. become childish
anís n.m. anise
aniversario n.m. anniversary
ano (anatomia) n.m. anus
año -a n. kid (sheep's offspring)
ano n.m. year
anoitecer v. grow dark
anónimo -a a, anonymous
anormal a. abnormal
anotar v. note, jot down, annotate
anoxar v. anger, vex, irritate
anque V. ainda que
ansia n.f. anxiety
antano adv. years past
ante prep. before, in front of
antefaz n.m. mask
antena n.f. antenna
anteollos n.m. pl. glasses

antepasado -a n. ancestor
anterior a. former, anterior
antes adv. before
anticipar v. anticipate
anticipo n.m. advance
antigo -a a. ancient, old
antiguiedade n.f. antiquity
antipático -a a. disagreable, uncongenial, unpleasant
antollo s.m. whim
antónimo -a a. antonym
antonte adv. the day before yesterday
antroito V. entroido
anual a annual
anubrar V. nubrar
anular a, & n.m. ring finger
anular a. anull
anunciar v. announce
anuncio n.m. announcement
anxina n.f. angina
anxo n.m. angel
apacentar v. tend grazing cattle
apadriñar v. act as a second in a duel
apagar v. extinguish, shut off
apaixonar v. inspire passion
apalabrar v. agree by word of mouth

apampado -a a, incapable of thinking
apañar v. pick up, catch
aparador n.m. cupboard
aparafusar v. secure something with screws
aparato n.m. apparatus, device
aparcamento n.m. parking lot
aparcar v. park
aparecer v. appear
aparecia n.f. appearance, aspect
aparejar v. get ready, harness, prepare
aparellador -a n. architect's aide
aparello n.m. apparatus
aparentar v. pretend, feign
aparición n.f. aparition, vision
apartado n.m. withdrawn; post office box
apartar v. separate, put aside
aparvado -a a, incapable of thinking
apatia. n.f. apathy
apear v. dismount
apegar v. attach, grow fond of
apego n.m. attachment; fondness
apeiro n.m. farm utensils, farm tools
apellido n.m. last name, surname
apéndice n.f. appendix
aperitivo n.m aperitif
aperta n.f. hug, embrace

apertar v. hug, embrace
apertura n.f. opening
apestar v. infect with a plague
apetecer v. fancy, feel like
apetito n.m. appetite
ápice n.m. apex
aplaudir v. applaud
aplauso n.m. applause
aplicar v. apply
apodecer V. podrecer
apodrentar v. make or become rotten
apoiar v. lean, rest, support
apoio n.m. rest, support
aposta n.f. bet, wager
apostar v. bet, wager
apóstolo n.m. apostle
apoucado -a a. spineless, feeble-minded, timid
apoxeo n.m. apogee, height, summit
aprazar v. postpone, put off, adjourn
apreciar v. appreciate
aprecio n.m. appreciation, esteem
apreixar v. press, tighten, squeeze
aprender v. learn
aprendiz n.m. apprentice
aprendizaxe n.f. apprenticeship
apresar v. seize, grasp, arrest

aprobado n.m. passed, as an examination
aprobar v. approve, pass an examination
apropiado -a a. appropriate, fit
apropiarse v. take possession of
aproveitar v. profit by
aproximar v. approximate, bring near
apto -a a, apt, fit, suitable
apuntar v. take notes
apurar v. hurry, push
apuro n.m. want, strait, in a tight spot
aquel pr. that one, the former
aquelo V. aquel
aquelotro pr. that other one
aquí adv. here
aquilo V. aquel
ar V. aire
árabe a. Arab
arado n.m. plow
arame n.m. wire
araña (xogo infantil) n.f. leap frog (children's game)
araña n.f. spider
arar v. plow
árbitro n.m. arbiter
árbore n. tree
arbusto n.m. shrub

arca n.f. chest, coffer, safe
arcebispo n.m. archbishop
arco n.m. arch
arder v. burn, blaze
área n.f. area
area n.f. sand
aresta n.f. edge, border; intersecting line
aresta n.f. stem of a spike
arestora adv. right now
argallar v. cheat, deceive
argalleiro -a a. cheater, deceiver
argola n.f. large ring, collar, hoop
argumento n.m. argument
árido -a a. arid, dry
aristocracia n.f. aristocracy
arma n.f. armament, weapon
armador -a a. outfitter, shipowner
armamento n.m. armament
armar v. arm
armario n.m. cupboard, wardrobe
armazón n.m. framework, skeleton, mounting
aro n.m. hoop
aroma n.m aroma, perfume, fragance
arpa n.f. harp
arquexar v. pant
arquexo n.m. pant, gasp

arquipélago n.m. archipelago
arquitecto -a n. architect
arquivo n.m. archive
arrabalde n.m. suburb
arraigar v. take or strike root
arrancar v. root out, pull out
arrandeadoiro n.m. swing
arranque n.m. sudden impulse
arranxar v. align, fix, arrange
arrapañar v. grasp, grab with greed
arrapiar v. terrify; ruffle hair or feathers
arrasar v. demolish, raze the ground
arrastrar v. drag
arredar v. take or put away
arredor adv. around
arrefecer v. cool, make cool
arrefriado n.m. cold (disease)
arrefriar V. arrefecer
arremangar v. tuck up
arrendar v. let, rent
arrendo n.m. letting, renting
arreo adv. without interruption or stopping
arrepañar V. arrapañar
arrepentimento n.m. repentance, contrition
arrepentirse v. repent, become contrite
arriba adv. above

arrimar v. bring or come near
arrincar V. arrancar
arriscado -a a. risky
arriscar v. be placed in danger
arrodear V. rodear
arrodeo V. rodeo
arroiar v. rain heavily
arroio n.m. rivulet, stream
arrolar v. lull
arrombar v. move aside; take up space
arrotar v. belch
arroto n.m. belch
arroupar v. dress, cover up, clothe, wrap
arroutada n.f. sudden jerk or start
arrouto n.m. pulling out
arroz n.m rice
arte n.f. art
artefacto n.m artifact
arteiro a a. skillful, astute, crafty, willy
artello n.m. ankle
artemisia n.f. sagebrush
arteria n.f. artery
artesá n.f. artisan
artesa n.f. kneading-trough
artesan n.m. artisan
articulación n.f. articulation

artificial a. artificial
artigo n.m. article
artista n. artist
arxila n.f. clay
as art.pl.f. the
as n.m. ace
as pr. they
asa n.f. handle
asado n. roast
asaltar v. assault
asasinar v. assassinate
asasinato n.m. assassination
asasino -a a. & n. assassin
ascander v. ascend, raise
ascenso n.m. ascent, ascending
ascensor n.m. elevator
asco n.m. cleanliness, neatness
asear v. clean
asegurar v. safeguard
asemblea n.f. assembly
asentar v. seat
asente n.m. wormwood, absinthe
asento n.m. seat
asexar v. spy
asfalto n.m. asphalt
asfixiar v. asphyxiate, suffocate

así adv. so, thus, this way
asiático -a a. Asiatic
asilo n.m. asylum, sanctuary
asinar v. sign
asistencia n.f. assistance
asoballar v. dominate
asociar v. associate
asomar v. show, stick out
asombrar v. shade
asombro n.m. astonishment, amazement
aspecto n.m. aspect, look, appearance
áspero -a a. rough, rugged
aspirador -a n. vacuum cleaner
aspirar v. aspirate, breath in
aspirina n.f. aspirin
associación n.f. association
astro n.m. heavenly body
astronauta n. astronaut
astucia n.f. cunning, craft
astuto -a a. astute, crafty
asubiar v. whistle
asubío n.m. whistle
asubiote n.m. basil
asunto n.m. matter, subject, affair, business
asustar v. frighten, scare
ata prep. till, until

atacar v. attack
atallar v. cut short, interrupt, intercept, stop
atallo n.m. interception
atar v. tie up, bind
atardecer n. grow late, towards evening
atascar v. stop up, plug in
ataúde n.m. coffin, casket
ate logo, até mais p. so long
atención n.f. attention
atender v. attend, be attentive
atento -a a attentive
ateo -a a. atheist
aterecer v. become numb
aterrar v. land a plane
aterrar v. terrify
aterraxe n.f. landing
aterse v. comply, conform
atinar v. hit the mark or the target
atlas n.m. Atlas
atleta n. athlete
atletismo n.m. athletics
atmósfera n.f. atmosphere
átomo n.m. atom
átono -a a, atonal
atopar v. find somebody or something by chance
atormentar v. torment

atracador -a n. hold up person, armed bandit
atracar v. hold up, rob
atracción n.f. attraction
atraco n.m. hold up, robbery
atractlvo -a a. attractive
atraer v. attract, lead, lure
atrancar v. bar, block up
atrapar V. trap, catch, grab, ensnare
atrás adv. back, behind, past
atrasar v. slow down, retard
atraso n.m. delay, lateness
atravesado -a a. awkward, nasty, difficult
atravesar v. stretch across, go through
atreverse n. dare, venture
atrevido -a a. daring, bold, audacious
atropelar v. trample down, run over
atún n.m. tuna
aturar v. support, endure
audaz a. audacious, bold, daring
audiencia n.f. audience
auga n.f. water
augardente n.f. fire water (alcoholic beverage);
    aqua vitae
aula n.f. lecture hall, class room
aulaga V. toxo
aumentar v. augment, increase, enlarge

aumento n.m. increase, enlargement
aurora n.f. dawn
ausencia n.f. absence
ausente a. absent
auténtico -a a. authentic
autobús n.m. bus
autoestrada n. highway
automático -a a. automatic
automobil n.m. automobil
autonomía n.f. autonomy
autopista n.f. highway
autor -a n. author
autoridade n.f. authority
autorizar v. authorize
auxiliar v. help, render aid or assistance
auxilio n.m. aid, help, assistance
avaliación n.f. evaluation
avaliar v. evaluate, assess
avance n.m. advance
avantaxar v. have the advantage
avanzar v. advance
avaría n.f. damage, breakdown
ávaro -a a. & n. greedy, avaricious
ave n. poultry
avea n.f. oats
avelá V. abelá

avelaiña n.f. moth
avellentar v. become or get old
avenida n.f. avenue
aveños n.m.pl. goods & shattels
aventura n.f. adventure
avergonzar v. shame, put shame
avésopora V. avespa
avespa n.f. wasp
aveztruz n.f. ostrich
aviación n.f. aviation
aviador -a n. aviator, pilot, flyer
avión n. airplane
avioneta n.m. small plane
avisar v. inform, advise
aviso n.m. notice, announcement
avó n.m. father
avoa n.f. mother
avogado -a n. lawyer attorney
avultar v. increase, augment, make bulky
axeitar v. accept, consent
axenda n.f. agenda
axente n. agent
axeonllar v. kneel down
áxil a. agile
axila n.f. axilla, armpit
axiña adv. afterwards

axitar v. shake
axóuxere n.m. small sleigh bell
axuda n.f. help
axudar v. help
axuntamento V. concello
axuntar V. xuntar
axustar v. adjust
azafrán n.m. saffron
azar n.m. chance, hazard, luck
azotea n.f. flat roof (of a house)
azouta n. f. spanking
azucre n.m. sugar
azul a. blue
azulexo n.m. glazed tile

B

baba n.f. saliva
babar v. dribble, slaver
babeiro n.m bib
babor n.m port side of a ship
baboso -a driveling, slavering
baca n.f. luggage rack (in a car)
bacadillo n.m. sandwich
bacallao n.m cod

bacelo n.m. grape vine

bache V. fochanca

bachelerato n.m. Bachelors Degree, first university degree in USA

bacoriño n.m. piglet, young sow

bácoro V. bacoriño

bacteria n.f. bacteria

baeta n.f. swadling clothes

bafexar v. gasp, pant

bafo n.m. breath

bagaño n.m bagasse

bagazo V. bagaño

bágoa n.m tear

baia n.f. bay

bailar v. dance

baile n.m. dance

baixa n.f. descent, decline

baixada n.f. lowering

baixar v. lower

baixo -a a. low

bala n.f. bullet

balancear v. balance

balanza n.f. balance

balcón n.m. balcony

baldar v cripple

balde n.m. bucket

baldeirar v. empty

baldeiro a a. empty

baldosa n.f. floor, paving tile

baldreu n.m. person with ragged, tattered appearance

balea n.f. whale

baleirar V. baldeirar

baleiro V. baldeiro

balón s.m. balloon, large ball

baloncesto n.m. basketball

balor n.m. crust formed when a substance begins rot

balsa n.f. raft

bambán n.m jumper (for children)

bambear v. oscillate

bañar v. bathe, wash

banco n.m. bench, pew

banda (costado, lado) n.f. edge

banda (feita estreita e longa) n.f. sash, band

banda (grupo de xente unida) n.f. gang, party

bandada n.f. covey, flock

bandeira n.f. flag, banner

bandexa n.f. tray

bandido n.m. bandit

bandullo n.m. belly, paunch

bañeira n.f. bathtub

baño n.m. bath
banqueta n.f. bench, stool
banquete n.m. banquet, feast
bar n.m. bar
baralla n.f. pack of cards
barallar v. shuffle cards
barato -a a. cheap, inexpensive
baraza n.f. cordon
barba n.f. beard
barbaridade n.f. barbarism, cruelty
bárbaro -a a. barbarian
barbeiro -a n. barber
barbería n.f. barbershop
barbudo a a. bearded
barca n.f. boat; bark
barco n.m. ship
barniz V. verniz
barómetro n.m. barometer
barón n.m. baron
baronesa n.f. baroness
barqueiro n.m. ferryman, boatman
barra n.f. bar, rod
barranco n.m. gully, gorge, ravine
barreira n.f. barrier
barrer V. varrer
barriga n.f. belly

barril n.m. barrel
barrio n.m. district, quarters (of a city)
barro n.m. mud, clay
barroco a a. baroque
barullo n.m. bustle, uproar, chaos
báscula n.m. platform scale; weighing machine
base n.f. base
básico -a a. basic
bastante a. sufficient, enough
basto -a a. coarse, rough, crude
bastón n.m. cane, stick, baton
bata n.f. dress, bathrobe
batalla n.f. battle
batea n.f. tray, washing trough
bater v. beat, pound
batería n.f. battery
baúl n.m. chest, trunk
bautismo n.m. baptism
bautizar v. baptize
bautizo n.m. baptism
bazar n.m. bazaar, market place
beato -a a. & n. blessed, pious
bebé n.m. baby
bébedo -a a. drunk
beber v. drink
bebida n.f. drink

beca s.f. scholarship
becerro -a n. young bull, calf
becho n.m. insect
bedel n. beadle, potter
beira n.f. edge, border, threshold
beirarrúa n.f. walkway
beixo n.m. kiss
beizo V. labio
belén n.m. manger
beleza n.f. beauty
beliscar v. pinch
belisco n.m. pinch
ben n.m. good
bendicir v. bless
beneficiar v. benefit
beneficio n.m. benefit
benestar n.m. well being
benigno -a a. benign
benvida n.f. welcome
berberecho n.m. clam
berce n.m. cradle
berexena n.f. eggplant
berrar v. bellow
berro n.m. bellow, lowing
besta n.f. beast
bevera n.f. fig

biberón n.m. bib
biblioteca n.f. library
bicar v. kiss
biceps n.m. biceps
bicicleta n.f. bicycle
bico n.m. beak
bidé n.m. bidet
bidón n.m. barrel, cask
bidueiro n.m. birch tree
bieiteiro V. sabugueiro
bigote n.m. mustache
bikini n.m. bikini
billa n.f. spigot
billar n.m. billiards, pool table
billete n.m. ticket, bank note
bioloxía n.f. biology
birollo -a a. cross-eyed, squinting, squint eyed
bisagra n.f. hinge
bisavó n.m. great-grandfather
bisavoa n.f. great-grandmother
biscoito n.m. biscuit
bisesto a. leap year
bisneto -a n. great-grandson, great-granddaughter
biso n.m. petticoat
bispo n.m. bishop
bisté n.m. beefsteak

blasfemia n.f. blasphemy
bloque n.m. block
blusa n.f. blouse
bo a.m. good
bo p. good morning
boa a.f. good
boa noite, boas noites p. good evening, good night
boa tarde, boas tardes p. good afternoon
bobo -a a. dunce, simpleton
boca n.f. mouth
bocha n.f. blister
boche n.m. lung (of an animal)
bochorno n.m. shame, embarrassment
bocio n.m. goiter
bocoi n.m. wine cask
boda V. voda
bodega n.f. warehouse, store house, wine cellar
boi n.m. ox
boia n.f. buoy
boina n.f. beret
bola n.f. ball
bolboreta n.f. butterfly
bolílgrafo n.m. ball point pen
bolo n.m. bump
bolo n.m. roll, bun, scone
bolsa n.f. purse, bag

bolso n.m. hand bag
bom dia, bons dias p. good morning
bomba n.f. bomb
bombardear v. bombard
bombeiro n.m. firefighter
bombilla n.f. light bulb
bombo s.m. drum
bombón s.m. chocolate
bombona s.f. gas tank, gas container
bondade n.f. kindness, goodness
boneca V. moneca
boneco V. moneco
bonito -a a. pretty
boquear v. gape, gasp
boqueira s.f. cold sore, mouth blister
borda n.f. gunwale
bordar v. embroider
bordear v. edge, skirt.
bordo n.m. edge
boroa n.f. corn bread
borra s.f. soot
borracho -a a. & n. inebriated, drunk
borrador n.m. eraser
borrador n.m. preliminary copy
borralla n.f. ash
borrancho n.m. scratch; ink blot

borrar v. erase
borroso -a a. blurred, illegible
bosque n.m. wood, forest
bosta n.f. animal excrement
bostela n.f. scab
bota n.f. boot
botafumeiro s.m. censer
botar v. throw away
bote n.m. boat
botella n.f. bottle
botica n.f. pharmacy, drug store
boticano -a n. pharmacist, druggist
botín n.m. loot
botiquín n.m. first aid kit
botoeira V. ollal
bou n.m. trawling
bourar v. strike
boxeo n.m. boxing
braga n.f. waist slip
branco -a a. white
brando -a a. soft
branquear v. whiten
branquia n.f. gills
brasa n.f. live coals, embers
braseiro n.m. brazier
bravio -a a. fallow

bravo -a a. brave
brazada n.f. arms full
brazo n.m. arm
breca (peixe) n.f. bleak (fish)
brétema V. néboa
breve a. brief, fleeting
brillante a. brilliant, shiny
brillo s.m. brilliance
brincar v. jump, bounce
brindar v. toast
brisa n.f. breeze
broa V. boroa
broca n.f. drill, bit
brocha n.f. brush for shaving or painting
broche n.m. clasp
broche V. xermolo
broma n.f. prank, joke
broma n.f. shipworm (mollusk)
bronce n.m. bronze
broncear v. sun tan, bronze
bronquio n.m. bronchus, bronchial tube
bronquite n.m. bronchitis
bruar v. low, bellow
brusco -a a. rude, peevish
bruto -a a. brute
bruxa n.f. witch

brúxula V. compás
bubela n.f. hoopoe (bird)
bucina n.f. snail shell
bufanda n.f. scarf
bufarda n.f. skylight
bufo n.m. owl
buiz n.m. net, snare (to catch birds)
bulbo n.m. bulb
bulebule n.m. restless
bulicioso -a a. noisy
buligar v. move rapidly from place place
bulir v. stir up
bulla n.f. noise, bustle
bulto V. vulto
buque n.m. vessel, ship
buraco n.m. hole
burato V. buraco
burbulla n.f. bubble
burgués -a n. bourgeois
burla s.f. mockery, sneer
burlar v. mock, laugh at
burrada n.f. asinine, crazy
burro -a n. ass, donkey
buscador n.m. searcher
buscar v. search
butaca n.f. armchair

butano n.m. butane
buxo n.m. yew tree

C

ca conj. than
cá contraction of conj, ca & art á
ca contraction of prep con, with, & art a, the
cabaleiro n.m cavalier
cabalgar v. ride, mount a horse
cabalgata n.f. cavalcade
cabaliños V. carrousel
cabalo n.m horse
cabana n.f cabin, hut, shack, hovel
cabaza n.f. pumpkin, gourd
cabazo n.m. silo
cabeceira n.f. upper part of a bed or of a table
cabelo n.m. hair
caber v. fit
cabeza n.f. head
cabezada n.f blow the head
cabezal n.m. pillow
cabezolo V. cágado
cabina n.f. cabin
cable n.m. cable

cabo n.m. cape
cabo n.m. corporal
cabodano n.m. death anniversary
cabra n.f. she-goat
caca n.f. excrement (human)
cacahuete n.f. peanut
cacao n.m. cocoa
cacarexar v. crow, cackle
cachar v. surprise
cacharro n.m. piece of crockery
cachear v. lower, bow down,
cacheira n.f. salted head of pork
cachelo n.m. boiled potato
cacho n.m. chunk, fragment
cachola V cacheira
cachón n.m. bubble
cachorro n.m puppy, cub, yelp
cacique n.m. cacique, chieftain
cacs n.m. chaos, confusion
cacto n.m. cactus
cada pr. each
cadanseu pr.m. each one
cadansúa pr.f. each one
cadaquén pr. each person
cadáver n.m. cadaver, corpse
cadea n.f. chain

cadeado n.m. chain, padlock
cadeira n.f. hip
cadela n.f. she dog
cadelo n.m. pup, puppy
caderno n.m. notebook
cadrado -a a. squared
cadrar v. coincide
cadril n.m. hip
cadro n.m. square
caducar v. expire, lapse
caduco -a a. senile, decrepit, in decline
caer v. fall
café n.m. coffee, coffee tree, coffee house
cafetería n.f. cafeteria
cágado n.m. tadpole
cagar v. defecate
cagarría n.f. diarrhea
cagote V. cágado
caida n.f. fall
cair V. caer
caixa n.f. box
caixón n.m. drawer
cal n.m. lime
cal pr. which
calafrio n.m. chill, shiver
calamidade n.f. calamity

calandra V. laverca
calar v. keep quiet
calcañar n.m. heel
calcaño V. calcañar
calcar v. copy
calcetar v. knit
calcetín n.m. sock
calcio n.m calcium
calcomanía n.f. decalcomania
calcular v. calculate
cálculo n.m. calculus
caldeira n.f. cauldron, boiler
caldeirada n.f. fish stew
caldeiro n.m. cauldron
caldo n.m. broth
calefacción n.f. heating
calendario n.m. calendar
calidade n.f. quality
cálido -a a. lukewarm, tepid
caligrafía n.f. calligraphy
callar v. curd, curdle, coagulate
callau V. seixo
callos n.m.pl tripe stew
calma n.f. calm
calmar v. calm
calmo -a a. quiet, calm, tranquil

calo n.m. callus, corn
calor n.f. heat
caloría n.f. calorie
calquera pr. whoever
caluga n.f. nape of the neck
calumnia n.f. calumny
calva n.f. baldness
calvo -a a. & n. baldheaded
calzada n.f. road paved with stones
calzado n.m. shoe
calzar v. put shoes on
calzón n.m. trousers, pants
cama n.f. bed
camada n.f. litter
cámara n.f. chamber
camareira n.f. waitress
camareiro n.m. waiter
camarón n.m. small prawn
camarote n.m. state room, berth, cabin of a ship
cambiar v. change, exchange
cambio n.m. change, exchange
cambra n.f. cramp
camelia n.f. camellia
camelo n.m. camel
camiñar v. walk
camiño de Santiago p. the way Santiago de
    Compostela

camiño n.m, road, lane, path; way, route

camión n.m. truck

camisa n.f. shirt

camiseta n.f. undershirt

camisón n.m. night shirt

camomila V. macela

campá n.f. bell

campaña n.f. campaign (military)

campanano n.m. bell tower

campesiño -a a. rural, rustic

campesiño -a n. peasant, countryman, countrywoman

campión a. & n.m. champion

campiona a. & n.f. champion

campionato n.m. championship

campo n.m. field

can n.m. dog

cana (pelo, cabelo) n.f. gray hair

cana n.f. cane, sugar cane

canalla a. & n. rabble, riffraff

canario n.m. canary

canastra n.f. basket

cancela n.f. front door, grating, screen

cancelar v. cancel

cáncer (enfermidade) n.m. cancer, malignant tumor

cáncer (zodiaco) n.m. cancer; fourth sign of
  the zodiac
cancha n.f. court, sports field or ground
canción n.f. song
canda prep. with you; at the same time
candea n.f. candle
candidato -a n. candidate
candil n.m. oil lamp
cando adv. when
canela n.f. cinnamon
canela n.f. shin
cangrexo n.m. lobster (cf. centola)
canino -a. canine
canle n.f. reservoir
cano n.m. pipe, duct, tube
canón n.m. canon
cansado -a a. tired
cansar v. tire
cansazo n.m. tired, fatigued
canso -a a tired
cantante n. singer
cantar v. sing
cántaro n.m. pitcher
canteira n.f. quarry
canteiro n.m. stone cutter
cantidade n.f. quantity

cántiga n.f. ancient poem designed be sung

cantimplora n.f. canteen, water bottle

cantina n.f. tavern

canto n.m. singing

canto pr. how much?

capa n.f. cape, cloak

capacidade n.f. capacity

capar v. castrate

caparucha V. caparucho

caparucho n m. crest, tuft of feathers

capaz a. able, capable

capela n.f. chapel

capelán n.m. chaplain

capicúa n.m. numbers that read the same in either direction

capital n.f. capital

capitalismo n.m. capitalism

capitán n.m. captain

capitana n.f. captain

capítulo n.m. chapter

capón n.m. capon

caprichoso-a a. capricious

cápsula n.f. capsule

capturar v. capture

caqui n.m. date plum

cara n.f. face

carabuña n.f. pit of fruits
caracol n.m. snail
carácter n.m. character
característico -a a. characteristic
carallada n.f. spree, carousing party
carallo (v.u.) n.m. penis
caramelo n.m. caramel
carantoña n.f. grimace,
carapucho V. caparucho
caravana n.f. caravan
caravel n.m. carnation
carballeira n.f. field of oak trees
carballo n.m. oak tree
carbón n.m. coal
carbono n.m. carbon (chemical element)
carburante n.m. fuel
cárcere ns.m. jail
cardíaco -a a. cardiac
cardinal a. cardinal
cardo n.m. thistle
carercer v. lack
careta n.f. mask
carga n.f. load, burden
cargar v. load
cargo n.m. freight
caricature n.f. caricature

caricia n.f. caress
caridade n.f. charity
carie n.f. tooth cavity
cariño n.m love, affection
carmesí a. & n. crimson
carne n.f. meat
carné n.m. official certificate or identification
carneiro n.m. sheep, mutton
carniceiro -a n. butcher
carnívoro -a a. & n. carnivore
caro -a a. expensive, dear
carozo n.m. pit
carpeta n.f. carpet
carpinteiro -a n. carpenter
carqueixa n.f. medicinal broom
carracha n.f. louse
carranchas adv. sitting down with legs spread out
carraspeira n.f. sore throat
carraxe n.f. vexation, annoyance
carreira n.f. sprint
carreiro n.m. foot way
carreta n.f. cart
carretar v. cart, convey in a cart
carricanta V. chicharra
carril n.m lane
carrizo n.m. wren

carro n.m. cart
carrusel n.m. carrousel
carta n.f. letter
cartabón n.m. triangle
carteira n.f. billfold
carteiro -a n. mailman
cartel n.m. bill board, cartel, agreement
cartilla n.f. spelling book
carto n.m. currency
cartolina n.f. thin cardboard
cartón n.m. cardboard
cartucho n.m. cartridge
casa n.f. house
casado -a a. married
casamento n.m. wedding
casar v. wed
casca n.f. skin of fruits
cascar v. break into pieces
casco n.m. helmet
case adv. almost
caseiro -a a. domestic, homely
caseta n.f. cabin, shed, hut
casino n.m. casino
caso n.m. case, occurrence, contingency
caspa n.f. dandruff
casta n.f. caste

castaña n.f. chestnut

castaño -a a. reddish brown

castelá a.f. Castilian

castelán a.m. Castilian

castelanismo n.m. use of Castilian words

castelo n.m. castle

castigar v. punish

castigo n.m. punishment

castiñeiro n.m. chestnut tree

castro n.m. prehistoric Galician village; hill top castle

casualidade n.f. change, coincidence

casula n.f. capsule

catalán -a a. Catalan

catálogo n.m. catalog

catar v. sample, taste

catarata n.f. cataract (eye disease)

catarata n.f. cataract, waterfall

catástrofe n.f. catastrophe

catecismo n.m. catechism

catedral n.f. cathedral

categoría n.f. category

caterreira n.f. cold

cativo -a a. captive

catolicismo n.m. Catholicism

católico -a a. Catholic

catorce pr. fourteen
catro pr. four
catrocentos -as pr. four hundred
causar v. cause
cavar v. dig
caveira n.f. skull
caverna n.f. cavern
cavilar v. ponder
caxato n.m. walking cane
caza n.f. hunt
cazador -a a. & n. hunter
cazar v. hunt
cazo n.m. cooking pot
cazola n.f. cooking pan
cazón (peixe) n.m. dog fish, god shark
cea n.f. dinner
cear v. dine
cebada n.f. barley
cebar v. fatten animals
cebo n.m. bait, feed, fodder
cebola n.f. onion
cecimbre V. hortelá
ceder v. yield
cedo adv. early
cegar v. blind
cego -a a. blind

cegoña n.f. stork
ceibar v. free
ceibe a. free
ceibo -a V. ceibe
celebrar v. celebrate
celeste a. celestial
cella n.f. eyebrow
celo n.m. zeal, ardor
celofán n.m. cellophane
celoso -a a. jealous
celta a. Celtic
célula n.f. cell
celulosa n.f. cellulose
cemento n.m. cement
cemiteno n.m. cemetery, graveyard
cempés n.m. centipide
cen pr one hundred
cenoria n.f. carrot
censo n.m. census
censurar v. censor
centeo n.m. rye
centímetro n.m. centimeter
cento pr. cien
centola n.f. crab (cf. cangrexo)
central a. central
centro n.m. center

ceo n.m. sky
cepa n.f. stump
cepillo n.m. brush
cepo n.m. wooden wedge
cera n.f. wax
cerámica n.f. ceramics
cerca adv. near
cerca n.f. fence
cerdeira n.f. cherry tree
cereal n.m. cereal
cerebro n.m. brain
cereixa n.f. cherry
cerimonia n.f. ceremony
cero pr. zero
cerradura s.f. locking or shutting up; lock
cerrar v. close
certeza n.f. certainty
certificado n.m. certificate
certo -a a. certain, sure
cerume n.m. ear war
cervexa n.f. beer
cervo -a n. deer, stag
cesar v. cease
céspede n.m. grass, lawn
cesta n.f. basket, hamper
cha contraction of pr. che & pr. a

chabola n.f. hovel, shepherd's hut

chafallada n.f. something done badly, without care or art

chafalleiro -a a. person who does things badly

chafullada V. chafallada

chafulleiro V. chafalleiro

chaga n.f. sore, wound, ulcer

chaira n.f. steppe

chalé n.m. chalet

chaleco n.m. vest

chama n.f. flame

chamar v. call

chambra n.f. house dress

champaña n.m. champagne

champiñón n.m. mushroom

champú n.m. shampoo

chamuscar v. singe

chan a. level

chan n.m. soil

chantar v. puncture, sting

chanzo n.m. step, rung

chapa n.f. metal plate

chapuzar v. splash

chaqueta n.f. jacket

chaquetón n.m. short overcoat

charamela n.f. cinder

charco n.m. pond, puddle
charla n.f. chat
charlar v. chat
charouvía n.m. parsnip
chasco n.m. joke, deceit, trick, disappointment
chasis n.m. frame, chassis
chatarra n.f. scrap iron
chato -a a. flat-nosed
chave n.f. key
che pr. you
chea n.f. raise, increase; flood; gluttony
chegada n.f. arrival
chegar v. arrive
cheirar v. smell
cheiro n.m. smell, odor, scent
cheminea n.f. chimney
cheo -a a. full, replete
chepa n.f. hump
cheque n.m. check
cheveiro n.m. key holder
chiar v. shriek, scream
chícharo n.m. pea
chicharra n.f. grasshopper
chifar v. play the horn
chifre n.m. horn
chimpancé n.m. chimpanzee

chimpar v. throw
chincha n.f. bed bug
chineiro n.m. china closet
chinela n.f. slipper
chinés -a a. Chinese
chintófano n.m. what-d'ye call it (v.u.)
chio n.m. squeak, shriek, shrill sound
chirlar v. sing (birds), squeak
chisca n. a little bit
chiscar v. wink
chisco V. chisca
chise n.m. joke
chisme n.m. gossip
chispa n.f. spark, sparkle
cho contraction of pr. che & pr. o
choca n.f. rattle, small bell, sleigh bell
chocallo V. choca
chocar v. crash, collide
chocar v. incubate; time for disease develop
chocho -a a. demented old person
choco -a a. fertilized egg; spoiled water
choco n.m. cuttlefish
chocolate n.m. chocolate
chofer n.m. chauffeur, driver
choia n.f. jackdaw
choiva V. chuvia

chojo n.m. small business
chopa (peixe) n.f. sea bream (fish)
chopo (árbore) n.m. poplar tree
chopo (coloquial) n.m. musket
chopo V. chocho
choque n.m. crash, collision
chorar v. cry
choricas a. & n. crybaby
choro n.m. cry
chorra n.f. good luck!
chorro n.m. jet, gush, flow
choscar V. chiscar
chosco -a a. one-eyed
chourizo n.m. pork sausage
choutar v. leap, jump,
chover v. rain
chuchamel n.m. honeysuckle
chuchar v. suck, draw
chufa (planta) n.m. earth nut
chumbeira n.f. fig tree
chumbo n.m. lead
chupamel V. chuchamel
chupeta n.f. baby's pacifier
chupete V. chupeta
churrasco n.m. barbecued meat
churro n.m. fritter

chutar v. shoot (football)
chuvascada s.f. squall
chuvia n.f. rain
chuvieira n.f. drizzle
chuzar v. prick, goad
cicatriz n.f. scar
ciclismo n.m. cycling
ciclo n.m. cycle
ciclón n.m. cyclone
cidadá a. & n.f. citizen
cidadán a. & n.m. citizen
cidade n.f. city
ciencia n.f. science
científico -a a. scientific
cifra n.f. cipher
cigala n.f, crayfish
cigarra V. chicharra
cigarro n.m. cigar
cilindro n.m. cylinder
cima n.f. summit, top
cimento n.m. foundation, base, basis, groundwork
cinc n.m. zinc
cinco pr. five
cincocentos -as pr. five hundred
cincuenta pr. fifty
cine n.m. cinema

cinguir v. gird
cínico -a a. cynical; cynic
cinsa n.f, ash(es)
cinseiro n.m. ashtray
cinta n.f. V. cinto
cinto n.m. girdle, belt, waist
cintura n.f. waist
ciprés n.m. cypress
circo n.m. circus
circuito n.m. circuit
circulación n.f. circulation
circular v. circulate
círculo n.m. circle
circunferencia n.f. circumference
circunstancia n.f. circumstance
cirio n.m. large wax candle used in churches
cirurxiá n.f. surgeon
cirurxian n.m. surgeon
cirúrxico -a a. surgical
ciruxía n.f. surgery
ciscar v. discard
cisne n.m. swan
ciste n.f. cyst
cisterna n.f. cistern, well
cita n.f. appointment, date
citar v. cite, make an appointment

cívico -a a. civic
civil a. civil
civilizacion n.f. civilization
clandestino -a a. clandestine
clara n.f. white (of an egg)
clarear v. clear up
claridade n.f. clarity
clarinete n.m. clarinet
claro -a a. clear
clase n.f class
clásico -a a. classical, classic
clasificación n.f. classification
clasificar v. classify
clausura n.f. closure, monastic life
clausurar v. close, terminate
clave n.f. key, code
clérigo n.m. clergy
clero n.m. member of the clergy
cliente -a n. client
clima n.m. climate
clínica n.f. clinic, physician's office
clínico -a a. clinical
cloro n.m. chlorine
clorofila n.f. chlorophyll
club n.m. club
có contraction of conj. ca & art a; pl. cos

coa contraction of prep. con & art a; pl. coas
coadoiro n.m. sieve
coágulo n.m. clot
coalición n.f. coalition
coandro n.m. coriander
coar v. sift
cóbado n.m. elbow
cobertor n.m. wrap, quilt
cobiza n.f. covetousness
cobrar v. collect
cobre n.m. copper
cocaína n.f. cocaine
cocer v. cook
coche n.m. car
cocho -a n. pig
cocido n.m. stew
cociente n.m. quotient
cociña n.f. kitchen
cociñar v. cook
coco (froito) n.m. coconut
coco n.m. bogy, bogeyman
cocote n.m. neck
codelo n.m. piece, slice of bread
codia n.f. crust
código n.m. code (law)
cogomelo n.m. mushroom

coherencia n.f. coherence
cohibir v. inhibit
coidado n.m. care, concern
coidar v. take care of, look after; watch
coincidencia n.f. coincidence
coincidir v. coincide
coio n.m. pebble
coiro n.m. leather
coitado -a a. miserable, pitiful
coitelo n.m. knife
col n.f. cauliflower
cola (zooloxía) n.f. tail
cola n.f. glue
colaboración n.f. collaboration
colaborador -a a. collaborator
colaborar v. collaborate
colar n.m. collar
colcha n.f. bedspread, quilt
colchón n.m. mattress
colección n.f collection
colectivo -a a. collective
colexio n.m. school, college; professional
    association
colgar v. hang
coliflor n.f. cauliflower
colleita n.f. harvest

collón n.m. (v.u.) testicles
colmea n.f. beehive
colo n.m. neck, throat
colocar v. place
colonia n.f colony
colono n.m. tenant farmer, colonist
coloquio n.m. colloquy
color V. cor
colorado -a a. colored, red
colorar v. color
columna n.f. column
coma conj. comma
coma n.f. coma
comadroa n.f. midwife,
comarca n.f. region
combate n.m. combat
combater v. battle
combinación n.f. combination
combinar v. combine
combustible a. combustible
comedia n.f. comedy
comedor n. person who eats too much; glutton
comedor n.m. dining room
comentano n.m. commentary
comentar v. comment
comenzar v. begin, start, commence

comer v. eat
comerciante n. merchant
comerciar v trade, deal
comercio n.m. commerce
comestible a. edible
comestible n. edible food
cometa n.m. comet
cometer v commit, charge
cómico -a a comic, comical
comida n.f. meal
comigo pr. with me
comiñas n.f.pl quotation marks
comisaría n.f police station
comisario -a n. chief of police
comisión n.f. commission
como adv. how
cómoda n.f dresser
cómodo -a a. comfortable, convenient
compadecer v. feel sorry for, sympathize
compaixón n.f. compassion
compañeiro -a n. companion
compañía n.f. company
comparación n.f. comparison
comparar v. compare
compartir v. share
compás n.m. compass

compaxinar v. arrange, combine, fit
compenetrarse v. get in tune with others
compensación n.f. compensation
competencia n.f skillfulness, ability
competición n. f. competition
competir v. compete
complemento n.m. complement
completar v. complete
completo -a a complete
complexo -a a. complex
complicación n.f complication
complicar v. complicate
cómplice n. accomplice
compoñente a. component
compoñer v. compose, put together
comportamento n.m. conduct, behavior,
　　deportment
comportar v. behave
composición n.f. composition
compositor -a n. composer
compostelá n.f. inhabitant of Santiago de
　　Compostela
compostelán n.m. inhabitant of Santiago de Com-
　　postela
composto -a a. compound
compota n.f. stewed fruit

compra n.f. buy
compracer v please
comprador n.m buyer
comprar v. buy
comprender v. understand
comprension n.f. understanding
comprimir v. compress
comprobar v. verify, check, test
comprometer v. compromise, jeopardize,
    endanger
compromiso n.m. compromise
computadora n.f. computer
común a. common
comunicación n.f. communication
comunicar v. communicate
comunidade n.f. community
comunismo n.m. communism
comuñón n.f. comunion
con prep with
con V. farallón
cona n.f. vulva (v u.)
cóncavo -a a concave
conceder v. concede
concelleiro -a n chancellor
concentración n.f. concentration
concentrar v. concentrate

concept n.m concept, idea
concertar v. arrange, make agree
concerto n.m concert
concesión n.f. concession
conciencia n.f conscience
conciso -a a concise
concluir v. end, finish
conclusión n.f. conclusion
concordar v. accord, agree, conform
concorrer v. meet
concreto -a a concrete
concursar v. enter a contest
concurso n.m contest, competition
conde n.m. count
condena n.f. sentence, penalty
condenar v. sentence, condemn
condesa n.f. countess
condición n.f. condition
condón (pl. condóns) n.m. condom
cóndor n.m. large vulture from the South
    American Andes
conducir v. conduct, drive a vehicle
conducta n.f. behavior, comportment, conduct
conductor -a n. conductor; driver
coñecemento n.m. knowledge
coñecer v. know

coñecido -a a. known
conectar v. connect
conejo -a n. rabbit
conexión n.f. connection
confección n.f. tailoring, preparation
confeiteria n.f. sweet-shop
conferencia n.f. conference
confesar v. confess
confesion n.f. confession
confianza n f. confidence, trust
confiar v. trust
configurar v. form
confirmación n.f. confirmation
confirmar v. confirm
conflicto n.m. conflict
conformar v. conform, resign
conforme a. agreeing, be in agreement with
confraría n.f. religious association
confrontar v. confront
confundir v. confuse
confusión n.f. confusion, bewilderment
congregar v. congregate, meet
congreso n.m. congress
congro n.m conger eel
conmover v. disturb
connosco pr. with us

cono n.m. cone
conquista n.f. conquest
conquistar v. conquer
consciencia n.f. conscience
consciente a. conscious, aware
consecuencia n.f. consequence
consecutivo -a a. consecutive
conseguir v. acquire, attain, obtain
conselleiro -a n. counselor, advisor
consello n.m. council, a body of people,
    municipal council
consello n.m. counsel, advice
consentir v. consent
conserva n.f. preserve
conservar v. keep, maintain
consideración n.f. consideration
considerar v. consider
consigo pr. with him
consistir v. consist
consoante n.f. consonant
consolar v. console
conspiración n.f. conspiracy
constante a. constant
constar v. be certain, be on record
constelación n.f. constellation
constipado n.m. constipated

constitución n.f. constitution
constituir v. constitute, set up
construcción n.f. construction
construir v. build, construct
consulta n.f. consultation
consultar v. consult
consumir v. consume
consumo n.m. consumption
conta n.f count
contacto n.m. contact
contado -a a. sparse, scarce, in low supply
contaminar v. contaminate
contar v. count
contarninación n .f contamination
contaxiar v infect
contaxio n.m. contagion
contaxioso -a a. contagious, catching, infectious
contemplar v. contemplate
contemporáneo -a a. contemporary
contento -a a. happy
conter v. contain
contestación n.f. answer
contestar v. answer, respond
contigo pr. with you
continente n.m. continent
continuación n.f. continuation

continuar v. continue
conto n.m. tale, story
contra n.f. blinds
contra prep. against, contrary
contrabando n.m. contraband
contracción n.f. contraction
contradicir v. contradict
contraer v. contract, limit, confine
contrano -a a. contrary
contraponer v. set against, compare
contraste n.m. contrast
contratar v. contract
contratempo n.m. mishap
contrato n.m. contract
contraventá V. contra
contribución n.f. contribution
contribuir v. contribute
control n.m control
controlar v. control
convencer v. convince
conveniente a. convenient
convento n.m. convent
conversa n.f. talk, chat
conversar v. talk, chat
converter v. convert
convexo -a a. convex

convidar v. invite
convir v agree
convivir v. coexist, live together
convocar v. convene, summon
convosco pr. with you
conxear v. limp
conxelador -a a. & n. freezer
conxelar v. freeze
conxestión n.f. congestion
conxugación n. conjugation
conxugar v. conjugate
conxuge n. married partner
conxunción n. conjunction
conxuncto -a a. joined
conxuntivo -a a. conjunctive
cooperar v. cooperate
coordinar v. coordinate
copa n.f. cup, goblet, wine glass
copia n.f. copy
copiar v. copy
copla n.f. couplet, stanza, ballad
cor n.f. color
coral a. coral
coraxe n.f. courage
corazón n.m. heart
corcova n.f. hump

corda n.f. cord, lace, string
cordal V. cordilleira
cordeiro -a n. lamb
cordial a. cordial
cordilleira n.f. mountain range
cordón n.m. rope, string
cordura n.f sanity, common sense
corenta pr. forty
coresma n.f lent
córnea n.f. cornea
corneta n.f. bugle, cornet
corno n.m. horn
coro n.m. choir, chorus
coroa n.f. crown
coronel n.m. colonel
corpo n.m. body
correa n.f. belt
corrección n.f. correction
corredoira n.f. berm
corredor -a n. runner
corredor n.m. corridor, aisle
corrente a. current
correo n.m. mail
correola n.f. rib-grass platain
correr v. run
corresponder v. correspond

corrixir v. correct
corrosco n.m. bread crust
corrupción n.f. corruption
cortadoría n.f. butcher's shop
cortar v. cut
cortauñas V. cortaúnllas
cortaúnllas n.m. nail clipper
corte de porcos V. cortello
corte n.f. court, royal house
corte n.m. cut, cutting, trimming
cortello n.m. pigsty
cortés a. kind, considerate
cortes n.m. legislative assembly in Spain
cortesia n.f. courtesy
cortina n.f. curtain
cortiza n.f. bark
coruñés a.m. native of the province Coruna, Galicia
coruñesa n.f. native of Corunna, Galicia
corvo marino n.m. diver (bird)
corvo n.m. raven
coser v. sew
cosmos n.m cosmos
costa n.f. coast
costado n.m. side, flank
costela n.f. rib
costume n.m. custom, habit

costura n.f. seam, needlework, sewing
costureira n.f. seamstress
cota (ferramenta)n.f. dull side of a cutting tool
cota (mallas de ferro) n. f. mail (flexible armor)
cota n.f. quota
cotizar v. quote, value, price
cotobelo n.m. elbow
cotovia V. laverca
cotra n.f. crust
couce n.m. kick
cousa n.f. thing
cova n.f. cave
covarde a. & n. coward
coxa n.f. thigh
cóxegas n.f.pl. tickling
coxín n.m. cushion, pillow
coxo -a a. & n. lame
coxote n.m. coyote
cranio n.m. skull, cranium
cravar V. nail
cravo n.m. nail
crear v. create
crebar v. break up
crecente a. growing
crédito n.m. credit
crego n.m. clergy

crema n.f. cream
cremalleira n.f. zipper
crer v. believe
creto n.m. credence, reputation
cría n.f. brood
criado -a n. servant, maid
criar v. breed, nurse, rear, foster, nourish
criba n.f. sifter
cribar v. sift
crime s.m. crime
crina n.f mane, horse hair
crise n.f. crisis
crista n.f crest
cristal n.m crystal
cristiá a.f. Christian
cristian a.m. Christian
cristianismo n.m. Christianity
crítica n.f. critique
criticar v. critizice
crítico -a a. critical
croar v. croak, caw,
croco V. azafrán
croia V. carabuña
croio V. coio
cromo n.m. colored pictures be collected
crónico -a a. chronic

croque n.m. bump, as in the head
croque n.m. foxglove
croqueta n.f. croquette
cruá a.f. raw
cruceiro n.m. cruiser (navy)
crucifixo n.m. crucifix
crue a.m. raw
cruel a. cruel
crustáceo n.m. crustacean
cruz n.f. cross
cruzamento n.m. crossing, as roads or streets
cruzar v. cross
cu n.m. buttocks
cualifiación n.f. qualification
cuartel n.m. barracks
cuarto -a a. fourth
cuarzo n.m. quartz
cuba n.f. earthen jar
cuberto -a a. covered
cúbico -a a. cubic
cúbito n.m. cubit
cubo n.m. cube
cubrir v. cover
cuco n.m cuckoo (bird)
cuestión n.f. question
culler n.f. spoon

cullerón n.m. ladle
culpa n.f. guilt
culpable a. & n. guilty
cultivacac n.m. cultivation
cultivar v. cultivate
cultivo V cultivacao
culto -a a cultured, educated
culto n.m. cult, worship
cultura n.f. culture
çume n.m top, summit, peak
cumprir v. fulfil, carry out
cun contraction of prep. con with art un (m)
cuña n.f. wedge
cuñada -a n. sister-in-law
cuñado n. brother-in-law
cunca n.f cup
cuncha n.f. shell
cuneta n.f. ditch
cunha contraction of prep. con, with, with art
    unha (f)
cuño n.m. die
cupón n.m. coupon
cura n.f. cure, healing
cura n.m curate, priest, prelate
curandeiro -a n. healer
curar v. heal

cúrcuman n.m. turmeric
curiosidade n.f. curiosity
curmá n.f. niece
curmán n.m. nephew
curral (pl. currais) n.m. enclosure (for domestic animals), yard
curruncho n.m. nook, corner of a room
curso n.m. course, term
curtir v. tan (hides)
curto -a a. short
curuxa n.f. owl
curvo -a a. curved
cuspe n.m. spit, spittle
cuspir v. spit
custar v. cost
custo n.m. cost
custoso -a a. expensive
cutre a. stingy, tight fisted
cuxo -a n. calf

D

D. n.m. abreviation for don, title of respect
da contraction of prep. de, of, & art a, the
dabondo adv. sufficient, enough

dado n.m. die; pl. dice

dalgun contraction of prep. de, of, & pr. algun, something

dalgunha contraction of prep. de, of, & with pr. algunha, something

dama n.f. dame, lady

danar v. cause damage

dano n.m. damage

danza n.f. dance

danzar v. dance

daquela contraction of prep de, of, & aquela, that one

daqueloutra contraction of prep. de, of, & aqueloutra

daqueloutro contraction of prep. de & aqueloutro

daquilo contraction of prep. de with prep aquilo.

dar a luz p. to give birth

dar v. give

data n.f. data

de prep. of

deavergonzado -a a. ashamed

debaixo adv. underneth

debate n.m. debate

débeda n.f. debt

deber n.m. obligation, duty

deber v. owe

débil a. weak
debilidade n.f. weakness
debruzarse v. lean
debullar v. chuck corn; shell chestnuts
debuxar v. draw
década n.f. decade
decandencia n.f. decadence
decatarse v. pay attention to, be aware of
decembro n.m. December
decena n.f. group of ten
decendente n descendant
decente a. & n. decent
decepción n.f. deception
decidir v. decide
decimal a. decimal
décimo -a a. tenth
decisión s.f. decision
declaración n.f. declaration
declarar v. declare
decomposición n.f. decomposition
decorado n.m, decoration
decorar v. decorate
decoro n.m. dignity, decorum
decreto n.m. decree
dedal n.m. thimble
dedaleira n.f. foxglove

dedicación n.f. dedication
dedicar v. dedicate
dedo n.m. finger
deducir v. deduce
defecto n.m. defect
defender v. defend
defensa n.f. defense
deficiente a. deficient
definición n.f. definition
definir v. define
definitivo a a. definitive
deforme a. deformed, disfigured, misshapen
defraudar v. defraud
defunto -a n. & a. defunct, dead, deceased
degoxar v. wish, yearn for
degracia n.f disgrace
degradar v. degrade
deica prep. till, until
deille corda o reloxo p. wind the clock
deitar v. lay down
deixar v. leave
del contraction of prep. de, of, & pr el, the (m)
dela contraction of prep. de, of, & pr ela (f)
delegación n.f. delegation
delegado -a a. & n. delegate
deletrear v. spell

delgado -a a. & n. thin
delicado -a a. delicate
delicia n.f. delight
delicto n.m. misdeed
delimitar v. delimit
delincuencia n.f. delinquency
delincuente n. delincuent
delirar v. rave, be delirious
delta n.m. delta (of a river)
demais pr. remaining, other
demasiado -a pr. too much
demo n.m demon
demoar v. delay
democracia n.f. democracy
demonstración n.f. demonstration
demostrar v. demonstrate
dende prep. from
denociña n.f. weasel
denominador -a & n. denominator
densidade n.f. density
dentadura n.f, set of teeth
dente n.m. tooth
dentista n. dentist
dentro adv. within
denunciar v. denounce
dependente a. dependent

depender v. depend, relay on

deporte n.m. sports

deportista a. & n. sports person

depósito n.m. deposit

depresión n.f. depression

deprimir v. depress

depurar v. cleanse, purify

deputación n.f. deputation

deputado a n. deputy

dereito -a a. right, straight

derivado -a a. & n. derivative

derradeiro -a a. final, last

derramar v. spill

derrear v. hurt one's shoulder or spine; become tired

derredor V. arredor

derreter v. melt

derribar V. derrubar

derrotar v. defeat

derrubar v. pull, throw, fling down

des prep. from

desabotoar v. unbutton

desabrochar v. unbutton, unfasten, unclasp

desacougo n. unrest, uneasiness

desafiar v. dare, defy, challenge

desafinar v. be or sing out of tune

desafío n.m. challenge, dare
desafogo n.m. relief
desagradable a. disagreeable
desagradecido -a a. ungrateful
desaire n.m. slight, rebuff, disdain, snub
desaloxar v. dislodge, evict
desamparar v. forsake, abandon
desangrar v. bleed
desanimar v. dishearten, discourage
desaparecer v. disappear
desaproveitar v. waste, misspend
desarmar v. disarm
desastre n.m. disaster
desatar v. lose, untie
desaugadoiro n.m. outlet, drain
desaxustar v. mismatch
desbandada n.f. rout
desbordar v. overflow, run over
descaizar v. take off the shoes
descalzo -a a. barefooted
descampado -a a. terrain free or trees or obstacles
descansar v. rest
descanso n.m. rest
descarado -a a. saucy, impertinent
descarga n.f. discharge
descaro n.m. impudent, sauciness

descarrilar v. derail

descartar v. discard

descender v. descend

descoidado -a a. careless, neglectful

descoido n.m. carelessness, neglect

descolgar v. take down

descompoñer v. decompose

desconfianza n.f. distrust, mistrust, suspicion

desconfiar v. distrust, mistrust

descoñocer v. not know

descontar v. discount

desconto n.m discount

describir v. describe

descrición (pl. descricións) n.f. description

descubrimento n.m. discovery

descubrir v. discover

desculpa n.f. excuse

desculpar v. excuse

desde prep. from

desembarcar v. disembark

desembocadura n.f. mouth of a river

desempatar v. settle a tied election or tie during a game

desempeñar v. redeem, take out of a pawn shop

deseñar v. design

desenfado n.m. ease, non-chalance

desenganar v. disillusion
desenganchar v. unhook
desenlace n.m. conclusion, end
deseño n.m. design
desentoar v. be out of tune
desentrañar v. disembowel
desenvoltura n.f. ease of manner of acting
desenvolver v. unfold, unwrap
desequilibrar v. unbalance
desertar v. desert
deserto -a a. deserted
deserto n.m. desert
desexar v. wish
desexo n.m. wish
desfacer v. undo
desfeita n.f. ruin, waste, havoc; cutting pork
    into pieces
desfilar v. parade
desfile n.m. parade
desgana n.f. lack of appetite
desgastar v. wear away or down
deshonesto -a a. dishonest
deshonrar v. dishonor
designar v. designate, name
desilusion (pl. desilusións) n.f. disillusionment
desinchar v. deflate

desinfectar v. disinfect

desinteresado -a a. uninterested

desmaiar v. faint, swoon

desmaio n.m. swoon, fainting spell

desmontar v. dismount

desnivel n.m unevenness

desobedecer v. disobey

desobediente a. disobedient

desocupado -a a. idle, unemployed

desorde n.f. disorder

desordenar v. disarrange, make untidy

desoutra (f) contraction of pre de, of, with esoutra, the other one

desoutro (m) contraction of pre de, of, with esoutro, the other one

despachar v. dispatch, send

despacho n.m. dispatch; room, study

despectivo -a a. scornful, derogatory

despedida n.f. farewell, good-bye

despedir v. say good-bye

despeitar v. ruffle the hair

despensa n.f. pantry, larder

desperdiciar v. waste

despertar v. wake up

despexar v. clear

despistar v. throw off the scent or track

desplumar v. fleece, skin
despois adv. after
despreciar v. scorn
desprecio n.m. scorn
despregar v. display
desprender v. detach, break away
despreocupado -a a. unconcerned, carefree
desprevido -a a. unprepared
desprezar v. scorn, despise, rebuff
desqustar v. displease, upset
desta contraction of prep. de, of, & esta, this
destacar v. make stand out, highlight, emphasize
destapar v. uncover, uncork
deste contraction of prep. de, of, & este, this
desterrar v. exile
destinar v. destine
destino n.m. destiny
destrucción n.f. destruction
destruir v. destroy
desuso n.m. disuse
desvantaxe n.f. disadvantage
desviar v. deviate
desvío n.m. deviation
detalle n.m. detail
detención n.f. detention
deter v. stop, detain

determinado -a a. determined
determinar v. determine
deterxente n.m. detergent
detestable a. hateful
detestar v. detest, hate
detrás adv. behind
deus n.m. God
deusa n.f Goddess
devacer v. yearn for
devalo n.m. low tide
devoción n.f. devotion
devolver v. return
devorar v. devour
devoto -a n. & n. devout
dexenerar v. degenerate
dez pr. ten
dia n.m. day
diabete n.f. diabetes
diagonal n.f. diagonal
dialecto n.m. dialect
diálogo n.m. dialog
diamante n.m. diamond
diámetro n.m. diameter
diante adv. before
dianteiro -a a. front
diapositiva n.f. negative

diario -a a. daily
diccionano n.m. dictionary
dicir v. say
dicta n.f. diet
dictado n.m. dictation
dictadura n.f. dictatorship
dictar v. dictate
diéresis n.m. dieresis
diferencia n.f. difference
diferenciar v. differentiate
diferente a. different
difícil a. difficult
dificultade n.f. difficulty
difundir v. diffuse, spread
dignidade n.f. dignity
dilatar v. dilate
dilema n.m. dilemma
diluvio n.m. deluge, flood
dimensión n.f dimension
diminuir v. diminish, lessen
diminutivo a. diminutive
dimitir v. resign
dinámico -a a dynamic
dinamita n.f. dynamite
diñeiro n.m. hard, metallic currency, money
diploma n.m diploma

diplomacia n.f. diplomacy
dique n.m. dyke, levee
dirección n.f. direction
directo -a a. direct
director -a n. director
dirixir v. direct
disciplina n.f. discipline
disco n.m. disc, record
discord n.m. discord, disagreement
discorrer v. think up, invent
discoteca n.f. discotheque
discreto -a a. discreet
discriminar V. discriminate
discurso n.m. discourse, speech
discusión n.f. discussion
discutir v. discuss
disfrace n.m. disguise
disfrazar v. disguise
disimular v. cover up, feign
disolver v. dissolve
disparar v. fire
disparo n.m. shot
dispersa v. disperse
dispoñer v. dispose, arrange, lay out
disposición n.f. disposition
disputar v. dispute

disque adv. It looks that way, rumor
distancia n.f distance
distante a. far, distant
distinción n.f. distinction
distinguir v. distinguish
distlnto -a a. distinct, different
distracción n.f. distraction
distraido -a a. distracted, absent minded
distribuir v. distribute
dito n.m. saying
ditongo n.m. diphthong
diurno -a a. diurnal
diversion n.f. amusement
diverso -a a. diverse
divertido -a a. amused, amusing
divertir v. amuse
dividir v. divide
divino -a a. divine
divisa n.f. foreign currency
division n.f. division
divorcio n.m. divorce
divulgar v. divulge, spread out, publish
dixestión n.f. digestion
dlstraer v. distract
do contraction of prep. de, of, with art o, the
do first note of the music scale

doado -a a. amenable
doar v. donate
dobra n.f. fold
dobrar v. fold
dobre a. & n.m. double
doce a. sweet
doce pr. twelve
docería n.f. sweet shop
documentación n.f. documentation
documentar v. document
documento n.m. document
doente a. aching, ailing, suffering
doenza n.f. ailment
doer v. ache, hurt
dolar n.m. dollar
dolmen n.m. dolmen
domador -a n tamer
domar v. tame, domesticate
doméstico -a a. domestic
domicilio n.m. domicile
dominar v. dominate
domingo n.m. Sunday
dominio n.m. dominion
don n.m. title of respect in front of a man's name;
abbreviated D.
doña n.f. title of respect in front of a woman's
first name

donativo n.m gift, endowment
doncela n.f. angel fish
donicela n.f. weasel
dono -a n. owner
donociña V. donicela
dor n.f. pain, ache
dormitorio n.m. dormitory
dorna n.f. small fishing vessel propelled by sails or oars
dose n.f. dose
dote n.m. dowry
dourado -a a. golden, gilded
dous pr. two
douscentos pr. two hundred
doutor -a n. doctor
doutra contraction of prep. de, of, & pr. outra, other
doutro contraction of prep. de, of, & pr. outro, other
dragar v. drag
dragón n.m. dragon
dragontea V. serpentaría
drama n.f. drama
droga n.f. drug, medicine
drogueria n.f. drugstore
dúbida n.f. doubt
dubidar v. doubt
ducha n.f. shower

ducia n.f. dozen
duna n.f. dune
dune -a a. & sm - double
duodécimo -a a. twelfth
duplicar v. duplicate
duque n.m. duke
duquesa n.f. duchess
duración n.f. duration
durante adv. during
durar v. last
dureza n.f. hardness
durmir v. sleep
duro -a a. hard

E

e conj. and
ebanista n. carpenter (of fine furniture)
eclesiástico a. ecclesiastic, ecclesiastical
eclipse n.f. eclipse
ecoloxía n.f. ecology
economía n.f economy
económico -a a. economical
ecuación n.f. equation
ecuador n.m. equator

edición n.f edition
edificar v. build
edificio n.m building
edil (pl. edís) n. Roman magistrate
editorial a. editorial
editorial n.f. publishing house
educación n.f. education
educar v. educate
efecto n.m. effect
efémero -a a. ephemeral
eficacia n.f. efficacy, efficiency
eficaz a. effective, efficient
egoísmo n.m. selfishness
egoísta a. selfish
egua n.f. mare
eiquí V. aquí
eira n.f. threshing floor, barn floor
eiruga n.f. caterpillar
eito n.m. plot (subdivision of arable land)
eivar v. disable totally or partially
eixada V. aixada
eixe n.m. axis
eixo V. eixe
el pr.m. the
elaborar v. elaborate
elástico -a a. plastic

elección n.f. election
electoral a. electoral
electricidade n.f. electricity
electricista n. electrician
eléctrico -a a. electrical
electrodoméstico n.m. electrical house appliance
electrón n.m. electron
electrónico -a a. electronic
elefante -a n. elephant
elegante a. elegant
elemento n.m. element
elevar v. elevate
eliminar v. eliminate
elixir v. elixir
ella pr.f. the
elo n.m. link (of a chain)
elocuencia n.f. eloquence
eloxio n.m. eulogy
embaixador -a n. ambassador
embaixo adv. below, underneath
embalar v. pack
embarazada a. pregnant
embarazo n.m. pregnancy
embarcar v. embark
embargo n.m embargo, seizure
embarrancar v. run aground, as a ship

embarrullar v. mix up things or ideas
embigo n.m. navel
emborrachar v. get drunk
embotellar v. bottle
embrague n.m. clutch
embrión n.m. embryo
embruxar v. bewitch
embude n.m. funnel
embuste V. mentira
embutido n.m. sausage
emerxencia n.f. emergency
emigración n.f. emigration
emigrante a. & n. emigrant
emigrar v. emigrate
emisor -a a. emitting, broadcasting
emitir v. emit
emoción n.f. emotion
emocionante a. moving, thrilling, exciting
empachar v. overeat
empacho n.m indigestion
empalme n.m. connection
empanada n.f. meat pie
empanar v. cover with flour before cooking
empanar v. fog up
empapar v. moisten
emparallar v. pair up, match

emparentar v be related by marriage
empaste n.m. filling of a tooth
empatar v. join, splice; tie a score during a game
empate n.m. tie (during a game)
empeña n.f. instep
empeñar v. pawn
empeorar v. worsen
emperador n.m. emperor
emperatriz n.f. empress
empezar v. begin, commence, start
empobrecer v. become or make poor
empoleirar v. climb into the chicken house
empreagado -a n. employed
empregar v. employ, use
empreñar v. impregnate
empresa n.f. enterprise
emprestar v. lend
empurrar v. push
empurrón n.m. push
en prep. in
encabezar v. head, lead
encadear v. chain
encaixar v. encase, enclose, insert
encaixe n.m. lace; act of encasing, of enclosing
encamiñar v. guide
encantador -a a. enchanting

encantar v. enchant
encapricharse v. get a whim or fancy
encargar v. entrust, put in charge
encarnado -a a. incarnate
encerado n.m. waxed; slate, writing surface
encerrar v. enclose, imprison
encestar v. place in a basket
encetar v. begin, start; try
encher v. fill; satisfy, saturate
enchufar v. plug in, connect
enciclopedia n.f. encyclopedia
encima adv. above
encoller v. shrink, contract, shorten
encontrar v. find
encontro n.m. finding
encordiar v. cause annoyance, nuisance
    or irritation
encrespar v. curl up (hair)
encubrir v. hide the truth
endereitar v. straighten, unbend
enderezo n.m. direction
endexamais adv. never
endurecer v. harden
enerxia n.f. energy
enfadar v. anger, annoy, vex
enfado n.m. anger, annoyance, irritation

énfase n.m. emphasis
enfermar n.m. become ill
enfermeiro -a n. nurse
enfermidade n. sickness, illness
enfermo -a a. sick, ill
enferruxar v. rust
enfeteizar v. cast an evil spell
enfiar v. thread a needle
enfoque n.m. focus
enfrontar v. confront
engadir v add
engado n.m. fish bait
engaiolar v. cage
enganar v. cheat
enganchar v. hook, connect
engano n.m. deceit, fraud, deception
engoa n.f. groin
engordar v. make or become fat
engraxar v. grease
engruñar v. limit, confine
engtrega n.f. delivery
engulir v. insert, stuff, pack tightly
engurra n.f. wrinkle
engurrar v. wrinkle
enlace n.m. link
enlatar v. tin

enlazar v. link
enlear v. tangle, get tangled, get embroiled in
enloquecer v. lose one's mind, go mad
enmudecer v. quiet somebody
enorme a. enormous
enoxar V. anoxar
enpadroar v. take a census
enquisa n.f. inquest
enredadeira n.f. ivy
enredar v. tangle
enredo n.m. tangle, entanglement
enriba adv. above
enriquecer v. become rich
enrolar v. enroll
ensaiar v. essay, try out
ensalada n.f. salad
ensalo n.m. essay
ensanguentar v. stain, cover with blood
ensinar v. teach
ensino n.m. teaching
ensuciar v. make dirty
enteiro -a a. entire, whole
entemés n.m. appetizer
entendemento n.m. understanding
entender v. understand
enterrar v. bury, inter

enterro n.m. burial

entidade n.f. entity

entón adv. then

entrada n.f. entrance

entragar v. deliver

entrambas contraction of pr. entre, between & pr. ambas, both

entrambos contraction of pr. entre, between & pr. ambos, both

entrañable a. deep, profound, intimate, close; very dear

entrañas n.f.pl. entrails

entrar v. enter

entre prep. between

entreabrir v. set ajar

entretemento n.m. amusement, pastime

entreter v. amuse, entertain

entrever v. catch a glimpse

entrevista n.f. interview

entrevistar v. interview

entristecer v. make or become sad

entroido n.m. period three days before Lent

entusiasmo n.m. enthusiasm

enumerar v. number

enunciado n.m. enunciation

envase n.m. container

envelenar v. poison
envexa n.f. envy
enviar v. send
envio n.m. sending, remittance, shipment
envoltono n.m. wrapping paper
envolver v. wrap
enxaboar v. lather, soap
enxame n.m. swarm, cluster of bees
enxebre a. regional customs unsoiled by foreign
    influences
enxeñeiro -a n. engineer
enxeño n.m. ingenious
enxerir v. graft
enxerto n.m. graft
enxiva n.f. gum (of the teeth)
enxoito -a a. dry
enxordecer v. make or become deaf
enxugar v. dry
enzoufarse v. speckle, stain
épico -a a. epic
epidemia n.f. epidemic
episodio n.m. episode
época n.f. epoch
equilibrio n.m. equilibrium
equipar v. equip
equipaxe n.f. luggage

equipo n.m. equipment, team (in sports)
equivalente a. & n. equivalent
equivocar v. be mistaken
era n.f. era
erbedeiro n.m. strawberry bush
érbedo V. erbedeiro
erguer v. erect, lift up
ermida n.f. hermitage
erosión n.f. erosion
erótico -a a. erotic
error n.m. error
eructar v. burp
erupción n.f. eruption
esaxerar v. exaggerate
esbardallar v. undo, take apart; talk senselessly
esbirro n.m. sneeze
esborrexer v. sneeze
esbozo n.m. sketch
esbucar v. bore, drill, pierce
escachar v. fragment
escacho V. miñato
escada n.f. ladder
escagallar v. smash, take apart
escaiola n.f. gypsum, plaster
escaiolar v. plaster
escala n.f. scale

escalafrío V. calafrío
escaldar v. scald
escaleira n.f. ladder
escama n.f. scale (of a fish or reptile)
escampar v. cease raining
escáncer n.m. amphisbaenian (tropical amphibian)
escándalo n.m. scandal
escano n.m. bench
escapar v. escape
escaparate n.m. glass display case
escaravellar v. scrape, scratch
escaravello n.m. scarab
escarmentar v. teach a lesson to
escarranchar v. open the legs
escarvar v. scratch
escasear v. be or become scarce
escaso -a a. scarce
escavación n.f. excavation
escavar v. excavate, dig
escena n.f. scene
escenario n.m. stage, scene, setting
escoar v. wring out, drain
escoba V. vasoira
escoitar v. listen
escola n.f. school

escolante n. school teacher
escolar a. scholar
escoller v. pick, choose
escolma n.f. selection, pick
escolta n.f. escort
escondeiro n.m. hiding place
esconder v. hide
escopeta n.f. shotgun
escornar v. gore
escorregar v. slide, slip
escorrentar v. shoo away
escorrer v. wring out, drain
escote n.m. low neck, décolletage
escravo -a n. & a. slave
escribir v. write
escrito -a a. written
escritor -a n. writer
escritorio n.m. desk
escritura n.f. writing
escrupuloso -a a. scrupulous
escuadro n.m. carpenter's square
escudo n.m. shield; Portuguese currency
escultura n.f. sculpture
escuma n.f. froth
escumadeira n.f. skimmer
escurecer v. make or become dark

escuridade n.f. darkness
escuro -a a. dark
escusa n.f. excuse
escusar v. excuse
ese pr. this
esencial a. essential
esfaragullar v. rend, shatter
esfarrapado -a a. broken
esfera n.f.sphere
esfiañar v. shred
esfolar v. skin (an animal)
esfollar v. defoliate
esforzo n.m. effort
esganar v. choke
esgarro n.m. sputum
esgazar v. tear
esgotar v. drain, exhaust, dry, empty, deplete
esixencia n.f. existence
esmagar v. crush, brush
esmalte n.m. enamel
esmeralda n.f. emerald
esmerarse v. take great pains, take care to
esmiuzar v. crumble, break into small pieces
esmola n.f. alms
esmorga n.f. orgy
esnacar V. esnaquizar

esnafrar v. break something with a single blow
esnaquizar v. tear into small pieces
eso V. ese
esófago s.m. esophagus
esoutro -a pr. this one
espacial a. spatial
espacio n.m space
espada n.f. sword
espalda n.f. back
espallar v. expand, extend
español -a a. Spanish
espantallo n.m scarecrow
espantar v. scare, shoo away
espanto n.m. apparition, fright
esparadrapo n.m. adhesive tape
esparagueira (planta) n.f. asparagus plant
espátula n.f. spatula
especial a. special
especialidade n.f. specialty
especialista n. specialist
especie n.f. species
especifico -a a. specific
espéctaculo n.m. spectacle
espectador -a n. spectator
espelido -a a. object or material full of holes
espello n.m. mirror

espera n.f. wait
esperanza n.f. hope
esperar v. wait
espeso -a a. thick
espetar v. nail
espeto -a n.m. spit for roasting meat
espiar v. spy
espido -a a. nude, naked
espiga n.f. spike or ear of grain
espiña n.f. thorn, fish bone
espiñazo n.m. spine
espiño n.m. hawthorn, buckthorn
espir v. take off the clothes
espiral n.f. spiral
espírito n.m. spirit
espléndido -a a. splendid
espontáneo -a a. spontaneous
esponxa n.f. sponge
espora n.f. spur
esposa n.f. wife
esposas n.f.pl. handcuffs
esposo n.m. husband
espreguizar v. stir into activity or action
espremedor n.m. squeezer
espremer v. squeeze
espulla n.f. pimple

espuma V. escuma
esquecer v. forget
esqueleto n.m. skeleton
esquema n.m. sketch
esquerdo -a a. left
esquina n.f. corner
esquivar v. dodge
estable a. stable
establecemento n.m. establishment
establecer v. establish
estaca n.f. stake, stick
estación n.f. station
estadio n.m. stadium
estado n.m. state
estafar v. cheat, swindle
estalar v. explode, burst
estalo n.m. crack, explosion, outburst
estálote V. croque
estampa n.f. print, stamp, mark
estampado -a a. print, stamping
estancar v. stanch, stop
estancia n.f. room
estanco n.m. store where state monopoly goods
    are sold
estaño n.m. tin
estanque n.m. pond, basin, reservoir

estante n.m. shelf
estar v. be
estarricar v. expand
estatal a. relative the state government
estático -a a. static
estatística n.f. statistics
estatua n.f. statue
estatura n.f. height
estatuto n.m. statute
este pr. this
esteiro n.m. estuary
estender v. extend
estercar V. fertilize
esterco n.m. dung, manure
estéril a. sterile
esterno n.m. sternum, breastbone
estético -a a. esthetic
estilo n.m. style
estimar v. estimate, appraise
estimular v. stimulate
estio V. verán
estirar v. stretch, pull
estómago n.m. stomach
estopa n.f. remnant of linen or flax after washing
estorbar v. hinder, hamper, get on the way
estorniño s.m. starling

estoupar v. explode
estoupido n.m. din, clamor
estourar V. estoupar
estoutro -a pr. that one
estrada n.f. road, highway, main road
estragar v. make or make worse
estramonio n.m. thorn apple
estrañar v. alienate
estrangular v. strangle
estraño -a a. alien, strange
estranxciro -a a. foreign
estrar v. spread straw on a stable floor
estratexia n.f. strategy
estrear v. use or wear for the first time
estreitar v. tighten
estreito -a a. tight
estrela n.f. star
estrelar v. shatter
estremecer v. shake, quiver, shudder
estribo n.m. stirrup
estribor n.m. starboard
estricto -a a. strict
estrofa n.f. strophe, stanza, verse
estrondo n.m. noise, boom, din, cracking, blast
estropallo s.m. dish scourer
estructura n.f. structure

estruga V. ortiga

estrume s.m. straw keep animals dry &
  collect waste

estudiante n. student

estudiar v. study

estudio n.m. study; learning

estufa s.f. stove

estufado n.m. stew

estupefaciente a. & n.m narcotic

estupendo -a a. fine, great, super

estúpido -a a. stupid

esvaecer v. cause vanish

esvaradoiro n.m. slippery

esvarar v. slide, slip

esvelto -a a. svelt

etapa n.f. stage

etcétera adv. etc

eternidade n.f. eternity

eterno -a a. eternal

ético -a a. ethical

etiqueta n.f. etiquette

eu pr. I

eucalipto n.m. eucalyptus

europeo -a a. European

eusquera n.m. Basque language

evanxeo n.m. Gospel

evaporar v. evaporate
evasión n.f. escape
evidencia n.f. evidence
evidente a. evident
evitar v. avoid
evolución n.f. evolution
exacto -a a. exact
exaltar v. exalt
exame n.m. examination
excelent a. excellent
excepción n.f. exception
excesivo -a a. excessive
excitar v. excite
exclamación n.f. exclamation
exclamar v. exclaim
exclusivo -a a. exclusive
excremento n.m. excrement
excursión n.f. excursion
executar v. execute
exemplar a. exemplary
exemplo n.m. example
exercer v. exercise, put into practice
exercicio n.m. exercise
exército n.m. army
exilio n.m. exile
existencia n.f. existence

existir v. exist
éxito v. success
expansión n.f. expansion
expedición n.f. expedition
experiencia n.f. experience
experimento n.m. experiment
experto -a a. & n. expert
explicación n.f. explanation
explicar v. explain
explorar v. explore
explosión n.f. explosion
explosivo -a a. explosive
explotación n.f. exploitation
explotar v. exploit
expoñer v. expose
exportar v. export
exposición n.f. exposition
expresar v. express
expresión n.f. expression
expulsar v. expel, eject
exquisito -a a. exquisite
extensión n.f. extension
exterior a. exterior
exterminar v. exterminate
externo -a a. external
extraer v. extract

extraordinario -a a. extraordinary
extravagante a. extravagant
extraviar v. mislead, lead astray
extremidade n.f. extremity
extremo -a a. extreme

F

fa n. fourth note of the musical scale
faba n.f bean
fabada n.f. Asturian stew of pork & beans
fábrica n.f. factory
fabricar v. manufacture, make
fábula n.f fable
fabuloso -a a. fabulous
face n.f. face
facenda n.f ranch, farm
facer v. make
fachada n.f. facade
fachenda n.f. arrogance, ostentation
facho n.m. torch, torch light
fácil a. easy
facilidade n.f. ease
factor n.m. factor
factura n.f. bill, invoice

facultade n.f. faculty
fada n.f. fairy
faena n.f. activity, work
faiado n.m. attic
faixa n.f. girdle
fala n.f. speech
falador -a a. blabber mouth
falar v. speak
falcatrua V. trasnada
falcatruada n.f. misdeed
falla n.f. fault (geology)
falla n.f. imperfection, error, failure
fallar v. fail
fallo n.m. failure, fault
falsificar v. falsify
falso -a a. false
falta n.f. want, lack, deprivation
faltar v. lack
fama n.f. fame
fame n.f. hunger
famento -a a. hungry,
familar a. familiar
familia n.f. family
famoso -a a. famous
fanático -a a. fanatic
faneca n.f. whiting pout

fantasia n.f. fantasy
fantasma n.m. phantasm
fantástico -a a. fantastic
faragulla n.f. crumb
farallón n.m. sharp rock sticking out of the sea
faraón n.m. Pharaoh
farelo n.m. bran
fariña n.f. flour
farinxe n.f. pharynx
farmacéutico -a a. pharmaceutical
farmacia n.f. pharmacy
faro n.m. beacon
farol (pl. farols) n.m. lantern
farola n.f. street lamp
faroleiro -a. pretentious
farrapeiro -a a. ill dressed
farrapo n.m. rag, shred, tattered clothing
farraxeria n.f hardware store
fartar v. gorge, sate, satiate
farto -a a. satiated, full
fartura n.f. satiety, fill, superabundance
fascinar v. fascinate
fascismo n.m. Fascism
fase n.f. phase
fatal a. fatal
fatiga n.f. fatigue, weakness

fatigar v. tire out, fatigue
fato n.m. ensemble
fauna n.f. fauna
favor n.m. favor
favorable a. favorable
favorito -a a. favorite
fazula n.f. cheek
fe n.f. faith
febra n.f. fibra
febre n.f. fever
febreiro n.m. February
fecundo -a a. fecund, fertile
feder v. stink
federación n.f. federation
feira n.f. fair
feirante n. fairgoer
feitizo n.m. charm, spell
feito n.m. fact, act, deed
feitura n.f. manufacture, making
feixe n.m. sheaf, bundle, faggot
fel n.m. gall, bile
felicidade n.f. happiness
felicitar v. congratulate
feliz a. happy
femia n.f. female
feminino -a a. feminine

femur n.m. femur
fender v. cleave, split
fenómeno n.m. phenomenon (pl. phenomena)
fento n.m. fern
feo -a a. ugly
ferida n.f. wound
ferir v. wound
fermento n.m. yeast
fermoso -a a. beautiful
feroz a. wild, fierce
ferrado n.m. measure for grain or surfaces
ferradura n.f. horse shoe
ferramenta n.f. tool
ferrar v. shoe a horse
ferreiro n.m. metal smith
ferro de pasar p. iron
ferro n.m. iron
ferrocarril n.m. railroad
ferrón n.m. sting, prick
ferruxe n.f. rust
fértil a. fertile
fervenza n.f. water rapids
ferver v. boil
festa n.f. feast
festeiro -a a. feast goer
festexar v. entertain, feast

festival n.m. festival
festivo -a a. festive
feto n.m. fetus
feudalismo n.m. feudalism
fiar v. sell on credit
fibela n.f. belt buckle
fibra n.f. fiber
ficción n.f. fiction
ficha n.f. index card
fichar v. file
fichero n.m. filing cabinet
fideo n.m. noodle
fiel a. faithful
fiestra n.f. window
figado n.m. liver
figo n.m. fig
figueira do demo V. estramonio
figueira n.f. fig tree
figura n.f. figure
figurado -a a. figurative, allegoric, metaphorical
fila s.f. file, queue
filba n.f. fritter, wafer, pancake
filla n.f. daughter
fillastro -a n. stepson, stepdaughter
fillo n.m. son
filosofía n.f. philosophy

filtrar v. filter
fin n. end
final a. final
finalizar v. finalize
finanzas n.f.pl. finances
fino -a a. fine; astute
finxir v. fake, feign
fio n.m. thread
firma n.f. industrial firm
firma n.f. signature
firmamento n.m. sky, firmament
firme a. firm
fiscal a. tax collector; public advocate
física n.f. physics
físico -a a. physical
físico -a n. physicist
fita n.f. tape, band, strip
fitar v. stare
fiúncho n.m. fennel
fixar v. fix
fixo -a a. fixed
flamengo n.m. flamingo
flan n.m. caramel or baked custard
flexible a. flexible
floco de millo p. popcorn
floco n.m. fluffy feathers, tuft

flor n.f. flower
flora n.f. flora
florecer v. flower
floreiro n.m. flower vase
flotador n.m. floating device
flotar v. float
fluído -a a. fluid
fluir v. flow
fluvial a. fluvial
fobia n.f. phobia
foca n.f seal
fochanca n.f. empty space
fochicar v. scrape, scratch, pick at
fociño n.m. snout
foco n.m. focus
foder (v.u.) v. engage in sexual intercourse
fogar n.m. kitchen range
fogo n.m. fire
fogueira n.f bonfire
foguete n.m. rocket
fol n.m. bellows
folclore n.m. folklore
folerpa n.f. snow flake
folerpar v. snow
folga n.f. strike
folgazán a. idle, lazy, slothful

folgo n.f. breath, respiration
foliada n.f. noisy night party
folio n.m. sheet
folla n.f. leaf
follaxe n.f. foliage
folleto n.m. pamphlet
fonda n.f. inn
fondo -a a. deep
fondo n.m. bottom
fontaneiro n. water works attendant
fonte n.f. fountain
fora adv. outside
forasteiro -a a. foreign
forca n.f. pitchfork
forma n.f. form
formación n.f. formation
formal a. formal
formar v. form
formidable a. formidable
formiga n.f. ant
formigón n.m. reinforced concrete
formigueiro n.m. ant hill
fórmula n.f. formula
fornada n.f. batch, baking bread
fornecer v. supply
fornicar v. have illicit sexual relations

forno n.m. oven
forrar v. cover
forro n.m. cover
fortaleza n.f. fortress
forte a. strong
fortuna n.f. fortune
forxa n.f. forge
forza n.f. strength
fosa n.f. grave
fósforo n.m. match
fósil a &. n.m. fossil
fotocopia n.f. photocopy
fotografía n.f. photography
fotógrafo -a n. photographer
fotosintese n.f. photosynthesis
fotoxénico -a a. photogenic
fouciño n.m. sickle
foxo n.m. pit, ditch
fozar v. dig a pit
fracasar v. fail
fracción n.f. fraction
fraco -a a. thin, slender
frade n.m. friar
fraga n.f. thicket of brambles
fragmento n.m. fragment
fragua n.f. forge

francés -a a. French
franxa n.f. fringe, band, strip
frasco n.m. bottle
frase n.f. phrase
fraternal a. fraternal
fraude n.m. fraud
frauta n.f. flute
fráxil a. fragile
frear v. brake
frecha n.f. arrow
frecuente a. frequent
fregar v. scrub, scour
fregona n.f. scrubbing brush
fregués -a n. person belonging a parish
freguesía n.f. parish
freira n.f. nun
freiro n.m. monk
freixo n.m. ash tree
freixó n.m. pancake
freo s.m. brake
fresco -a a. cool
friame n.m. cold meat
friaxe n.f. coldness
frigorífico -a n. refrigerator
frio -a a. cold
fritir v. fry

frixideira n.f. frying pan
froita n.f. fruit
froitero -a a. & n. fruit
fronte n.f. forehead
fronteira n.f. frontier
frouxo -a a. weak, feeble, timid
frustrar v. frustrate
fuga n.f. escape, flight
fulano -a n. John Doe
fumador -a a. & n. smoker
fumar v. smoke
fume n.m. smoke
fumegar v. expel smoke
fumeiro n.m. place smoke sausages
fumigar v. fumigate
función n.f. function
funcionar v. function
funda n.f. slip, sheath
fundación n.f. foundation
fundamental a. fundamental
fundar v. found
fundir v. melt
fúnebre a. mournful
funeral (pl. funerais) n.m. funeral
fungar v. mutter, grumble, whimper
fungo n.m. fungus

funil (pl. funis) n.m. funnel
funxicide n.f. fungicide
furacán (pl. furacáns) n.m. hurricane
furado n.m. hole
furar v. drill, bore, pierce
furgoneta n.f. van
furia n.f. fury
furioso -a a. furious
furón (pl. furóns) n.m. ferret
furtivo -a a. furtive
furuncho n.m. boil
fusco -a a. sullen
fuselaxe n.m. fuselage
fusil (pl. fusís) n.m. rifle
fusilar v. execute by firing squad
futbol (pl. futboles) n.m. football
futbolist n. football player
fútil (pl. fútiles) a. futile
futuro -a a. future
fuxir v. flee, escape
fuxitivo -a a. & n. fugitive

G

gabán (pl. gabáns) n.m. overcoat
gabanza n.f praise, eulogy, laud

gabar v. praise, laud

gabardina n.f. gabardine, raincoat

gabeta n.f. drawer

gabia n.f trench

gabián n.m hawk

gabinete n.m. ensemble of government ministers

gabinete n.m. studio

gadaña n.f. scythe

gaditano -a a. pertaining or inhabitant of Cadix

gado V. gando

gaélico -a a. Celtic languages spoken in Ireland and Scotland

gafas V. lentes

gaio n.m. jay (bird)

gaita n.f. bagpipe

gaitero -a n. bagpipe player

gaivota n.f. gull, sea gull

gala n.f. gala, elegance; full or court dress

galardón n.m. reward, recompense, prize

galaxia n.f. galaxy

galbana n.f. idleness, loafing, sloth

galego -a a. Galician; language spoken in Galicia

galeguismo n.m. beliefs & actions in defense of Galicia

galés -a a. pertaining or inhabitant of Wales

galgo n.m. greyhound

galiña de rio n.f. grouse
galiña n.f. hen
galiñeiro n.m. hen house
galiñola V. galiña de rio
galla n.f. branch (of a tree)
galleta n.f. biscuit
galo -a a. pertaining Gallia (Gaul), or modern France
galo n.m. rooster
galopar v. trot
galope n.m. trot
galopín -a a. & n. rascal, scoundrel
gama n.f. gamut, scale, series or range
gama n.f. third letter of the Greek alphabet
gamba n.f. crawfish, prawn
gana n.f. wish
ganancia n.f. earning
gañar V. ganar
ganar v. win
gancho n.m. hook, hairpin
gandeiro -a a. concerning livestock
gandería n.f. animal husbandry
gando n.m. cattle
ganga n.f. bargain
gaño n.m. gain
ganso -a n. goose
gaoila n.f. cage

garabato n.m. scribble, scrawl
garabullo n.m. kindling wood
garantía n.f. guarantee
garantir v. guarantee
garavanzo n.m. garbanzo
garaxe n.m. garage
garda n.f. guard
gardacostas n.m. coast guard
gardameta n. goal keeper
gardar v. guard
gardería n.f. day-nursery
garfo n.m. hook
gargallada n.f. guffaw
garganta n.f. throat
garrafa n.f. carafe, decanter
gas n.m. gas
gasa n.f. gauze, muslin
gaseoso -a V. gasoso
gasolina n.f, gasoline
gasolineira n.f. gas station
gasoso -a a. gaseous
gastar v. spend
gasto n.m. expenditure
gastronomía n.f. gastronomy
gatear n.m. crawl
gatiño n.m. kitten

gato -a n. cat

gaucho -a a. & n. inhabitant of South American pampas

gavela n.f. armful

gavilán V. gabián

gheada n.f. sound of the letter g in Galician

glaciar s.m. glacier

glándula n.f. gland

globo n.m. globe

glóbulo n.m. globule

gloria n.f. glory

gobernador -a n. governor

gobernar v. govern

gobierno n.m. government

gol n.m. goal (in sports)

golfiño n.m. dolphin

golfo n.m. golf

golpe n.m. fox in northern Galicia

golpe n.m. strike, blow

golpear v. strike, hit

goma n.f. gum

gordo -a a. fat, obese

gordura n.f. fatness

gorida n.f. den, lair

gorila n.m. gorilla

gorra n.f. cap

gorrión V. pardal
gorro n.m. cap, bonnet
gorza n.f. throat, gullet
gota n.f. drop
gotear v. drop, drip
gótico -a a. Gothic
gozar v. enjoy
grabar V. gravar
gracia n.f. grace
gracioso -a a. funny
grade n.f. grille, grate
graduar v. graduate
gralla (ave) n.f raven, rook (bird)
gramo n.m. gram
grampa n.f. clamp, clasp
gran a. grand
gran n.m. grain
granate a. garnet; dark red
grande a. big
grandeza n.f. bigness
graneiro n.m. granary, barn
granito n.m. granite
granxa n.f. grange, farm, farmhouse
grao n.m. grade
gratis a. free
grato -a a. pleasant, pleasing, agreeable

gratuito -a a. free of charge; without base or reason
grava n.f. gravel
gravar v. engrave
gravata n.f. tie
grave a. grave, serious, burdensome
gravidade n.f. gravity, seriousness
graxo -a a. greasy
grego -a a. Greek
grella n.f. grill
greta n.f. crevice, crack
grilo n.m. cricket
grima n.f. malaise or uneasiness
gripe n.f. influenza
gris a. grey
gritar v. shout
grito n.m. shout
grolo n.m. sip
groseiro -a a. gross, rude, coarse
groso -a a. thick
grosor n.m. girth
grou (ave) n.m. crane (bird)
gruta n.f. grotto
guante n.m. glove
guapo -a a. good looking
guardia V. garda
guarida V. gorida

guedella n.f. mop of unruly, long hair

gueixa n.f. geisha

guerla n.f. one of gills in fish

guerra n.f. war

guerrear v. make war

gueto n.m. gheto

guía n. guide

guiar v. guide, lead

guinche V. guindastre

guinda n.f. cherry

guindar v. throw

guindastre n.m. crane

guindeira n.f. cherry tree

guión (pl. guións) n.m. script (as for a movie)

guisar v. stew

guiso n.m. stew

guitarra n.f. guitar

gula n.f. gluttony

gume n.m. edge, cutting or sharp edge of a
cutting tool

gustar v. like

gusto n.m. taste, flavor

H

habano -a a. & n. pertaining or inhabitant of Havana, Cuba

habano n.m. cigar made in Cuba

habelencia n.f. ability, dexterity

haber n.m. property, income

haber v. happen, take place

hábil a. able, skillful

habilidade n.f. ability

habitante n. inhabitant

habitar v. inhabit, dwell

habitual a. habitual

halar v. pull

hamaca n.f. hammock

harén (pl. haréns) n.m. harem

harmonía n.f. harmony

harmoninioso -a a. harmonious

hastra V. ata

hebreo -a a. Hebrew

hectárea n.f. hectare

hedra n.f. ivy

hélice n.f. helix, spiral

helicóptero n.m. helicopter

hemisfeno n.m. hemisphere

hemorraxia n.f. hemorrhage

hepatite n.f. hepatitis
herba aguilleira n.f. dill
herba de San Xoan V. croque
herba do demo V. estramonio
herba n.f. herb
herba paxareira n.f. chickweed, stitchwort
herbivoro -a a. herbivore
herdar v. inherit
herdeiro -a n. heir, heiress
hermético -a a. hermetic
hernia n.f. hernia
heroe n.m. hero
heroína n.f. heroine
hidroavión n.m. hydroplane
hidróxeno n.m. hydrogen
himno n.m. hymn
hindú a. & n. Hindu
hipnotizar v. hypnotize
hipócrita a. & n. hypocrite
hipódromo n.m. race track
hipopótamo n.m. hippopotamus
historia n.f. history
historico -a a. historical
hixiene n.f. hygiene
homaxe V. homenaxe
hombro V. ombro

home n.m. man
homenaxe n.f. homage
homicide n.f. homicide
homosexual a. & n. homosexual
homoxéneo -a a. homogeneous
honesto -a a. honest
honra n.f. honor
honrado -a a. honorable, decent
hora n.f. hour
horario n.m. schedule
horizontal a. horizontal
horizonte n.m. horizon
horóscopo n.m. horoscope
hórreo n.m. silo
horta n.f. vegetable garden
hortaliza n.f. vegetable
hortelá n.f. mint
hortensia n.f. hydrangea
hospede n. lodger
hospital n.m. hospital
hostal n.m. hostel, inn
hostia n.f. host (church liturgy)
hostil a. hostile
hotel n.m. hotel
hoxe adv. today
hucha n.f. chest, trunk

hule n.m. oil cloth
humanidade n.f. humanity
humano -a a. human
húmedo -a a. humid
humidade n.f. humidity
humilde a. humble
humillación n.f. humiliation
humillar v. humiliate, humble
humor n.m. humor
huno -a a. & n. Hun

I

iarda n.f. yard
iate n.m. yacht
ibérico -a a. Iberian, pertaining the Iberian peninsula
iceberg n.m. iceberg V. also tempano
icona n.f. icon
idade n.f. age
idea n.f. idea
ideal a. ideal
idéntico -a a. identical
identidade n.f identity
identificar v. identify

ideoloxía n.f ideology
idioma n.m. language
idiota a. idiot
ídolo n.m idol
idóneo -a a. fit, suitable
ignorancia n.f. ignorance
ignorante a. ignorant
ignorar v. ignore
igrexa n.f. church
igual a. equal
igualar v. equalize
il pr. he
ilegal a. illegal
ileso -a a. unhurt, uninjured
illa n.f. isla
illar n.m. flank
illar v. isolate
iluminación n.f. illumination
ilusión n.f. illusion
ilusionar v. fill with hope & expectation
ilustración n.f. illustration
ilustre a. illustrious
imán n.m magnet
imaxe n.f. image
imaxinación n.f. imagination
imaxinar v. image

imbécil a. imbecile
imitar v. imitate
impaciente a. inpatient
impar a. odd, unven
impar v. pant, sob
imparcial a. impartial
impecable a. impeccable
impedir v. impide, hinder, obstruct
imperativo -a a. imperative
imperdible n.m. safety pin
imperfecto -a a. imperfect
imperio n.m. empire
impermeable a. impermeable
impertinente a. & n. impertinent
implicar v. implicate
imponer v. impose
importación n.f. import
importancia n.f. importance
importante a. important
importar v. import
imposible a. impossible
imposto n.m. tax
impreciso -a a. imprecise, vague
imprenta n.f. printing
imprescindible a. indispensable
impresión n.f. impression, printing

impresionar v. impress, affect deeply
impreso n.m. printed matter
imprevisto -a a. unforeseen, unexpected
imprimir v. print
improvisar v. improvise
impulsar v. impel, urge on
impulso n.m. impulse
inauguración n.f. inauguration
inaugurar v. inaugurate
incapaz a. incapable, unable, unfit
incendiar v. set on fire
incendio n.m. fire
incerto -a a. uncertain
inchar v. swell
incident n.m. incident
incisivo -a a. incisive
incitar v. incite
inclinación n.f. inclination
inclinar v incline
incluir v. include
incluso adv. including
incógnito -a a. unknown
incoherent a. incoherent
incoloro -a a. colorless
incómodo -a a. inconvenient
incompleto -a a. incomplete

inconsciente a. flimsy, unconscious
inconveniente a. inconvenient
inconvinte V. inconveniente
incorporar v. incorporate
incorrecto -a a. incorrect
incrementar v. increment
incrible a. incredible
incubadora n.f. incubator
incubar v. incubate
inculto -a a. uneducated
indecente a. & n. indecent
indeciso -a. indecisive
indefinido -a a. indefinite
indemnizar v. indemnify, compensate
independencia n.f. independence
independente a. independent
indeterminado -a a indeterminate
indicación n.f. indication
indicar v. indicate
índice a. & n.m. index
indición V. inxección
indiferent a. indifferent
indignación n.f. indignation
indigno -a a. unworthy,
indio -a a. Hindu, pertaining India; original inhabitant of the Americas

indirecto -a a. indirect
indiscreto -a a. indiscreet
indisposto -a a. indisposed
individual a. individual
individuo n.m. individual
indíxena a. & n. indigenous
indixestión n.f. indigestion
indulxente a. indulgent, lenient
industria n.f. industry
inercia n.f. inertia
inestable a. unstable
inevitable a. inevitable
infancia n.f. infancy
infantil a. infantile
infarto n.m. infarct
infección n.f. infection
infectar v. infect
inferior a. inferior
inferioridad n.f. inferiority
inferno n.m. hell
infiel (pl. infieis) a. unfaithful, infidel
infinito -a a. infinite
inflamable a. flammable
inflamar v. inflame
inflar v. inflate
influencia n.f. influence

influir v. influence
información n.f. information
informar v. inform
infusión n.f. infusion
inglés -a a. English
ingrato -a a. ungrateful
ingrediente n.m. ingredient
ingresar v. enter, join
ingreso n.m. entrance, admission
inhumano -a a. inhuman
inicial a. initial
iniciar v. initiate
iniciativa n.f. initiative
inimigo -a a. & n. foe, enemy
inmediato -a a. immediate
inmenso -a a. immense, huge
inmigrar v. immigrate
inmóbil a. immovable
inmoble a. immovable (real estate)
inmortal a. immortal
innovación n.f. innovation
innumerable a. innumerable
inocencia n.f. innocence
inocent a. innocent
inodoro -a a. odorless
inodoro n.m. toilet

inofensivo -a a. inoffensive
inoportuno -a a. inopportune
iñorar V. ignorar
inprudencia n.f. imprudence
inquedo -a a. restless
inquilino -a n. renter
inquitude n.f. restlessness
insá (pl. insás) a.f. insane
insán (pl. insáns) a.f. insane
inscrición n.f. inscription
insecticida a. & n.f. insecticide
insecto n.m. insect
inseguro -a a. insecure
insensato -a a. & n. crazy, wild
insignia n.f. decoration, badge
insignificante a. insignificant
insinuar v. insinuate
insípido -a a. tasteless, insipid
insistir v. insist
insolación n.f. sunstroke, heat stroke
insólito -a a. unusual
insomnio n.m. insomnia
insoportable a. intolerable
inspector -a n. inspector
inspirar v. inspire, inhale
instalación n.f. installation

instalar v. install
instant n.m. instant
instantáneo -a a. instantaneous
instinto n.m. instinct
institución n.f. institution
instituir v. institute
instituto n.m. institute
instruir v. instruct
instrumento n.m. instrument
insuficiente a. insufficient
insultar v. insult
insulto n.m. insult
integrar v. integrate
intelectual a. intellectual
intelixencia n.f. intelligence
intelixente a. intelligent
intención n.f. intention
intenso -a a. intense
intentar v. try, attempt
intento n.m. attempt, try
intercambiar v. interchange
interesante a. interesting
interesar v. interest
interese n.m. interest
interior a. interior
intermedio -a a. intermediate

intermitente a. intermittent
internacional a. international
internar v. intern, detain
interno -a a. internal
intérprete n. interpreter
interrogación n.f. interrogation
interrogar v. interrogate
interromper v. interrupt
interruptor -a a. & n.m. circuit breaker, switch
intervalo n.m. interval
intervención n.f. intervention
intervir v. intervene
intestino n.m. intestine
intimidade n.f. intimacy
íntimo -a a. intimate
intoxicar n. poison
intransixente a. intransigent, uncompromising
introducción n.f. introduction
introducir v. introduce
intuición n.f. intuition
inundación n.f. flooding
inútil a. useless
invadir v. invade
inválido -a a. invalid
invasor -a a. & n. invader
inventar v. invent

invento n.m. invention
inventor -a a. & n. inventor
invernadoiro n.m. hot house
inverno n.m. winter
inverso -a a. inverse
invertebrado -a a. & n.invertebrate
inverter v. invert, reverse
investigar v. investigate
invisible a. invisible
invitación n.f. invitation
invitar v. invite
involuntarlo -a a. involuntary
inxección n.f. injection
inxenuo -a a. naive
inxustiza n.f. injustice
inxusto -a a. unfair
inzar v. reproduce
iodo n.m. iodine
iogur n.m. yogurt
ir v. go
ira n.f. ire
iris n.m. iris (of the eye)
irma n.f. sister
irmán n.m. brother
ironía n.f. irony
irreal a. unreal

irregular a. irregular
irritar v. irritate, vex, annoy
ise pr. V. ese
islamismo n.m. Islam
iso pr. V. ese
istmo n.m. isthmus
isto pr. V. este
italiano -a a. Italian
iuca n.f. yucca

L

la art.f. the
la n.f. wool
la n.m. sixth note of the musical scale
la pr.f. her
labarada n.f. flame
labazada n.f. slap on the face
laberinto n.m. labyrinth
labio n.m. lip
labor n.m. labor, work
laboratorio n.m. laboratory
labrador -a V. labrego
labranza n.f. farming,
labrar v. work, plow, cultivate

labrego -a n. farm hand, peasant
laca n.f lacquer
lacaio n.m. foot soldier; lackey
lacazán -a a. & n. idle, slothful, lazy
lacena n.f. cupboard
lacón n.m. front leg of pork, salted or cured
lácteo -a a. milky, lactic
ladear v. tilt, tip, turn on one's side
lado n.m. side
ladrar v. bark
ladrillo n.m. brick
ladroa n.f. thief
ladrón n.m. thief
lagarta n.f. small lizard
lagartixa V. lagarta
lagarto n.m. small lizard
lago n.m. lake
lagoa n.f. small lake,
lagosta n.f. locust (insect), crab (marine animal)
lagostino n.m. giant or king prawn
lagrima n.f tear
laiar v. moan, groan
laido n.m. yell, howl, scream
lama n.f. mud, mire
lamber v. lick
lamberetada n.f. tasty

lambetada V. lamberetada
lamboa a. & n.f. glutton
lambón a. & m.n. glutton
lameiro -a a. muddy place
lamentar v. lament, mourn, bewail
lámina n.f. plate, sheet
lámpada n.f. lamp, lantern
lampo n.m. lightning
lamprea n.f. lamprey
lan V. la
lancha n.f. launch
landra n.f. fruit from the oak tree
langosta V. lagosta
langostino V. lagostino
lanterna n.f. lantern
lanza n.f. lance
lanzar v. launch
lapa (molusco) n.f limpet (mollusk)
lapa n.f. limpet (type of sea shell)
lapa n.f. smoke
lapada n.f. slap
lapar v. swallow, gulp
laparada n.f. flame
lapela n.f. lapel
lápida n.f. memorial stone
lapis n.m. pencil

lapón V. larpeiro
lapote V. lapada
lar n.m. hearth, home
larada n.f. bonfire
laranxa n.f. orange (fruit & color)
laranxeira n.f. orange tree
lareira n.f. space devoted eating in Galician
    kitchens
largo -a a. long
largura n.f. length
larinxe n.f. larynx
larpar V. lapar
larpeirada n.f. tasty morsel
larpeiro -a a. tasty
larva n.f. larva
lastre n.m. ballast (ship)
lata n.f. tin
latar v. miss (a class), be negligent
lateral a. lateral
latexar v. beat
latifundio n.m. large landed estate
latín (pl. latins) n.m. Latin
latitude n.f. latitude
latón (pl. latóns) m. brass
latricar v. chatter, jabber
lava n.f. lava

lavabo n.m. washstand, basin
lavadoiro n.m. washing place
lavadora n.f. washing machine
lavalouza n.f. dish washing machine
lavanda n.f. lavender
lavandeira n.f. laundry
lavar v. wash
laverca n.f. lark (bird)
laxe n.f. flag stone, slab
lazada n.f. shoe lace
lazo n.m. ice cap
lazo n.m. lasso
lear v. tackle, (try) cope or deal with
lebre n.m. hare
lección n.f. lesson
lectura n.f. lecture
ledicia n.f. delicacy, delight
ledo -a a. happy, ecstatic
legal a. legal
legua n.f. league, measurement equivalent 5½ km.
legume n.m. legume
lei n.f. law
leira s.f. farm
leite s.m. milk
leiteiro -a a. dairy
leito n.m. cama

leitón (pl. leitóns) n.m. piglet, suckling pig
leituga n.f. lettuce
lembranza n.f. remembrance, memory
lembrar v. remember
leña n.f. fire or kindling wood
lena n.f. idle chit chat
lenda n.f. legend, tradition
lendia n.f. nit
lene a. soft, tactful
lente n.f. lens
lentella n.f. lentil
lento -a a. slow
lenzo n.m. canvas, linen
leoa n.f, lioness
león n.m. lion
lepra n.f. leprosy
ler v. read
lercho -a a. & n. (v.u.) shameless person, a failure
lesbiana a. lesbian
lesión n.f. lesion
lesma n.f. snail, slug
leste n.m. east
letargo n.m. lethargy
letra n.f. letter
letreiro n.m label, sign, notice
levantar v. raise

levante n.m. Levant

levar n. carry

levedar v. raise as a result of fermentation

lexia V. lixivia

léxico n.m. lexicon

lexítimo -a a. legitimate

lexos V. lonxe

liberal a. & n. liberal

liberar v. liberate

libertade n.f. liberty

libra (unidade de mocda) n.f. pound (unit of currency)

libra (unidade de peso) n.f. pound (unit of weight)

librar V. liberar

libre a. free

libreiro -a a. bookseller

librería n.f. bookstore

libreta V. caderno

libro n.m. book

licencia n.f. license

licor n.m. liquor

lider n. lider

liga n.f. league

ligar v. link

lila n.f. lilac

lima (ferramenta) n.f. file (tool)

lima (froita) n.f. lime (fruit)
limar v. file one's nails
limitar v. limit
límite n.m. limit
limoeiro n.m. lemon tree
limón s.m. lemon
limpar v. clean
limpo -a a. clean
liña n.f. line
liñaceiro V. pintarroxo
lince V. lobo cerval
lindar v. border, be contiguous
lindeiro n.m. contiguous, bordering
lingaxe n.f. language
lingua n.f. tongue
linguado n.m. sole (fish)
liño n.m. flax, linen
lintel n.m. lintel
liorta n.f. squabble
líquido -a a. & n. liquid
lírico -a a. lyric
lirio (animal) n.m. dormouse
lirio (planta) n.m. lily
lis n.m. iris, fleur-de-lis
liscanzo V. escáncer
liso -a a. smooth

lista n.f. list
listo-a a. ready
literario -a a. literary
litoral n.m. litoral
litro n.m. litter
lixa n.f. sand paper
lixeiro -a a. fast
lixivia n.f. liquid starch
lixo n.m. speck of dirt
lla pr contraction of lle & a
llama n.f. llama (South American mammal)
llas pr contraction of lle & as
lle pr.sing. he
llela sing. contraction of pr. lles & pr. as
llelo pr. contraction of pr. lles & pr. a eles, a elas
llo pr. contraction of lle & o
llos pr contraction of pr. lle & os
loar v. praise, eulogize
lobo ceval n.m. lynx
logo adv. then, next, afterwards
lograr v. attain
loiro V. louro
loita n.f. fight
loitar v. fight
loito n.m. mourning
lombo n.m. back

lombriga n.m. worm
lona n.f. canvas
longo -a a. long
lonxa n.f. fish market
lonxe adv. remote, distant, far away
lonxitude n.f. longitude
lostregar v. flash with lightning
lostrego n.m. lightning
lote n.m. lot
lotería n.f. lottery
louco -a a. & n. crazy
loucura n.f. madness
loureiro n.m. laurel tree
louro -a a. blond
lousa n.f. flagstone, slab
louvar v. loar
louza n.f. china, earthenware
lóxico -a a. logical
lúa de miel n. honeymoon
lúa n.f. moon
luar n.f. lunar
lucecú (pl. lucecús) n.m. firefly
luceiro n.m. bright star
lucio n.m. pike
lucir v. light up, display
lugar n.m. place

lugués -a a. inhabitant of Lugo
lumbago n.m. lumbago
lumbrigante n.m. lobster
lume n.m. flame
luminoso -a a. luminous
lunar a. lunar
luns n.m. Monday
lupa n.f. magnifying glass
lura n.f. octopus
luscofusco n.m. dusk
lusquefusque V. luscofusco
lustro n.m. period of five years
luva n.f. glove
luxo n.m. luxury
luxoso -a a. luxurious
luz n.f. light

M

ma contraction of pr. me & art. a
macaco n.m. monkey, macaque
macarrón n.m. macaroon
macedonia n.f. fruit cocktail
maceira n.f. apple tree
macela n.f. chamomile

maceta n.f. flower pot
machado n.m. ax, axe
machete n.m. machete
macho n.m. male
macizo -a a. solid, massive
madeira n.f. wood, timber
madeixa n.f. skein
madrasta n.f. stepmother
madre n.f. mother
madreselva n.f. honeysuckle
madriña n.f. godmother
madrugada n.f. early morning
madrugar v. rise or get up early
maduro -a a. ripe
maestro -a V. mestre
magnético -a a. magnetic
magnífico -a a. magnificent
magnolia n.f. magnolia
mago -a n. magician
mágoa n.f. sorrow, grief
magoar v. hurt, wound, bruise
magosto n.m. bonfire (to roast chestnuts), meal
    of roasted chestnuts & wine
mai V. nai
maila contraction of conj. mais, more, & art la, the
mailo contraction of conj. mais, more, & art lo, the

maimiño -a a. tender, small

maimiño n.m. small toe

maino -a a. soft

mainzo V. millo

maio n.m. May

maionesa n.f. mayonnaise

maior a. mayor

maioría n.f. majority

mais conj. more

malúsculo a a. & n. capital letter

mal n.m. evil

mala herba V. xoio

maldade n.f. wickedness, evil

maldicir v. damn, curse

maldito -a a. cursed

maleducado -a a. & n. impolite

malentendido n.m. misunderstood

malestar n.m. malaise, uneasiness

maleta n.f. suitcase, valise

maleteiro n.m porter at a train station

malgastar v. misspend, squander

malia conj. in spite of

malicia n.f. malice

malicioso -a a. malicious

malla s.f. act of separating the wheat from the chaff

mallar v. separate the wheat from the chaff

malleira n.f. beating, thrashing
malo -a a. bad
malpocado -a a. lacking resolution, timid
maltratar v. ill treat
malva n.f. mallow
mamá n.f. mother
mama n.f. udder
mamadeira n.f. nursing bottle
mamar v. suckle
mamífero -a a. & n. mammal
mamiño V. maimiño
man n.f. hand
mañá n.f. morning
maña n.f. skill, knack, cleverness
manancial n.m. flowing, running
mañancina n.f. early morning hours
manar v. pour forth
mancar v. main, cripple, disable
mancha n.f. spot, stain, blot
manchar v. stain
manco -a a. & n. one-handed, one armed person
mandado -a n. errand
mandamento n.m. commandment
mandar v. order, command
mandarina n.f. mandarin (fruit)
mandato n.m. mandate

mandíbula n.f. mandible
mandilón n.m. smock
mandilón.m. apron
mando n.m. command, order
maneira ns.f. manner
manexar v. manage, handle
manga n.f. sleeve
mango n.m. handle
mangonear v. act in a selfish manner
mangueira n.f. hose
manía n.f mania
maniático -a a. & n. maniacal, crazy
manicomio n.m. mental hospital
manifestación n.f. manifestation, declaration
manifestar v. manifest, show
maniño V. maimiño
maniotas n.f.pl. muscle strains
manipular v. manipulate
manivela n.f. crank, handle
manobra n.f. maneuver
manopla n.f. gauntlet, mitten
mañoso -a a. skillful, clever, crafty, cunning
manoxo V. monllo
manso -a a. meek, tame
manta n.f. blanket
manta n.f. manta (fish)

manteiga n.f. lard
mantel n.m. table cloth
mantenza n.f. feed, fodder
manter v. feed
mantido a. well fed, sated
manto n.m. mantle
manual a. manual
manuscrito -a a. manuscript
manzanilla V. macela
mao V. man
mapa n.m. map
maqueta n.f. model (architectural)
maquillaxe n.f. make-up
máquina n.f. machine
maquinaria n.f. machinery
mar n.m. sea
marabilla n.f. marvel
marabilloso -a a. marvelous
marca n.f. mark
marcar v. mark
marchar v. march
marco n.m. frame
marear v. get seasick
marelo V. amarelo
mareo n.m. seasickness
marfil n.m. marble

margarida n.f. margarita (flower)
maricas a. & s.m. homosexuals
maricón V. maricas
marido n.m. husband
mariñeiro -a n. sailor
mariño -a a. maritime
marioneta n.f. puppet
marisco n.m. shellfish
marítimo -a a. maritime, marine
marmelada n.f. marmalade, jam
marmeleiro n.m. quince tree
marmelo n.m. quince
mármore n.m. marble
marmota n.f. woodchuck
marmular V. murmurar
marqués n.m. marquis
marquesa n.f. marchioness
marrón a. brown
marta n.f. marten, pine marten, minx
marta zibelina n,f. sable
martelo n.m. hammer
martes n.m. Tuesday
martir n. martyr
martuza V. marta
maruca n.f. bass
marusia n.f. agitation, tossing of sea waves

marxe n.f. margin, border, edge
marxinal a. marginal
marzo n.m. March
masa s.f. mass, dough
masaxe n.f. massage
mascar v. chew
máscara n.f. mask
masculino -a a. masculine
maseira n.f. feeding trough
mastigar v. chew
mastro n.m. mast
masturbar v. masturbate
matadoiro n.m. slaughter house, abattoir
matanza n.f. killing
matapiollos V. polgar
matar v. kill
maté (arbusto) n.m. maté, herba mate
matemático -a a. mathematical
materia n.f. matter
material a. material
materno -a a. maternal
matinar v. mull over
matiz (diferencia de grao) n.m. nuance
matiz (gradacions de mesma cor) n.m. tint,
   hue, shade
matrícula n.f. register, list

matricular v. enroll
matrimonio n.m. matrimony
matriz n.f. chief, head; womb
mau V. man
maxia n.f. magic
máxico -a a. magical
maxilar a & s.m.
máximo -a a. & s.m. maximum (sing), maxima (pl)
maxín n.m. imagination
maxinar v. imagine
maxistrado -a n. magistrate
mazá (froita) n.f. apple
mazá n.f. mace
mazaira V. maceira
mazapán n.m. marzipan
mazar v. pound, crush, mash
mazarico (paxaro) n.m. woodpecker (bird)
mazo n.m. mallet, maul
mazorca n.f. ear or spike of grain
me pr. me
meandro n.m. meander
mear v. bleat
mecánico -a a. mechanical
mecánico -a n. mechanic
mecanismo n.m. mechanism
mecanografía n.f. typing

mecha n.f. wick, fuse
meda n.f. stack, heap, pile
medalla n.f. medallion, medal
medeiro V. meda
media n.f. stocking
medianiño V. anular
mediano -a a. middling, moderate, mediocre, average
mediante prep. intervening
mediar v. mediate, intervene
medicina n.f. medicine
médico -a a. physician
medida n.f. measurement
medieval a. medieval
medio -a a. half
mediodia n.m. midday
mediterráneo -a a. Mediterranean
medo n.m. fear
medoñento -a a. fearful
medrar v. grow
medula n.f. medulla, bone marrow
meiga -a a. coy
meixela n.f. cheek
mel n.m. honey
melancolía n.f. melancholy
melena n.f. mane

melga (peixe) n.f. fox shark
mélica (planta) n.f. melic
melisa n.f. lemon or garden balm
mellor a. better
mellora n.f. improvement, betterment
melocotoeiro n.m. peach tree
melocotón n.m. peach
melón n.m. melon
membrana n.f. membrane
membro n.m. member
memoria n.f. memory
menciña n.f. medicine, medicinal substance
menciñeiro -a n. healer
mendigo -a n. beggar
mene n.f. mind
meneiro a. miner
meniño -a n. infant
meninxite n.f. meningitis
menor a. minor
menos adv. less
mensaxe n.s. message
menstruación n.f. menstruation
mensual a. monthly
menta n.f. mint
mental a. mental
mentalidad n.s. mentality

mentir v. lie
mentira n.f. lie, falsehood, fib
mentireiro -a a. liar
mentres conj. & a while
mercado n.m. market
mercadoría n.f. merchandise
mercar v. acquire
mercería n.f. dry good store
mércores de cinzas p. Ash Wednesday
mércores n.m. Wednesday
merda n.f. shit (v.u.)
merecer v. merit
merenda campestre p. picnic
merenda n.f. afternoon snack
merendar v. have a snack
merengue n.m. meringue
meretriz V. prostituta
mergullador -a n. diver
meridiano n.m. meridian
mérito n.m. merit
merla V. merlo
merlo -a n. blackbird
mes n.m. month
mesa n.f. table
mesmo -a a. & pr. same
mesto -a a. mixed

mestra n.f. teacher
mestre n.m. teacher
mestura n.f. mixture
mesturar v. mix
meta n.f. goal, aim
metade n.f. half
metal n.m. metal
metálico -a a. metallic
metamorfose n.f. metamorphosis
meteoro n.m. meteor
meter v. put, place, shove, stick
método n.m. method
metralladora n.f. machine gun
metro n.m. meter
metro n.m. subway
meu pr. my
mexar v. urinate
mexillón n.m. mussel
mexo V. urina
mi n.m. third note of the musical scale
miañar v. mew
microbio n.m. microbe
micrófono n.m. microphone
miga n.f. crumb
migala V. miga
mil pr. one thousand

milagre n.m, miracle
milímetro n.m. millimeter
militar a. military
millar s.m. one thousand
milleiro V. millar
millo n.m. corn
millón n.m. one million
millor V. mellor
mimosa n.f. mimosa
mina pr. f. mine
miñato (peixe) n.m. flying gournard (fish)
miñato n.m. hawk
mincha n.f. sea snail
mineral n.m. mineral
minguante a. & n.f. diminishing, decreasing
mínimo -a a. & s.m. minimum
ministerio n.m. ministry
ministro -a n. minister
miñoca n.f. earthworm
minoría n.f. minority
minúsculo -a a. minuscule
minusválido -a a. invalid
minuto n.m, minute
miola n.f. marrow
miolo (anatomía) n.m. cerebrum, brain; medula
miolo (botánica)n.m. pith (spongy tissue of plants)

miolo (panadería) n.m. interior, soft part of the bread

miope a. & n. near sighted

miquiño n.m. kitten

mirada n.f. look

mirar v. look

mirasol n.m. sunflower

mirto n.m. myrtle

misa n.f. mass

miseria n.f. misery

misil n.m. missile

misión n.f. mission

misteno n.m. mystery

misto n.m. match

mitade V. metade

miúdo -a a. small

mixto -a a. mixed

mm pr. m. my

mo contraction of pr. me & pr o

moa n.f. molar tooth

móbil a. movil

mobilano n.m. furniture

moble n.m. piece of furniture

mochila n.f. knapsack

mocidade n.f. youth

moco n.m. mucus

moda n.f. mode, fashion
modelo n.m. model
moderno -a a. modern
modestia n.f. modesty
modesto -a a. modest
modificar v. modify
modo n.m. mode, manner, way
moeda n.f. coin
moedeiro n.m. purse
moer v. grind
mofo n.m. mold
moi adv. very
moito -a a. much
mol a. soft; having little energy or incentive
molde n.m. mold
molécula n.f. molecule
moleira n.f. fontanel
molestar v. bother
molestia n.m bother
molete n.m. whole wheat roll
mollar v. wet, get wet
molo V. miolo
molusco n.m. mollusk
momento n.m. moment
mona n.f. ape
monarquía n.f. monarchy

monda n.f. skin (of vegetables)
mondar v. peel
moneca n.f. doll
moneco n.m. doll
monicreque n.m. puppet
monitor -a n. monitor, coach, instructor
monllo n.m. sheaf
mono n.m. ape
moño n.m. bun, chignon
monótono -a a. monotonous
monstro n.m. monster
montar v. mount
monte n.m. hill, mount
montón n.m. heap, pile
montura n.f. mount, saddle
monumento n.m. monument
monxa n.f. nun
monxe n.m. monk
moqueta n.f. wall paper
mora V. amora
morado -a a. purple
moral a. moral
morcego n.m. bat
morcilla n.f. black pudding
morder v. bite
morea (peixe) n.f. moray eel

morea n.f. pile, heap, moraine (geology)

moreira n.f. mulberry tree

moreno -a a. brown

morno -a a. lukewarm

morodeira V. amorodeira

morodo V. amorodo

morrer v. die

morriña n.f. nostalgia, homesickness

mortadela n.f. mortadella

mortal a. mortal

mortalidade n.f. mortality

morte n.f. death

morteiro n.m. mortar

morto n. dead, deceased

mosca s.f. fly

mosquito s.m. mosquito, gnat

mosteiro s.m. monastery

mosto n.m. fermented beverage with low alcohol content

mostra n.f. sample

mostrador n.m. counter

motivo n.m. motive

motocicleta n.f. motorcycle

motor n.m. motor

moucho n.m. little owl

mouro -a a. & n. Moor; having dark skin

move v. move
movemento n.m. movement
mozo -a a. & n. young person
muda n.f. change
mudar v. move
mudo -a a. & n. mute
mudo past participle of moer, grind
muelle V. peirao
muelle V. resorte
muiñeiro -a n. miller
muiño n.m. mill
mulato -a a. & n. mulatto
muleta n.f. crutch
muller n.f. woman
mulo -a n. mule
multa n.f. fine
multidud n.f. multitude, mob
multiplicación n.f. multiplication
multiplicar v. multiply
múltiplo -a a. & n. multiple
mundial a. wordly
mundo n.m. world
munguir V. muxir
municipio n.m. municipality
mural a. & n. mural
muraño n.m. shrew mouse

murcho -a a. withered
muricego V. morcego
murmurar v. mutter, murmur
muro n.m. wall
murralla n.f. wall, rampart
muscaraña V. muraño
músculo n.m. muscle
museo n.m. museum
música n.f. music
músico -a a. musical
mustélido n.m. musteline
musulmán a. & s.m. Moslem
musulmana a. & s.f. Moslem
mutuo -a a. mutual
muxe (peixe) n.m. stripped mullet
muxica n.f. cinder
muxir v. milk an animal
muxo (peixe) n.m. mullet

N

na contracción of prep. en, in, & art a. the (f)
nabiza n.f. young, tender turnip shoots
nabo n.m. turnip
nacemento n.m. birth

nacer v. be born

nacho -a a. & n. person with a prominent nose

nacíón n.f. nation

nacional a. national

nada pr. nothing

Nadal n.m. Christmas

nadar v. swim

nádega n.f. buttocks

nai n.f. mother

nalgún contraction of prep. en, in, & algun, someone

nalgunha contraction of prep. en, in, & algunha, someone

namorado -a a. lover, be in love

namorar v. cause fall in love

naquel (m) contraction of prep. en, in, & aquel, that one

naquela (f) contraction of prep. en, in, & aquella, that one

naqueloutra contraction of prep. en, in, & prep aqueloutra

naqueloutro contraction of prep. en, in, & prep aqueloutro

naquilo contraction of prep. en, in, & prep. aquilo

nariz n.m. nose

narrar v. narrate

nasa n.f. net, basket (to catch fish)

nasal a. nasal
nata n.f. cream
natación n.f. swimming
natal a. related birth or a birthday
natureza n.f. nature
naufragar v. be or become shipwrecked
náutico -a a. nautical
navalla n.f. knife
nave n.f. ship, vessel
nave n.m. nave (space between walls, arcades, etc)
navegar v. navigate
navío n.m. ship, vessel
nazismo n.m. Nazism
néboa n.f. fog
nebra V. néboa
necesario -a a. necessary
necesidade n.f. necessity
necesitar v. need
nécora n.f. small sea, ten-legged crab
néctar s.m. nectar
negar v. deny
negativo -a a. negative
negociar v. negotiate, deal, trade
negocio n.m. trade, business
negro -a a. black
nel contraction of prep. en, in, & pr. el, the

nela contraction of prep. en, in, & pr. ela

neno -a n. child

nervioso -a a. nervous

nervo n.m. nerve

nesa contraction of prep. en with pr.f. esa

nese contraction of prep. en with pr. m. ese

nesoutra contraction of prep. en with pr. esoutra

nesoutra contraction of prep. en with pr. estoutra

nesoutro contraction of prep. en with pr. esoutro

nesoutro contraction of prep. en with pr. estoutro

nespeira n.f. nedlar tree

néspera n.f. medlar (fruit)

nesta contraction of prep. en with pr. esta

neste contraction of prep. en with pron. este

neto -a n. grandson, granddaughter

neumático V. pneumático

neutral a. neutral

neutro -a a. neuter

neutrón n.m. neutron

nevada n.f. snow fall

nevar v. snow

neve n.f. snow

neveira n.f. refrigerator

nicho n.m. niche

nicolao V. ouriolo

nin conj. neither

niña V. meu
niñada n.f. brood
ninguén pr,m. nobody
ningunha pr.f. not any
ningures adv. no place
niño n.m nest
nitróxeno n.m. nitrogen
nivel n.m. level
no contraction of prep. en with art. 0
nó n.m. knot
no pr.m. we
nobre a. & n. noble, aristocrat, aristocratic
noceira V. nogueira
nocello n.m. knee cap
noción n.f. notion
nocivo -a a. noxious, harmful
nocturno -a a. nocturnal
nogueira n.f. walnut tree
noite n.f. night
Noiteboa n.f. Christmas eve
noitiña n.f. twilight, dusk
noivo -a n. bridegroom, bride
nola contraction of prep.
nolo contraction of pr. nos & art o, the
nome n.m. name
nomear v. name, mention by name; nominate

non adv. no
nora n.f. daughter-in-law
norma n.f. norm, standard
normal a. normal
norte n.m. north
nos, nós pr.pl. we
noso -a pron.sing. ours
nosoutros -as pr. we
nota n.f. note
notar v. note
notario -a n. notary
noticia n.f. notice, news
noutra contraction of prep. en, in, & prep. outra
noutro contraction of prep. en, & prep. outro
novato -a a. novice
nove pr. nine
noveano -a. ninth
novecentos -as pr. nine hundred
novela n.f. novel
novelo n.m. ball of yarn, skein
novembro n.m. November
noventa pr. ninety
novidade n.f. novelty
novo -a a. new
noxo n.m. nausea
noz moscada n.f. nutmeg

noz n.f. nut
nube n.f. cloud
nuboso -a a. cloudy
nubrar V. cloud over
núcleo n.m. nucleus
nudez n.f. nudity
nudo V. nó
nugallá a.f. lazy, slothful
nugallán a.m. lazy, slothful
numerador n.m. numerator
numeral a. numeral
número n.m. number
nun contraction of prep. en, in, & art. un
nunca adv. never
nuncio n. papal representative
nunha contraction of prep. en with art. unhua
nutrición s.f. nutrition
nutriz (pl. nutrices) n. wet nurse

O

o art.sing.m. the
ó contraction of prep. a & art. o. the
obedecer v. obey
obediente a. obediente

obeso -a a. obese
obra n.f. work, task
obrar v. work, carry out, perform
obreiro -a n worker
obriga n.f. obligation
obrigación V. obriga
obrigar v. force, compel
observación n.f. observation
observar v. observe
obsesión n.f. obsession
obstáculo n.m. obstacle
obtener v. obtain, to
obtuso -a a. obtuse
obvio -a a. obvious
obxección n.f. objection
obxecto n.m object
obxetivo -a a. objective
oca n.f. ganso
ocasión n.m. occasion
occidente n.m. occident, west
océano n.m. ocean
ocio n.m. idleness, leisure
ocorrencia n.f. idea, happening, occurrence
ocorrer v. occur, happen
oculista n. ophthalmologist
ocultar v. hide

ocupación n.f. occupation
ocupar v. occupy
odiar v. hate
odio n.m. hatred
oeste n.m west
ofender v. offend
ofensivo -a a. offensive
oferta n.f. offer
oficial a. official
oficina n.f. office
oficio n.m. work, occupation
ofrecer v. offer
ogallá V. ¡oxalá!
ogro n.m. ogre
oido n.m. ear
oir v. hear
oitavo -a. eighth
oitenta pr. eighty
oito pr. eight
oitocentos -as pr. eight hundred
ola inter. hello
ola n.f wave
ola n.f. cooking pot
óleo n.m. oil
olfato n.m. sense of smell
olimpíada n.f. olympiad

oliva n.f. olive

oliveira n.f. olive tree

ollada n.f. glimpse

ollal n.m. button-hole

ollar v. glimpse

olleiras n.f.pl. dark rings around the eyes

ollo n.m. eye

olor n.m. smell, odor, scent

ombreiro V. ombro

ombro n.m. shoulder

omnívoro -a a. omnívorous

once pr. eleven

onda n.f. wave

onde adv. where

ondular v. wave, make waves

onte adv. yesterday

onza (animal) n.f. ounce (carnivorous mammal)

onza n.f. ounce, weight equivalent 287 decigrams

opaco -a a. opaque

opción n.f. option

ópera n.f. opera

operación n.f. operation

operar v. operate

opinar v. opine

opinión n.f. opinion

opoñer v. oppose

opor V. opoñer
oportunidade n.f opportunity
oposición n.f. opposition
oposto -a a. opposite
oprimir v. oppress
óptica n.f. optics
óptico -a a. optical
optimismo n.m. optimism
ora conj. now
oración n.f. prayer
oráculo n.m. oracle
oral a. oral
orar v. pray
orballo n.m. drizzle
orbellar v. drizzle
órbita n.f. orbit
orde n.f. order
ordenar v. order
ordinal a. ordinal
orella n.f. ear
orfo -a a. & n. orphan
orgánico -a a. organic
organismo n.m. organism
organizar v. organize
órgano n.m. organ
orgasmo n.m. orgasm

orgullo n.m. pride
orientar v. orient, give guidance to
oriente n.m. orient, east
orixe n.f. origin
orixinal a. original
orizo V. ourizo
ornear v. bellow
orquestra n.f. orchestra
ortiga n.f. poison ivy, nettle, sting nettle
ortigueira n.f. field of poison ivy
ortografía n.f. spelling
orxía n.f. orgy, bacchanal
orzamento V. presuposto
os art.pl.m. the
osa n.f. she bear
oscilar v. oscilate, fluctuate
óseo -a a. bony, osseous
osíxeno n.m. oxygen
oso n.m. bear
óso n.m. bone
ostentar v. show, display
ostra n.f. oyster
ou conj. or
ourego n.m. marjoram
ourensá a.f. native of Ourense
ourensán a.m. native of Ourense

ouriñal n.m urinal
ouriolo (ave) n.m. oriol, oriole
ourizo n.m. chestnut bur
ouro n.m. gold
ousado -a a. daring
ousar v. dare
outeiro n.m. mesa, plateau
outo -a V. alto
outono n.m. autumn, fall
outorgar v. grant, reward
outro -a pr. other, another
outubro n.m. October
ouvear v. howl
oval a. oval
ovano n.m. ovary
ovella n.f. ewe, sheep
ovíparo -a a. oviparous
ovo n.m. egg
oxalá V. ogallá
oxidar v. rust
óxido n.m. oxide, rust
ozone n.m. ozone

P

pa n.f. shovel, spade
pacaraídas n.m. parachute
pacer v. pasture, grace
pachoulí n.m. patchouli
paciencia n.f. patience
pacífico -a a. pacific, peaceful
pacto n.m. pact
padal n.m. palate
padecer v. suffer, endure
padiola n.f. stretcher, gurney
padrasto n.m. stepfather
padre n.m. father
padrino n.m godfather
padrón n.m. census, electoral list
paella n.f. dish typical of Valencia based on rice &
    sea food
paga n.f. payment
pagar v. pay
pai n.m. father
pailán -a a. & n. uncouth person
país n.m. country
paisano -a a. from the same area or country
paisaxe n.f. landscape, scenery
paixón n.f. passion

palabra n.f. word

palangana n.f. basin

palco n.m. orchestra pit; balcon (of a theater)

paleta n.f. spade

pálido -a a. pallid, pale

palíndromo n.m. palindrome

palisandro n.m. rosebud

palla n.f. hay

pallaso n.m. clown

palleira n.f. storage silo

palleiro n.m. hay stack

palmeira n.f. palm tree

palpar v. touch, feel, grope

pálpebra n.f. eyelid

pampillo n.m. chickweed

pan n.m. bread

pana n.f. corduroy

panadeiro -a n. baker

panadería n.f. bakery

panal n.m. beehive

panca n.f. lever

pancarta n.f. poster

panda n.f. leap frog

panda n.f. panda (animal)

pandar (xogo infantil) v. play hide & seek
(children's game)

pandeireta n.f. small tambourine
pandeiro n.m. tambourine
pano de mesa n.m. napkin
pano n.f. cloth
panorama n.m. panorama
pantalla n.f. screen
pantalón n.m. trouser(s)
pantano n.m. marsh, swamp
pantasma V. fastasma
panteón n.m. pantheon
panxoliña n.f. Christmas carol
pao n.m. stick, pole
papá n.f. father (colloquial)
papa n.m. the Pope, the Holy Father
papada n.f. double chin
papagaio n.f. parrot
papas n.f.pl. potatoes
papel n.m. paper
papeleira n.f. stationary store
papo n.m. chin
paporroibo n.m. bullfinch
paquete n.m. package
par n.m. pair
para prep. for, to
parabéns n.m. pl. congratulations
parabrisas n.m. windshield

parachoques n.m. bumpers
parado a. slow, diffident, lifeless
parafuso n.m. screw
paraíso n.m. paradise
paralama n.m. hubcap
paralelo -a a. parallel
parálise n.f. paralysis
paralizar v. paralyze
parar v. stop
pararraois n.m. lightning rods
parasito -a a. & n. parasite
paraugas n.m. umbrella(s)
parcela n.f. parcel
parche n.m. plaster, patch
parchís n.m. Parcheesi
pardal n.m. sparrow
pardo -a a. grey
parecer v. appear, seem, look
parede n.f. wall
parella n.f. pair, couple
parello -a a. equal, similar, even
parente n. relative
parentesco n.m. kinship, family relationship
paréntese n.m. parenthesis
parexa V. parella
parir v. give birth

parlamento n.m. parliament
paro n.m. work stoppage
parque n.m. park
parra n.f. vine
parrocha n.f. sardine
parroquia n.f. parish
parrulo -a n. duck
parsimonia n.f. moderation, parsimony
parte n.f. part
participar v. participate
partícula n.f. particle
particular a. particular
partida n.f. departure; consignment
partidiario -a a. & n. adherent, supporter, follower
partido n.m. party; game, match (in sports)
partir v. depart
parto n.m. childbirth
parva n.f. snack before lunch
parvo -a a. small, little
párvulo -a n. infant
pasa n.f raisin
pasado -a a. past
pasadomañá adv. day after tomorrow
pasa-lo ferro v. iron
pasamáns n.f. railing
pasaporte n.m. passport

pasar v. pass, cross, go across
pasatiempo n.m. pastime, amusement, hobby
pasaxe n.f. passage, fare
pasaxeiro -a n. passenger
pascua n.f. Easter
pasear v. take a stroll
paseo n.m. walk,. stroll
pasivo -a a. passive
pasmar v. stun, amaze
paso n.m. step
paspallás n.m. grouse
pasta n.f. paste, batter
pastel n.f. cake, pastry
pasteleria n.f. pastry shop
pastilla n.f. tablet
pastor -a n. shepherd
pata n.f. leg
pataca n.f. Jerusalem artichoke
patada n.f. kick
patear v. kick
paterno -a a. paternal
patilla n.f. sideburns
patin n.m. skate
patinar v. skate
patio n.m. patio, courtyard
pato -a n. duck

patria n.f. mother country
patrimonio n.m. patrimony
patroa n.f. patroness, owner
patrocinar v. patronize, sponsor
patrón n.m. patron, owner
pausa n.f. pause
pavía n.f. peach
pavillón n.m. pavilion
pavo n.m. turkey
paxara n.f. spleen
paxarela V. paxara
paxaro carpinteiro n.m. woodpecker
paxaro n.m. bird
paxaro pescador V. picapeixe
paxe n.m. page
paxel V. breca
páxina n.f. page
paz (pl. paces) n.f. peace
pazo n.m. palace
pé n.m. foot
peatón (pl. peatóns) n. pedestrian
peaxe n.f. toll
pebida n.f. pebble, nugget
peca V. penca
pecado n.m. sin
pechadura n.f. lock

pechar v. lock
peculiar a. peculiar
pedagoxía n.f. pedagogy
pedal n.m. pedal
pedante a. & n. pedantic
pediatría n.f. pediatrics
pedir v. ask, ask for
pedra n.f. stone
pega (paxaro) n.f. magpie (bird)
pega (peixe) n.f. remora (fish)
pega n.f. cementing
pegada n.f. sticking plaster
pegamento n.m. cementing, sticking
pegar v. stick, glue
pegar v. strike somebody
peido n.m. fart
peirao n.m. pier
peitar v. comb
peite n.m. comb
peito n.m. chest
peituga n.f. breast of fowl
peixe espada n.f. swordfish
peixe n.m. fish
peixe sapo V. rabada
peixe voador n.m. flying fish
peixeria n.f fish market

pel n.f. skin
pela n.f. bark; skin (of a fruit or vegetable)
pelar v. pare, peel
pelexa n.f. quarrel
pelexar v. quarrel, fight
película n.f. film
pellejo n.m. hide, pelt
pelo n.m. hair
pelota n.f. ball
pelouro n.m. pebble
peludo -a a. hairy
pelve n.f. pelvis
pementa n.f. pepper
pemento n.m. paprika, red pepper
pemento n.m. pigment
pena n.f. boulder
pena n.f. penalty
penalti n.m. penalty (during a sports event)
penca n.f. freckle
pendello n.m. good-for-nothing
pendente a. hanging, pending
pendurar v. hang
pene n.m. penis
penedo n.m. large stone, rock
peneira n.f. pannier, bread basket
penicilina n.f. penicillin

península n.f. peninsula
penitencia n.f. penance, penitence
pensamento n.m. thought
pensar v. think
pensión n.f. boarding house; pension
pensionista n. retired
penso n.m. hay
pente V. peite
pentear V. peitear
penúltimo -a a. next the last
peon a n.f. peony
peón n.m. laborer
peor a. worse
pequeñino V. maimiño
pequeno -a a. small
perca (peixe) n.f. perch (fish)
percebe n.m. barnacle
percha n.f. cloth hanger
percibir v. perceive
percorrer v. go through, transverse, travel
perda n.f. loss
perder v. lose
perdiz n.f. partridge
perdoar v. forgive
perdón n.m. pardon
peregrinar v. make a pilgrimage

peregrino -a n. pilgrim
pereira n.f. pear tree
perenne a. perennial
perexil (pl. perexís) n.m. parsley
perfección n.f. perfection
perfecto -a a. perfect
perfil n.m. profile
perforar v. perforate
perfume n.m. perfume
periodico -a a & n. periodical, newspaper
periferia n.f. periphery
perigo n.m. danger
perigoso -a a. dangerous
periodista n. journalist
período n.m. period
perla n.f. pearl
permancer v. remain
permanente a. permanent
permiso n.m. permission
permitir v. allow, permit
perna n.f. leg
pernil n.m. ham, leg of pork
pero conj. but
pero n.f. pear
perpendicular a. perpendicular
perpetuo -a a. perpetual

perrencha n.f. temper tantrum
perruca n.f. wig
perseguir v. persecute; pursue, chase
persiana n.f. blind(s)
persignarse v. make the sign of the cross
persoa n.f. person
persoal a. personal
personalidade s.f. personality
personaxe n. personage
perspectiva a. perspective
persuadir v. persuade
pértega n.f. pole
pertencer v. belong
perturbar v. disturb, perturb
perverso -a a. perverse
pervertir v. pervert
pervinca n.f. periwinkle
perxudicar V. prexudicar
perxuizo V prexuiso
pesadelo n.m. nightmare
pesado -a a. heavy
pésame n.m. condolence
pesar n.m. condolence
pesar v. weigh
pesca n.f. fishing
pescada n.f. hake

pescadiña n.f. haddock

pescador -a n. fisherman, fisherwoman; angler

pescozo n.m. neck

peseta n.f. currency in Spain before the euro

pesimismo n.m. pessimism

peso n.m. weight

pesqueiro -a a. related fishing

pestana n.f. eyelash

pestanexar v. blink

peste n.f. pest

pétalo n.f. petal

petar v. knock

petardo n.m. petard, firecracker

peteiro n.m. beak

petiscar v. sip food, taste it

peto n.m. piggy bank

peto n.m. woodpecker

petrel (ave marina) n.m. petrel (sea bird)

petrina n.f. fly (of trousers)

petróleo n.m. petroleum

pexego n.m. peach

pexegueiro n.m. peach tree

peza n.f. piece

pezuño n.m. hoof

pía bautismal n.f. baptismal font

pía n.f. large container contain water

piano -a a. plane, level, flat
piano (instrumento musical) n.m. piano
piar v. chirp
picada n.f. puncture, prick
picadura V. picada
picante a. hot, spicy
picapeixe s.m. kingfisher
picaporte n.m. latch
picar v. prick, pierce, puncture
picardo V. xilgaro
pícaro -a a. & n. rogue
pico n.m. beak; peak
piedade n.f. piety
pila n.f. battery
pildora (ave) n.f. plover (bird)
pillabán -a a. & n. roguish., rascal
pillar v. catch, grab
piloto n.m. pilot
pílula n.f. pill, pellet
piña n.f. pineapple
pincel n.m. artist's brush
pinchacarneiro s.m. jumping on one's head
pinchar v. prick, pierce, puncture
pincho n.m. nipper(s)
piñeiro n.m. pineapple tree
pingüín.in n.m. penguin

pingar v. drip, trickle, drizzle; leak
pingueira n.f. drizzle, drip, leak
piñon n.m. pinion
pinta n.f. spot, mark
pintar v. paint, draw
pintarroxo n.m. sparrow
pintasiligo V. xílgaro
pintega n.f. salamander
pinto -a a. spotted, speckled
pintor -a n. painter
pintura n.f. painting
pinza n.f. pincers
pio n.m. chirping
piollo n.m. louse
piolloso -a a. lousy
pipa n.f. pipe
pipote s.m. small pipe
piquete n.m. picket
pirámide n.f. pyramid
pirata n.m. pirate
pirixil V. perexil
pirola (v.u.) n.f. penis
piropo n.m. complementary or flattering remark
pisada n.f. footstep, footprint
pisar v. step, tread on
piscina n.f. swimming pool

pisco V. paparroibo
piso n.m. floor
pista n.f. track, trail; clue
pistola n.f. pistol
pita n.f. hen
pito (paxaro) n.m. woodpecker (bird)
pito (cría da galiña) n.m. chick
pito n.m. whistle
pitón (serpe) n.m. python
pixama n.m. pajamas
pixota (peixe) n.f. hake (fish)
pizarra n.f. dark slate used for writing
placa n.f. plaque
plan n.m. plan
plancha V. ferro de pasar
planchar V. pasa-lo ferro
planear v. plan
planeta n.m. planet
planta n.f. plant
planta (anatomía) n.f. sole (of the feet)
plantar v. plant, sow
plástico -a a. plastic
plataforma n.f. platform
plátano n.m. plantain
plebe n.f. common people
pleite V. peite

pleno -a a. full, complete
pluma n.f. feather
plural a. & s.m. plural
pneumático -a a. pneumatic
po n.m. powder
pobación n.f. population
pobo n.m. town
pobre a. & n. poor
pobreza n.f. poverty
podar v. prune
poder n.m. power
poder v. be able to
poderoso -a a. powerful
podre a. rotten
podrecer v. rot
poema n.m. poem
poesía n.f. poetry
poeta n.m. poet
poetisa n.f. poetess
poidro -a n. colt, foal
pois conj. then
pola contraction of prep. por with art. la
pola (árbore) n.f. branch (of a tree)
pola n.f. chicken
polar a. polar
polbo n.m. octopus

pole n.m. pollen
poleiro n.m. chicken coop
polémico -a a. controversial
polgar a. & s.m. thumb
policía n.f. police
polígono n.m. polygon
polísilabo -a a. polysyllable
político -a a. political
polo contraction of prep. por & art. lo
polo (ave) n.m. chicken
polo (xeografía) n.m. pole, one of the ends of the earth, North or South
polo n.m. pole, post
pólvora n.f. powder
pomada n.f. pomade
pomba n.f. domestic fowl
pombal n.m. chicken house
pomelo n.m. grapefruit
pompa n.f. pomp
pómulo n.m. cheek
poncentaxe n.f. percentage
ponche n.m. punch (beverage)
poñer v. put, set, lay
ponte n.f. bridge
ponteaerán -a a. & n. inhabitant of Ponteareas

pontecaldano -a a. & n. inhabitant of
  Pontecaldelas
pontecasano -a a. & n. inhabitant of Ponteseco
pontedumés -a a. & n. inhabitant of Pondedeumes
pontevedés -a a. & n. inhabitant of Pontevedes
pontevedrés -a a. & n. inhabitant of Pontevedra
pontón n.m. pontoon
popa n.m. stern (of a ship)
popular a. popular
por prep. for, by
porca n.f. screw
porcelana n.f. porcelain, chinaware
porción n.f. portion
porco -a n. pig
porfiar v. persist
porfillar v. become a godfather or a godmother
pormenor n.m. retail
poro n.m. pore
porque conx. because
porra n.f. wooden hammer
porrón n.m. earthenware jug keep fresh water
porta n.f. door
portal n.m. portal
portar v. bear, carry
portátil a. portable
portavoz n.m. spokesperson

portavultos n.m. luggage carrier
porteiro -a n. porter, janitor
portela n.f. opening, gap, gate
portelo V. portela
portería n.f. goal area (sports)
porto s.m. port
portugués -a a. Portuguese
posesivo -a a. & n. possessive
posibilidade n.f. possibility
posible a. possible
posición n.f. position
positivo -a a. & n.m. positive
pospoñer v. postpone
postal a. postal
poste n.m. pole, post, pillar
posterior a. later, subsequent
postizo -a a. wicket
posto -a a. look
postre V. sobremesa
postura n.f. posture
posuir v. possess
pota n.f. cooking pot
potable a. potable
potaxe n.f. porridge, stew
pote n.m. three-legged cooking pot made of iron
potencia n.f. power, dominion

pouco -a pr. little
pousada n.f. inn
pousar v. lay, set down
pouso n.m. dregs, sediment; resting place
pouta n.m. claw
poxo n.f. auction
poza n.f. puddle
pozo n.f. well
pra V. para
pracer n.m. pleasure
practicar v. practice
práctico -a a. practical
pradairo n.m. maple tree
prado n.m. meadow
praga n.f. plague
praia n.f. beach
prata n.f. silver
prato n.m. dish
praza n.f. plaza, square
prazo n.m. term; space of time, time limit
prea n.f. carcass
precaución n.f. precaution
precavido -a a. forewarned
precedente a. precedent, antecedent
precintar v. strap, seal
precio V. prezo

precioso -a a. precious
precipitación n.f. precipitation
precisar v. specify
preciso -a a. precise
precursor -a a. & n. precursor
predicar v. preach
predicir v. forecast
predisponer v. predispose
predominar v. predominate
preferir v. prefer
prefixo n.m. prefix
pregar v. fold
pregón n.m. proclamation by crier
preguiza n.f. laziness
pregunta n.f. question
preguntar v. ask
prehistoria n.f. prehistory
preito n.m. litigation, lawsuit
prematuro -a a. premature
premer v. squeeze
premiar v. reward
premio n.m. prize
prenda n.f. garment
prender v. seize, grasp
prensa n.f. daily publication, newspaper
prensa (maquinaria) n.f. press (machinery)

preocupar v. worry
preparar v. prepare
preposición n.f. preposition
presa n.f. prisoner
présa n.f. speed
presebe n.m. manger
presencia n.f. presence
presentar v. present
presente a. present
presentimento n.m. foreboding, premonition
preservar v. preserve
preservativo n.m. condom,
president -a n. president
presidir v. preside
presión n.f. pressure
preso -a a. captive, prisoner
préstamo n.m. loan
prestar v. lend
presumido -a a. conceited
presumir v. presume, assume
presuposto n.m. budget
pretender v. pretend
pretexto n.m, pretext
preto adv. near
prever v. foresee
previo -a a. previous

previr v. anticipate, foresee
prexudicar v. damage, injure, impair
prexuizo n. detriment, damage, harm
prezo n.m. price
primano -a a. primary
primavera n.f. Spring
Primeira Comuñón n.f. First Communion
primeiro -a a. first
primitivo -a a. primitive
primo -a n. cousin
princesa n.f. princess
principal a. principal, main
príncipe n.m. prince
principio n.m. beginning
prisión n.f. prison, jail
prisioneiro -a n. prisoner
privado -a a. private
privar v. deprive
privilexio n.m. privilege
proa n.f. bow, prow
proba n.f. proof, evidence
probable a. probable
probar v. prove, test
problema n.m. problem
procedemento n.m. procedure
proceder v. proceed

procesión n.f. procession
proceso n.m. process
procurar v. procure
producción n.f. production
producir v. produce
producto n.m. product
profanar v. profane, blaspheme
profano -a a. & n. profane
profesión n.f. profession
profesional a. professional
profesor -a n. professor
profundo -a a. deep
prognóstico n.m. forecast
programa n.f. program
progresar v. progress
progreso n.m. progress
prohibir v. forbid
prólogo n.m. prolog
promesa n.f. promise
prometer v. promise
promoción n.f. promotion
pronome n.m. pronoun
pronto adv. quick
pronunciar v. pronounce
propaganda n.f. propaganda; advertising
propagar v. propagate, spread, disseminate

propenso -a a. propense, inclined, prone
propiedade ns.f. property
propietario -a a. & n. owner, proprietor
propina n.f. tip
propio -a a. one's own; proper
proponer v. propose
propor V. proponer
proporción n.f. proportion
propósito n.m. purpose
proposta n.f. proposal
prórroga n.f. postponement
prosa n.f. prose
prospecto n.m. prospect
prosperar v. prosper
prostituta n.f. prostitute, harlot, whore
protagonista n. protagonist
protección n.f. protection
protesta n.f. protest
protestar v. protest
protexer v. protect
protón n.m. proton
proveito n.m. advantage, benefit
providencia n.f. providence
provir n. arise, originate
provisión n.f. provision
provisional a. provisional

provocar v. provoke
proxectar v. project
proxectil n.m. projectile
proxecto n.m. project
próximo -a a. near
prudente a. prudent, cautious
psicoloxía n.f. psychology
psiquiatría n.f. psychiatry
pube n.f. pubic area
pubertade n.f. puberty
publicar v. publish
publicidade n.f. publicity
público -a a. public
pucha n.f. shawl
pucheiro n.m. earthenware cooking pot; stew
puir v. polish
pulga n.f. flea
pulir V. puir
pulmón n.m. lung
pulmonía n.f. pneumonia
pulpo V. polbo
pulseira n.f. bracelet
pulso n.m. pulse
puñado n.m. hand full
puñal n.m. dagger
punta n.f. point

puntada n.f. stitch
puntería n.f. aim
puntilla n.f. small point; narrow lace edging
punto n.m. point, period
puntual a. punctual
puntuar v. punctuate
pupila n.f. pupil (of the eye)
puré n.m. purée
purgatorlo n.m. purgatory
puro -a a. pure
pus n.m. pus
puta n.f. whore, harlot
puxar v. pull

Q

que pr. that, which
quebrado n.m. fraction (arithmetic)
quebrar V. crebar
quece v. warm up
queda n.f. curfew
quedar v. stay
quedo -a a. quiet, still
queimada n.f. Galician beverage made up by
　　burning sugar & rum

queimadura n.f. burn
queimar v. burn
queixa n.f. complaint
queixada n.f. jawbone
queixarse v. complain
queixeira n.f. covered dish keep cheese
queixo (alimento) n.m. cheese
queixo (anatomia) n.m. chin
quemarroupa adv.p. point blank
quen pr. who
quenlla n.f. canal, aqueduct
quenlla (peixe) n.f. shark
quentador -a a. heater
quentar v. warm up
quente a. warm
quepis n.m. kepi(s)
querer v. like
querido -a a. dear
querubín (pl. querubíns) n.m. cherubim
quieto -a V. quedo
quilate n.m. karat
quilla n.f. keel
quilo n.m. kilo
quilogramo n.m. kilogram
quilómetro n.f. kilometer
quilovatio n.m. kilowatt

química n.f. chemistry
químico -a a. & n. chemical, chemist
quince pr. fifteen
quincena n.f. fifteeth
quiniela n.f. football pool
quintal (pl. quintais) n.m. ancient weight, about 50 kilograms
quinto -a a. fifth
quiosco s.m. kiosk
quirófano n.m. operating room
quirúrgico V. cirúrxico
quiste V. ciste
quitar v. remove, take away
quitina n.f. chitin
quixotesco -a a. quixotic
quizá adv. perhaps
quizabes V. quizá
quizais V. quizá
quizás V. quizá

R

ra n.f. frog
rabada n.f toad fish
rabaño n.m flock

rabelo -a a short tailed or without tail

rabeno V. rabelo

rabia n.f rage, fury; rabies

rabiar v. have rabies; rage, be furious, hopping
mad

rabisaco V. xineta

rabo n.m. tail

rabudo -a a long or thick tailed

rabuñada n.f scratch

rabuñadura V. rabuñada

rabuñar v. scratch

racha n.f. small pieces of wood or stone

rachar v tear, rend, rip, slash

rachón n.m rent, tear, rip, slash

ración n.f. ration

racional a. rational

racismo n.m. racism

radar n.m radar

radiador n.m. radiator

radio n.f. radio

radiografía n.f. X-rays

raia (peixe) n.f. ray (fish)

raia espiñosa (peixe) n.f. thorback (fish)

raia n.f. ray

raiar v. rule, line, scratch

rail n.m. rail

raiña n.f. queen

raio n.m. beam, ray

raiola n.f. sun rays

raiz s.f. root

rama n.f. branch, bough

ramal n.m. branch, off-shoot

ramaxe n.f. ramada

ramo n.m. branch, bough; section, division, department

rampla n.f. ramp, slope

rañaceos n.m.pl. skyscrapers

rañar v. scratch

rancho -a n.f. piglet

rancio -a a. rancid, stale

rancor n.m. rancor, grudge

randear V. arrendar

randeeira V. bambán

raño n.m. adz

rapa n.f. scrape, coarse file

rapante n.m. edible sea fish, with an oval & flat shape

rapar v. scrape

rapaz -a a. & n. rapacious, predatory

rapidez n.f. speed

rápido -a a. fast

rapina n.f. rapine, plundering, looting

raposo -a n. fox
raqueta n.f. racket
raquítico -a a. rickety
raro -a a. rare
rascadura n,f. scratching, scraping
rascar v. scratch, scrape
raso -a a. clear, open, flat
rastrear v. trace, track, trail
rastro n.m. trace, track, scent, sign
rata n.f. rat
rateira n.f. mouse trap
rato -a n. mouse
raxo n.m. pork shoulder
raza n.f. race
razoable a. reasonable
razoar v. reason
razón n.f. reason
re n.m. second note of the musical scale
reacción n.f. reaction
real (realeza) a. royal
real a. real
realididade n.f. reality
realización n.f. realization; fulfillment
realizar v. realize, fulfill
reanimar v. revive
rebaixa n.f. lowering, reducing

rebaixar v. lower, reduce, cut down
rebanda n.f. slice
rebaño V. rabaño
rebelar v. rebel
rebelde a. & n. rebel
rebentar v. burst, explode
rebezo n.m. chamois
rebulir v. begin move, show signs of life
rebumbio n.m. mixture
rebuscar v. search, look
recadar v. collect
recado n. errand, message
recaer v. fall back, relapse
recaída n. relapse
recalcar v. emphasize, stress
recambio n.m. re-exchange
recanto n. recant
receita n.f. prescription; recipe
recender v. smell good
recente a. recent
recepción n.f. reception
receptor -a a. receptor
rechamante a. colorful, brilliant
recheo n.m. dough
recibir v. receive
recibo n.m. receipt

recinto n.m. enclosed area, site, precinct

recíproco -a a. reciprocal, mutual

recitar v. recite

reclamar v. reclaim

recluir v. shut up, put away; keep in

recobrar v. recover

recolledor n.m. dust pan

recolleita n.f. harvest

recoller v. pick up, gather

recomendar v. recommend

recompensa n.f. reward

reconciliar v. reconcile

recoñocer v. recognize

reconstruir v. rebuild

reconto n.m. retelling

recordar v. remember

recordo n.m. remembrance, memory

recorrer v. cross, traverse; travel over

recortar v. cut away

recostar v. recline

recrear v. delight, amuse

recreo n.m. recreation, amusement

recruta n.m. recruit

rectángulo n.m. rectangle

recto -a a. straight, right

recua n.f. drove, string (of animals)

recuar v. back down
recuncho n.m. nook
recuperar v. recover, recuperate
recurso n.m. recourse, resort
redacción n.f. editing
redactar v. edit
rede n.f. net
rédito n.m. interest, revenue
redondear v. round, make rounds
redondo -a a. round
reducir v. reduce
reembolso n.m. reimbursement
refacer v. redo
refaixo n.m. petticoat
refén n. hostage
referencia n.f. reference
referendo n.m. referendum
referir v. refer
reflectir v. reflect, show, reveal
reflexar v. reflect
reflexionar v. reflect, think it over
reflexo -a a. reflex
reformar v. reform
reforzar v. reinforce
reforzo n.m. reinforcement
refrán n.m. saying, proverb, adage

refrescar v. refresh
refresco n.m. refreshment
refrexar V. reflectir
refucir v. tuck up one's pants or dress
refugallo n.m. remains
refuxiar v. shelter
refuxio n.m. shelter
rega n.f. sprinkle
regadeira n.f. watering can
regado n.m. irrigation
regalar v. give away, give presents
regalo n.m. gift
regaña n.f. scolding
regañar v. scold
regar v. sprinkle
regatear v. haggle over
regato n.m. rivulet, brook
regazo n.m. lap
rego n.m. irrigation
regra n.f. ruler
regresar v. return
regueiro n.m. trickle, stream
regular a. regular
regular v. regulate
rei n.m. king
reinar v. reign

reino n.m. kingdom
reiseñor n.m. nightingale
reistencia n.f. resistance
reivindicar v. make a bid, recover
reixa n.f. plowshare; grating, grille
relación n.f. relation
relacionar v. relate, connect
relampo n.m. lightning
relar v. divide into small pieces
relativo -a a. relative
relato n.m. tale, narrative
relaxar v. relax
relevante a. relevant
relevo n.m. relief; relay; change
relixión n.f. religion
relixioso -a a. religious
relón n.m. chaff
reloxería n.f. watch, clock maker shop
reloxo n.m. watch, clock
relucir v. shine, glitter, glisten, gleam
remangar V. arremangar
remar v. row, paddle
rematar v. finish off
remate n.m. auction, public sale
remedio n.f. remedy
remendar v. mend, patch, darn

remendo n.m. patch, mending piece
remexer v. stir, turn around
remitir v. send
remo n.m. oar
remoer v. grind again
remolacha n.f. beet, sugar beet
remolcar v. tow
remollo n.m. act of softening up
remollo (zooloxía) n.m. cow's udder
remolque n.m. towing
rémora (peixe) n.f. sucking fish, remora
remordimento n.m. remorse
remoto -a a. remote
remover v. remove
remuiño n.m. mill
renacemento n.m. rebirth
renda n.f. rent
rendemento n.m. yield
render v. render
renegar v. deny
reno -a n. reindeer
renome n.m. renown
renovar v. renovate
renquear v. limp
renunciar v. renounce
renxer v. creak

reo (peixe) n.m. species of river or sea trout
reo -a n. prisoner
reparación n.f. reparation
reparar v. repair
reparo n.m. repair
repartir v. share
repasar v. review
repenicar v. ring the bells
repente n.m. suddenly
repentino -a a. sudden
repercutir v. rebound
repertorio n.m. repertory
repetir v. repeat
repleto -a a. replete
replicar v. replicate
repolo n.m. cabbage
repoñer v. replace, put back, restore
reportaxe n.f. report, reporting
repousar v. settle, rest
reprender v. reprimand
represa n.f. water dam
represalia n.f. reprisal, retaliation
representación n .f. representation
representante n. representative
representar v. represent
reprimir v. repress, check, curb

reprochar v. reproach
reproducción n.f. reproduction
réptil a. & n.m. reptile
república n.f. republic
repugnar v. disgust, nauseate; reject
requeixo n.m. whey; serum
requentar v. reheat
res n.f. head of cattle
resaca n.f. undertow
resaltar v. bounce, rebound
rescate n.f. rescue
resentimento n.m. resentment
resentirse v. be resentful
reserva n.f. reserve
reservar v. reserve
reseso -a a. stale
resfriado V. arrefriado
resgardar v. defend, protect, shield
residencia n.f. residence
residir v. reside
residuo n.m. residue
resignación n.f. resignation
resina n.f. resin
resistir v. resist
resolver v. resolve
resorte n.m. spring

respaldo n.m. backing
respectivo -a a. respective
respecto n.m. respect
respiración n.f. respiration
respirar v. breathe
resplandor s.m. brilliance, radiance
responder v. answer
responsable a. & n. responsible
resposta n.f. answer
resta n.f. subtraction
restablecer v. re-establish
restar v. subtract
restaurante n.m. restaurant
resto n.m. remainder, residue
restra n.f. braided vegetables hang
restringir v. restrict, limit
resucitar v. resuscitate, resurrect, revive
resultado n.m. result
resumir v. summarize, abridge
resumo n.m. abridgment, summary
retar v. challenge a duel
retellar v. retile a roof
retener v. retain
retina n.f. retina
retirado -a a. withdrawn, retired
retirar v. retire

reto n.m. dare
retoque n.m. retouch, touching up
retorcer v. wring, twist
retranca n.f. ill will, ill intention
retransmitir v. relay
retratar v. portray, take a picture
retrato n.m. painting, picture
retrete n.m. lavatory; boudoir
retroceso n.m. going back
retrovisor n.m. rear view mirror
reuma n.f. rheumatism
reunión n.f. reunion
reunir v. unite
revelar v. reveal
reverso n.m. reverse
reverter v. revert
revés n.m. back, reverse
revirar v. turn, twist around
reviravolta n.f. spin around, pirouette in dancing
revisar v. revise
revista n.f. magazine
revivir v. revive
revolta n.f. revolt
revoltoso -a a. turbulent, rebellious
revolución n.f. revolution
revólver n.m. revolver

revolver v. revolve
rexeitar v. reject
rexer v. rule, govern
réxime n.m. regime
rexión n.m. region
rexional a. regional
rexistar v. register
rexoubar v. bad mouth or speak evil of another
rexurdimento n.m. resurgence
rexurdir v. reappear, arise
rezar v. pray
ría n.f. estuary
ribeira n.f. shore, bank
rico -a a. & n. rich
ridículo -a a. ridiculous
rifa n.f. raffle
rifar v. raffle
ril n.m. kidney
rillar v. chew
rima n.f. rhyme
rinchar v. neigh, whine
ringleira n.f. file, queue
rinoceronte n. rhinoceros
rito n.m. rite
rival a. & n. rival
rivalidade n,f. rivalry

ríxido -a a. rigid
rizo n.m. curly hair
rob n.m. roll
robaliza s.f. sea bass
robalo n.m. sea bass
rocha n.f. rock
roda n.f. wheel
rodaballo n.m. turbot (fish)
rodar v. roll
rodear v. surround
rodeira n.f. tire track
rodeo n.m. short cut
roedor -a a. & n. rodent
roer v. gnaw
rogar v. plead
roibo -a a. blonde
rola V. rula
rolada n.f. brood
rolda n.f. round, night patrol
roldana n.f. winch
rolla n.f. cork
romana n.f. balance
románico -a n. Romanesque
romanticismo n.m. romanticism
romaría n.f. pilgrimage
romaxe V. romaría

rombo n.m. rhomb
romeu n.m. rosemary (plant)
romper v. break
roñar v. grunt
roncar v. snore
ronda V. rolda
rosa n.f. rose
rosario n.m. rosary
rosca n.f. twisted loaf
roseira n.f. rose bush
rostro n.m. face
rotación n.m. rotation
rótula n.f. rotula, knee cap
rotulador n.m. fountain pen
rotura n.f. breaking
roubar v. steal
rouco -a a. hoarse
roupa n.f. clothing
roupeiro n.m. wardrobe
roxo -a a. red
roxón s.m. remains after removing fat from a pig
rozadura n.f. friction, rubbing
rozar v. weed, clear
rúa n.f. street
rubio -a a. blond
ruborizar v. make blush

rubrica n.f. signature
rudo -a a. rude
ruido s.m. noise
ruidoso -a a. noisy
ruin a. mean, low, base
ruina n.f. ruin
rula n.f. turtle dove
rumbo n.m. course, direction, bearing
rumiante a. & n. ruminant
rumor n.m. rumor
rural a. rural
ruso -a a. Russian
rustrido n.m. mixture oil, lard, condiments fried
    together
ruta n.f. route
rutina n.f. routine
ruxir v. roar
ruzo -a a. white-haired person

S

sa a.f. healthy
saba n.f sheet (of a bed)
sábado s.m. Saturday
saber n.m. knowledge

saber v. know
sabina (árbore) n.f savin (tree)
sabio -a a. & n. sage, wise person
sabor n.m. flavor, taste
saborear v. savor, taste
sabre n.m. sable
sabugueiro n.m. elder tree
sabuxo (can de caza) n.m. hound
sacar v. take out, pull out
sacarina n.f. sacharine
sacerdote n.m. priest, clergyman
sachar v. remove earth using a mattock or a hoe
sacho n.m. matlock, hoe
saco n.m. sack
sacramento n.m. sacrament
sacrificio n.m. sacrifice
sacristán V. sancristán
sacristía V. sancristía
sacudir v - shake, shake off, beat
sagrado -a a. sacred
saia n.f. skirt, petticoat
saída n.f. exit
sair v. exit, leave
sal n.m. salt
sala n.f. hall, drawing room
salario n.m. salary

salchicha n.f. sausage
salchichón n.m. salami
saldo n.m. balance, settlement, liquidation
saleiro n.m. salt shaker
salema (peixe) n.f. gilt head (fish)
salgado -a a. salty
salgar v. salt
salgueiro n.m. willow tree
salitre n.m. saltpeter, sea salt
saliva n.f. saliva
salmón n.m. salmon
salón n.m. drawing room
salouco n.m. sob
salpicar v. sprinkle
salsa (música) n.f. salsa (music)
salsa n.f. sauce
saltar v. jump
salteado -a a. in here & there, all over the place
salto n.m. jump
saltón n.m. grasshopper
salvar v. save
salvavidas n.m. life jacket
salvaxe a. savage
salvia n.f. sage (plant)
salvo -a a. unhurt, unharmed, unscathed
sambesuga n.f leech

samesuga V. sambesuga

san (relixión) a. saint

san a.m. healthy

sanatorio n.m. sanatorium

sanción n.f. sanction

sancristán n.m. saxton (of a church)

sancristía n.f. sacristy

sandalia n.f. sandal

sandar V. heal

sandia n.f. watermelon

sangrar v. bleed

sangría (bebida) n.f. sangria (diluted & spiced wine)

sangría n.f. blood letting

sangue n.m. blood

sanidade n.f. health

santanderino -a n. inhabitant of Santander, Spain

Santiago de Compostela n. city in Galicia

¡santiago! n.m. battle cry of the Spaniards
    attacking the Moors

Santiago n.m. Saint James

Santiagués -a n. inhabitant of Santiago, Galicia

Santiagués a. pertaining the order of Santiago

santo -a a. & n. saint

sapo n.m. toad

sarabia n.f. hail

sarabiar v. hail

saraiba V. sarabia
sarampelo n.m. measles
sardiña n.f. sardine
sarna n.f. mange
sarno n.m. sediment
sarxa V. salvia
sarxento n. sergeant
satélite n.m. satellite
satisfacción n.f. satisfaction
satisfacer v. satisfy
saudar v. greet
saúde n.f. health
saúdo n.m greeting
saxofón n.m. saxophone
sazón n.f. seasoned, ripe
se. conx. if
sebo n.m. tallow, suet, fat, grease
seca n.f. drought
secador -a n.m. dryer
secar v. dry
sección n.f. section
seco -a a. dry
secretario -a n. secretary
secreto -a a. secret
secuencia n.f. sequence
secuestro n.m. kidnapping

século n.m. century
secundario -a a. secondary
secura n.f. dry
seda n.f. silk
sede n.f. thirst
seducir v. seduce
sega n.f. harvest, reaping season
segar v. harvest, reap, mow
segmento n.m. segment
segredo n.m. secret
seguida (de) adv. at once, immediately, without
    delay
seguido -a adv. without interruption, follow
seguinte a. & n. following
seguir v. follow
según prep. according to
segundo -a a. second
seguranza n.f. security, safety
seguridade V. seguranza
seguro -a a. secure, safe
seica adv. may be
seis pr. six
seiscentos -as pr. six hundred
seixo n.m. pebble
selar v. seal
seleccionar v. select

selo n.m. seal
selva n.f. forest, jungle
semáforo n.m. traffic light
semana n.f. week
Semana Santa n.f. Holy Week
semellante a. similar
semellanza n.f resemblance, similarity, likeness
semellar v. resemble, be alike
sementar v. sow, seed
semente n.f. seed
seminatio n.m. seminary
sempre adv. always
sen n.f. temple (of the face)
sen prep. without
senado n.m. senate
senil (pl. senís) senile, old
senlleiro -a a. alone, solitary
seno -a a. serious
senon conj. but
señor -a a. & n.m. mister (Mr.)
señora a.f. & n. Mrs., married woman
sensación n.f sensation
sensato -a a. sensible,
sensible a. sensitive
sentar v. sit down
sentencia n.f sentence

sentido -a a. sensitive, deeply heart-felt
sentimento n.m. feeling
sentir v. feel
seo n.m. breast
separar v. separate
sepultura n.f. tomb, grave
ser n.m. being
ser v. be
serán n.m. dusk
serea n.f. siren
sereno -a a. serene, calm
serie n.f. serie, set
sermón (pl. sermóns) m. sermon
serodio -a a. overripe; late
serpe de cascabel n.m. rattlesnake
serpe de crótalo V. serpe de cascabel
serpe n.f. serpent
serpentería n.f. dragon tree, green dragon
serra n,f. saw
serra n.f. mountain range
serraduras n.f.pl. saw dust
serrar v. saw
serrín V. serraduras
servicio n.m. service
servilleta V. pano de mesa
servir v. serve

sesenta pr. sixty
sesión n.f. session
sesta n.f afternoon nap
sete pr. seven
setecentos -as pr. seven hundred
setembro n.m. September
setenta pr. seventy
sétimo -a a. seventh
seu pr. m. yours
sexo n.m. sex
sexto -a a. sixth
sexual a. sexual
si (música) n. seventh letter of the musical scale
si adv. yes
sicómoro n.m. sycamore tree
siderurxia n.f. iron & steel industry
sidra n.f. cider
sifón n.m. siphon
sigla n.f. initials used as abbreviation
significado n.m. significance
significar v. signify, mean, declare
signo n.m. sign
sílaba n.f. syllable
silencio n.m. silence
siluro n.m. cat fish
silva n.f. blackberry bush

silveira n.f. copse of blackberry bushes
silvestre a. wild
símbolo n.m. symbol
simpatía n.f. sympathy
simpático -a a. congenial, likable
simple a simple
sin V. sen
sinai n.m. signal
sinalar v. signal
sinatura n.f. signature
sincero -a a. sincere
sindicato n.m. trade union
singular a. singular
sinónimo -a a. & n.m. synonymous
síntoma n.m symptom, sign of illness
sinxelo -a. simple
sirena n.f. siren
sistema n.m. system
sitio n.m. site, place
situación n.f situation
só a.m. alone
soa a.f. alone
soament adv. only
soar v. sound
sobaco n.m. axilla, arm pit.
sobar v. rub, neck, pet, paw

soberano -a a & n. sovereign
soberbia n.f. pride, arrogance
sobor V. sobre
sobornar V. subornar
sobra n.f. surplus, excess
sobrar v. be left over, be in surplus
sobre n.m. envelope
sobre prep. on
sobrecama n.f. quilt, bedspread
sobreira n.f. cork oak
sobreiro V. sobreira
sobremesa n.f. desert
sobrenome V. alcume
sobresair v. stand out, protrude
sobresaliente a. outstanding, excellent
sobrevivir v. survive
sobriña n.f. niece
sobriño n.m. nephew
social a. social
socialismo n.m. socialism
sociedade n.f society
socio -a n. partner, member, fellow
socorro n.m. help, aid
sofá n.m. sofa
sofraxe n.f. popliteal area (back of the knee)
sogra n.f mother-in-law

sogro n.m. father-in-law
soidade n.f. solitude
soio V. só
sol (música) n.m. fifth note of the musical scale
sol n.m. sun
sola n.f. sole (of the shoes)
solapa n.f. lapel
soldado n.m. soldier
soldar v. weld
soldo n.m. salary
solfexo n.m. sol-fa, solmization
solicitar v. solicit
solidario -a a. jointly liable
sólido -a a. & n. solid
solitario -a a. solitary, alone
solla (peixe) n.f. flounder (fish)
sollo (peixe) n.m. pickerel (fish)
solpor n.m. time of sun setting
soltar v. untie, unfasten, loosen
solteiro -a a. & n. bachelor
solto -a a. loose
solución n.f. solution
sombra n.f. shade
sombreiro n.m. hat
sombrío -a a. gloomy, somber, sullen; dark
sombrizo V. sombrío

someter v. submit

somnámbulo -a a. & n. sleep walker

son n.m. sound

sona n.f. knowlegeable

soñar v. dream

soño n.m. dream

sono n.m. sleep; state of being sleepy

sonoro -a a sonorous

sopa n.f. soup

soportar v. support

soprar v. blow

sopro n.m. blow

sorber v. sip, suck

sorna n.f. sarcasm, irony

soro n.m serum

sorprender v. surprise

sorpresa n.f. surprise

sorrir v. smile

sorte n.f. luck, fate, fortune

sorteo n.m. raffle, drawing, casting lots

sospeitar v. suspect

sospeitoso -a a. & n. suspect

soster v. support, hold up, sustain

sotana n.f. cassock (worn by priests)

soto n.m. basement

souto n.m. field of chestnut trees

súa pr.f. yours
suar v. perspire, sweat
suave a. soft
subida n.f. ascent, going up
subir v. climb, go up
sublevar v. raise up rebellion
submarino -a a. under, below the sea
submarino n.m. submarine (navy)
subnormal a. & n. below normal
subordinado -a a. subordinated
subornar v. bribe, suborn
subriñar v. underline
subscribir v. subscribe
substancia n.m. substance
substantivo n.m noun
substituir v. substitute
substituto -a n. substitute
subterráneo -a a. subterranea, underground
subvención n.f. subvection, subsidy
subxectivo -a a. subjective
suceder v. happen; suceed
sucesión n.f. succession
suceso n.m. success
sucesor -a a & n. successor, heir
sucidade n.f. suicide
sucio -a a. dirty

sucursal n.f. branch (of a commercial enterprise)

suficiente a. enough

sufixo n.m. suffix

sufraxe V. sofraxe

sufraxio n.m. suffrage

sufrir v. suffer

suicidio n.m. suicide

suma n.f. sum

sumar v. add

sumidoiro n.m. drain, sewer

suor n.f. sweat

superar v. surpass, excel

superficie n.f. surface

superior -a a. superior

supermercado n.m. supermarket

supersticioso -a a. superstitious

supeto p. term used in the phrase **de supeto,** suddenly

suplemento n.m. supplement

suplicar v. beg, plead, entreat

supoñer v. suppose, assume

supor V. supoñer

suposición n.f. supposition, assumption

supositorio n.m. supository

supremo -a a supreme

suprevivente a. & n. survivor

suprimir v. suppress
sur n.m. south
suspender v. suspend
suspenso -a a. hung, hanging, suspended
suspirar v. sigh
suspiro n.m. sigh
sustento n.m. sustenance, support, maintenance
susto n.m. freight
suxeitador -a a. fastening
suxeitar v. fasten, keep hold of
suxeito -a a. subject
suxerencia V. suxestion
suxerir v. suggest
suxestión n.f. suggestion

T

tab n.m. stalk, stem
tabaco n.m. tobacco
tabán n.f. gad fly, horse fly
taberna n.f. tavern
tabique n.m. partition, wall
táboa n.f. board, plank
taboleiro n.m. blackboard
tabú n.m. taboo

tacaño -a a. stingy, tight fisted

taco n.m. wad, plug, stopper

tacto n.m. tact; touch, feel

tal pr. such

talco n.m. talc

talento n.m. talent, cleverness

tallar v. carve, cut

talle n.m. figure, waist, fit

talleja n.f. slice

taller n.m workshop

tallo n.m. stool

tallón n.m. graft, grafting

talón n.m. heel

talonario n.m. stub book

tamaño n.m. size

tambor n.m. drum

tamén adv. also, too

tampa n.f. cover

tampouco adv. either

tan adv. so, as

tanque n.m. tank

tanto -a pr. so, as

tapa n.f. cover (of a book)

tapa (alimento) n.f. snack go along with wine

tapadeira n.f. lid

tapar v. cover

tapete n.m. small carpet, rug
tapón n.m. cork, stopper, plug
taquilla V. portela
tara n.f. tare
tarabelo -a a. & n. haired-brained, thoughtless
tardar v. take a long time
tarde n.f. late
tardiña n.f. late afternoon, early evening
tarefa n.f. task
tarifa n.f. tariff
tarro n.m. jar, bottle
tarta V. torta
tartamudo V. tatexo
tartaruga n.f. turtle
tarteira n.f. large earthen jar
tarxeta de crédito p. credit card
tarxeta n.f. card
tarxeta postal p. post card
tatexar v. stutter
tatexo -a a. & n. stutterer
taxa n.f. tax
taxi n.m. taxi
taza V. cunca
té n.m. tea
te pr. you (informal)
tea n.f. cloth

tear n.m. weave
teatro n.m. theater
tebras n.f.pl. darkness, gloom; tenebre (church)
teca n.f. teakwood
tecer v. weave, knit
tecido n.m. weave, textile, cloth
tecla n.f. key (of a piano, computer, typewriter, etc)
técnico -a a. technical
tecnoloxía n.f. technology
teima n.f. theme
teito n.m. roof
teixo n.m. badger
teixugo V. teixo
telefonar v. telephone
teléfono n.m. telephone
telégrafo n.m. telegraph
telescopio n.m. telescope
televisión n.f. television
tella n.f. roof tile
tellado n.m. roof
tema n.m. theme; harmony; base of a musical
    composition
temer v. fear
temible a. fearful, formidable
temón n.m. helm, rudder
temor n.m. fear, dread, apprehension

tempada n.f. season, spell of time
temperá a.f. early crops
temperán a.m. early crops
temperatura n.f. temperature
tempestad n.f. tempest
templo n.m. temple
tempo n.m. time
temporada V. tempada
temporal a. temporary, temporal
tenaces n.f.pl. pincers, claws
tenaz a. tenacious
tenca (peixe) n.f. tench (fish)
tenda n.f. store, shop
tendeiro -a n. store clerk
tendencia n.f. tendency
tender v. spread out, spread out
tendón n.m. tendon
tenedor V. garfo
tener v. have, possess, own
tenis n.m. tennis
tenro -a a. tender
tensión n.f. tension
tentación n.f. temptation
tentativa n.f. tentative
tento n.m. feel, careful, touch, care
teoría n.f. theory

teórico -a a. theoretical
tépedo -a a. lukewarm, tepid
terceiro -a a. third
tercio n.m. third
termar v. keep a hold of, hold fast or tight
terminar v. end, finish
término V. termo
termo n.m. end
termórnetro n.m. thermometer
terra n.f. land, earth
terraplén n.m. terrace, mound, embankment
terraza n.m. terace
terreo n.m. land, ground, terrain
terrestre a. terrestrial
terrible a. terrible
territorio n.m. territory
terrón n.m. clod or lump of earth
terror n.m. terror
terrorismo n.m. terrorism
teso -a a. stiff
tesoira n.f. scissors
tesouro n.m. treasure
testamento n.m. testament
testemuña n.f, witness
testemuño n.m. testimony
testículo n.m. testicle

testo n.m. lid

teta n.f. udder, breast

teto n.m. teat

teu pr. yours

téxtil a. textile

texto n.m. text

ti pr. you (informal)

tiburón V. quenlla

tiduo V. título

tigre n.m. tiger

tileiro n.m. flower from the linden or lime tree

tilo n.m. linden tree

timbre n.m. bell, chime; timber of a musical instrument

tímido -a a. timid, shy

timón V. temón

tímpano n.m. ear drum

tina n.f. large earthen jar, vat, tub

tinguir v. dye

tino n.m. skillful touch, tact

tinto -a a. deep colored, dark red

tintureria n.f. dyer's shop

tinxir V. tinguir

tío -a n. uncle, aunt

típico -a a. typical

tipo n.m. type, category, class

tira n.f. strip, thong
tirano -a a. & n. tyrant
tirar v. throw, cast, fling
tiritar v. shake, shiver from the cold
tirizó n.m. sty (eye)
tiro n.m. shot; team of draft animals
titor -a n. guardian, tutor
título n.m. title
tixeira V. tesoira
tixela n.f. frying pan
tixola V. tixela
toalla n.f. towel
tobeira n.f. nozzle
tobogán n.f. slide, chute
tocadiscos n.m. record player
tocar v. touch; play a radio or record player
tódalas contraction of pr. todas, all, & art las, the
todo -a a. all
tódolos contraction of pr. todos, all & art los, the
toldar v. make muddy or cloudy
toldo n.m. awning, canopy
tolear v. become mad or insane
tolemia n.f. madness
tolerar v. tolerate
tolleito -a a. crippled
tolo -a a. & n. crazy, insane

tomar v. take, take hold of
tomate n.m. tomato
tombar v. topple, knock down
tómbola n.f. game of chance
tomiño n.m. thyme
ton n.m. tone, tune
tona n.f. skin of fruits & vegetables
tonelada n.f. ton
tónico -a a. tonic
topar V. atopar
tope n.m. top; stop
toquear v. nod, in response music or being sleepy
toquenear V. toquear
torada n.f. timber
tórax n.m. thorax, chest
torcedura n.f. twisting
torcer v. twist
tormenta n.f. torment, tempest, disturbance
tornar v. return, give back
tornecelo n.m. patella, knee cap
torneo n.m. tournament
tornillo V. parafuso
torno n.m. lathe
torpe a. & n. clumsy, awkward
torrada n.f. toast
torrar v. toast

torre n.f. tower

torresmo n.m. piece of bacon

torta n.f. cake, pie

tortilla n.f. omelet

torto -a a. twisted

tose n.f. cough

toser V. tusir

tostar V. torrar

total a. total

touciño n.m. bacon

toupa n.f. mole

touro n.m. bull

tóxico -a a. toxic

toxo n.m. furze, gorse

traballar v. work

traballo n.m. work

trabar v. bind, clasp, join, shackle, fetter

trabe n.f. beam, rafter, girder

trabucar v. upset, confuse; mix up

tractor v.m. tractor

tradición n.f. tradition

traducir v. translate

traer v. bring

trafegar V. trasfegar

traficar v. traffic, deal, trade

tráfico n.m. trafic

tragar v. swallow
traidor -a a. & n. traitor
traizón n.f. treason
trala(s) contraction of prep. tras & art. la, las, the
tralo(s) contraction of prep. tras & art. lo, los, the
tramallo V. trasmallo
tramar v. plot, hatch
tramo n.m. stretch of a road, strip of ground
trampa n.f. trap, snare, pitfall
trampolín n.m. springboard
tranca n.f. cross-bar
tranquilidade n.f. tranquillity
tranquilo -a a. tranquil, calm
transeúnte n. transient
transferencia n.f. transference
transformar v. transform
transición n.f. transition
tránsito n.m. transit
transmitir v. transmit, send
transparente a. transparent
transplantar v. transplant
transportar v. transport
transporte n.m. transport
trapallada n.f. worthless object created without art
trapecio n.m. trapeze
trapo n.m. rag

tras prep. behind
trascendental a. transcendental
traseiro -a a. back, hind, rear
trasfegar v. transfer
trasgada V. trasnada
trasladar v. move, remove, transfer
trasmallo n.m. bag net (for fishing)
trasnada n.f. knavish trick
traspasar v. transfer, cross, go over, go beyond
trastorno n.m. upset, upheaval, disorder, trouble
tratamento n.m. treatment
tratar v. treat; deal with; discuss
trato n.m. treatment, manner
traxe n.m. dress
traxedia n.f. tragedy
trazar v. plan, design, outline
trazo n.m. outline
treboada n.f. sudden downpour
trebón V. treboada
trece pr. thirteen
tremer v. tremble, shake
tremor n.m. trembling, tremor
tren n.m. train
trenza n.f. braid, tresses
tres pr. three
trescentos -as pr. three hundred

trevo n.m. clover
triángulo n.m. triangle
tribo n.f. tribe
tribunal n.m. tribunal
trigo n.m. wheat
trincar v. chop with the teeth
trinta pr. thirty
tripa n.f. tripe
triple a. triple
tripulación n.f. crew
triste a. sad
tristeza n.f. sadness
triturar v. triturate, mash, crush
triumfo n.m. triumph
trobisco n.m. flax-leaved daphne
trobisqueira V. trobisco
trobo n.m. bee hive
trocar v. exchange, barter
trofeo n.m. trophy
troita n.f. trout
trola n.f. fib, lie
trompeta n.f. trumpet
tronada n.f. thunder
tronar v. thunder
tronco n.m. trunk
trono n.m. thunder

tronzar v. slice, cut through

tropezar v. stumble, trip out

tropical a. tropical

trote n.m. trot

troular v. make merry, go on a spree

troulear V. troular

truco n.m. trick

trufa n.f. truffle

tubería n.f. tubing, piping

tubo n.m. tube

tufo n.m. vapor, offensive smell

tulipán n.m. tulip

tumbar V. tombar

tumor n.m. tumor

tunda n.f. a batch

tunel n.m. tunnel

tupir v. stuff; pack tight

turbio -a a. turbid, cloudy, muddy

turismo n.m. tourism

turista n.m. tourist

turrar v. butt, push or knock down with the head

turrón n.m. sweet made with almond paste at
   Christmas

tusir v. cough

tutor V. titor

túzaro -a a. sullen

U

ubre n.m. udder
ulir V. cheirar
último -a a. last
ultramarino -a a. ultramarine
ultraxar V. aldraxar
ultraxe V. aldraxe
un art. & pr.m. a, an
uña n.f. nail
uñada n.f. meal prepared with pig's knuckles
ungüento n.m. oitment
unha art. & pr.f. a, an
único -a a. unique
unidade n.f. unit
uniforme a. uniform
unión n.f. union
unir v. to unite
universidade n.f. university
universo n.m. universe
unlla V. uña
untar v. annoint, spread, smear
unto n.m. grease, fat
urbanización n.f. urbanization
urbano -a a. urban
urdir v. to warp

urina n.f. urine
urizo V. ourizo
urna n.f. urn
urticaria n.f. urticaria
urxencia n.f. urgency
urxente a. urgent
usar v. use
uso n.m. use
usté pr. you
usuario -a n. user
utensilio n.m. utensil, tool
útero n.m. uterus
útil (útiles) a. useful
utilizar v. utilize, use
uva n.f. grape
uz n.m. heather

V

va a.f. empty
vaca n.f. cow
vacación n.f. vacation
vacaloura n.f. stag beetle
vacilar v. vacillate, hesitate
vacina n.f. vaccination

vacúa n.f. bovine
vacún n.m. bovine
vagabundo -a a. vagabond
vagalume n.m. firefly
vagar v. wander, roam about
vago -a a. lazy, idle; vague
vago -a n. wanderer
vaixela n.f. table or dinner service
val n.m. valley
valado n.m. stone fence
valente a. valiant, courageous
valer v. be useful
válido -a a. valid
valor n.m. valor
valorar v. value, appraise
válvula n.f. valve
van a.m. empty
vantaxe n.f. advantage
vapor n.m. vapor
vaqueiro -a a. & n. cowboy, cowgirl
vara n.f. rod, pole, staff
varanda n,f. rail
varear v. shake a tree bring down its fruits
varexar V. varear
variable a. variable
variación n.f. variation

variar v. vary
varicela n.f. chicken-pox
variedade n.f. variety
varios -as pr. several
varrer v. sweep
vasco -a a. Basque
vaso n.m. glass
vasoira n.f. broom
vasto -a a. vast
vea n.f ore (mining)
vea n.f. vein (anatomy)
veciño -a a. neighboring
vecino -a n. neighbor
vehículo n.m. vehicle
veiga n.f. fertile low land or plain
vela n.f. sail
vela n.f. watch, vigil
vela V. candea
velaí adv. here it is
velar v. watch over; guard
vélaro de ouro p. golden fleece
vélaro n.m. fleece
veleiro n.m. sailing vessel
veleno s.m. poison
vellez n.f. old age
vello -a a. old

velocidade n.f. speed
veloz a. fast
veludo n.m. hairy cloth, downy
vencer v. vanquish, conquer
venda (enfermería) n.f. bandage
venda n.f. sale
vendar v. bandage, blindfold
vendaval n.m. gale, hurricane
vender v. sell
vendima n.f. vintage, grape harvest
veneno V. veleno
venres n.m. Friday
ventá n.f. window
ventanilla V. portela
ventar v. smell, scent, sniff
ventas n.f.pl. opening of the nostrils of animals
ventaxa V. vantaxe
ventear V. ventar
ventilar v. ventilate
vento n.m. wind
ventre n.m. belly
ver v. see
verán n.m. Summer
veratro n.m. hellbore
verbena n.f. verbena, fair, festival
verbo n.m. verb

verdade n.f. truth
verde a. green
verdura n.f. vegetables
vergonza n.f. shame
verme de seda n.m. silkworm
verme n.m. worm
vermello -a a. red
verniz n.m. shellac
verruga n.f. wart
versión n.f. version
verso n.m. verse
vértebra n.f. vertebra (anatomy)
vertebrado -a a. & n. vertebrate
vertebral a. relating the vertebra
vertedeiro n.m. kitchen sink; garbage can
vertedoiro V. vertedeiro
verter v. pour, shed, spill
vertical a. vertical
vértice n.m. vertex, apex, top
verxa V. reixa
verza n.f. cabbage leaf
vesgo -a a. crosseyed
vespa V. avespa
véspera n.f. eve, the day before
vestido n.m. dress
vestimenta n.f. garments, clothing

vestir v. dress, get dressed
veterano -a a. & n. veteran
veterinario -a n. veterinarian
vexetación n.f. vegetation
vexetal n.m. vegetable
vexiga n.f. bladder, gall bladder
vez n.f. turn, time, ocassion
veza (planta) n.f. vetch (plant)
vía n.f via, way
viaxar v. travel
viaxe n.f. trip
viaxeiro -a n. traveller
vibrar v. vibrate
vicario (planta) n.m. periwinkle
viceversa adv. vice versa
vichelocrego V. ouriolo
viciño V. vecino
vicio n.m. vice
vicioso -a a. & n. licentious, addicted vice
victima n.f. victim
victoria n.f. victory
vida n.f. life
vidalia n.f. temple (on each side of the forehead)
vide n.f. vine, grapevine
videira V. vide
vidro n.m. glass

vieira n.f. scallop

viga n.f. beam, rafter, girder

vigués -a n. inhabitant or pertaining Vigo

vila (arquitectura) n.f. Roman country house

vila n.f. village

vilagarcián -a (pl. vilagarciáns, nas) a pertaining
Vilagarcía de Arousa

vimbio n.m. wicker

vime V. vimbio

viña n.f. vineyard

vinagre n.m. vinegar

vincha V. vexiga

vínculo n.m. link

vindeiro -a a. next, near

viñeta n.f. vignette

vinganza n.f. revenge

viño n.m. wine

vinte pr. twenty

violación n.f. violation

violencia n.f. violence

violeta n.f. violet

violín n.m violin

vir v. go

virar v. turn

virilla n.f. groin

virollo V. birollo

virtude n.f. virtue
virus n.m. virus
virxe a. & n. virgin
viseira n.f. viscera
visible a. visible
visita n.f. visit
visitar v. visit
víspera V véspera
vista n.f. sense of sight
vital a. vital
vitalidade n.f. vitality
vitamina n.f. vitamin
viuva de xardin n.f. mourning bride
viuva n.f. widow
viuvo n.m. widower
viveiro n.m. fish pond; nursery
vivenda n.f. dwelling, housing
víveres n.m.pl. provisions, comestibles
vivir v. live
vivo -a a. alive
vixiante a. vigilant
vixiar v. watch, keep
vixiga V. vexiga
voar v. fly
vocabulano n.m. vocabulary
vocal a. vocal

voceiro -a n. spoke person
voitre n.m. vulture
vola contraction of pr. vos
volante n.m. steering wheel
volcán n.m. volcano
volo contraction of pr. vos
volta n.f. turn
volume n.m. volume
voluntario -a a. volunteer
volver v. return
vomitar v. vomit, throw up
vontade n.f. will, willpower, willingness
voo n.m. flight
vos pr.f.& m. you
vosa pr.f. yours
voso pr.m. yours
vosoutros -as pr. you
votar v. vote
voto n.m. vote
voz n.f. voice
vulgar a. vulgar
vulto n.m. bulk, lump
vulva n.f. vulva

X

xa adv. already
xabaril n.m. wild boar
xaboeira n.f. soapwort
xabón n.m soap
xabrón V. xab n
xadrez n.m. chess
xaguar n.m. jaguar
xamais adv. never
xamón n.m ham
xaneiro n.m. January
xanela n.f. window
xantar v. have lunch
xaponés -a a. Japanese
xaque s.m. checkmate (chess)
xaqueca n.f. migraine headache
xarampón V. sarampelo
xarda n.f. mackarel
xardín n. m. garden
xardón V. acivro
xargón V. xergón
xarope n.m. syrup
xarra V. xerra
xarrete n.m. plopiteal area (back of the knee)
xarro V. xerra

xarsa V. salvia
xasmín n.m. jasmine
xastre -a n. tailor
xastrería n.f. tailor shop
xaula V. gaiola
xaxuar v. fast
xaxún n.m. fasting
xeada n.f. freezing
xeado n.m. ice cream
xear v. freeze, congeal
xefe -a n. chief, boss
xeira n.f. batch, shift during a working day
xeito n.m. plan, design
xeitoso -a a. capable, apt
xelado V. xeado
xelín n.m. shilling
xema n.f. yolk (of an egg)
xemelgo -a a. & n. twin
xemer v. groan, whine
xenebra n.f. gin (drink)
xenebreiro n.f. juniper (tree)
xeneral n. general (army rank)
xeneralizar v. generalize
xénero n.m. kind, sort, genre
xeneroso -a a. generous
xénese n.f. genesis

xenial a. genial
xenio n.m. genius
xenital a. genital
xenocidio n.m. genocide
xenofobia n.f. xenophobia
xenreira n.f. phobia, fear
xenro n.m. brother-in-law
xente n.f. people
xenxibre n.f. ginger
xeo n.m. ice
xeografía n.f. geography
xeoloxía n. geology
xeometría n.f. geometry
xeonllo n.m. knee
xeración n.f. generation
xeral a. general
xeranio n.m. geranium
xerarquía n.f. hierarchy
xerente n.m. manager
xerez n.m. sherry
xerga n.f. jargon
xergón n.m. straw mattress
xerife n.m. sheriff
xerme n.f. germ
xermolar v. germinate, sprout
xermolo n.m. bud, sprout, rosebud, young tree
xeroglífico -a a. &. n. hieroglyphic

xerra n.f. pitcher, jug
xersei n.m. jersey
xerundio n.m. gerund, present participle
xesta n.f. genista, broom (shrub)
xestación n.f. gestation
xesto n.m. gesture
xiba n.f. cuttlefish
xigante a. giant
xílgaro n.m. goldfinch (bird)
ximnasia n.f. gymnastics
ximnasio n.m. gymnasium
ximnasta n. gymnast
xinecoloxía n.f. gynecology
xineta n.f. genet
xinete n.m. horseman, rider
xio V. xeo
xirafa n.f. giraffe
xirar v. rotate, turn
xirar (moeda) v. send (as money)
xirasol n.m. sunflower
xiringa n.f. syringe
xiro n.m. turn, gyration, revolution
xitano -a a. & n. gypsy
xiz n.m. white clay
xoaniña n.f. lady bird (insect)
xoenllo V. xeonllo
xofre n.m. sulfur

xogador -a a. player
xogar v. play
xogo n.m. play
xoguete n.m. toy
xoia n.f. jewelry
xoio n.m. weed
xordeira n.f. deafness
xordo -a a. & n. deaf
xordomudo a. & n. deaf & mute
xornada n.f. working day
xornal n.m. day's work, day's wages; newspaper
xornalista n. journalist
xorneleiro -a n. day laborer
xoroba V. chepa
xouba n.f. small sardine
xove a. & n. young, youth
xoves n.m. Thursday
xubilar v. retire (from work)
xudeu a.m. Jewish
xudia a.f. Jewish
xudicial a. judicial
xugo n.m. yoke
xuia V. doncela
xuíz -a n. judge
xuizo n.f. judgement, trial
xulgado n.m. court of justice
xulgar v. judge

xullo n.m. July
xunca n.f. rush, bulrush
xunco V. xunca
xunguir v. yoke (oxen)
xuño n.m. June
xunta n.f. junta
xunta prep. near
xuntar v. join, bring together
xunto -a a. near, next to
xurado n.m. jury
xuramento n.m. oath
xurar v. swear
xurdir v. rise, spring forth
xurelo n.m. jack fish
xustificar v. justify
xustiza n.f. justice
xusto -a a. just
xuventude n.f. youth

Z

zamarra n.f. sheepskin, coat, jacket
zamburiña n.f. species of scallops
zanca n.f. shank, long leg
zanco n.f. leg of birds or mammals

zanoria V. cenoria

zanxa V. gabia

zapateiro -a n. shoe maker

zapatería n.f. shoemaker's shop

zapato n.m. shoe

zarabeto -a a. person who lisps

zarangalleiro -a a. & n. bungler

zarapalleiro V. zarangalleiro

zarrar V. cerrar

zoar v. buzz, hum

zoca n.f. sabot

zoco n.m. boot

zodíaco n.m. zodiac

zona n.f. zone

zooloxía n.f. zoology

zorza n.f. pork meat ground and seasoned to make sausages

zoupar v. beat, strike

zugar v. suck, draw, sap; absorb

zumaque n.m. poison ivy

zume n.m. sap (of plants)

zumegar v. exude, ooze

zunido n.m. buzz

zurcir v. mend

zurdo -a a. left handed

zurrar v. spank

ENGLISH-GALICIAN DICTIONARY

A

a, an art. ur, um (m), umha (f)
abandon v. abandonar, deixar, desocupar
abbess n. abadesa
abbey n. abadía, mosteiro, convento
abbot n. abade
abbreviate v. abreviar
abbreviation n. abreviatura
abdicate v. abdicar, renunciar, ceder
abdomen n. abdome
abnormal a. anormal
abolish v. abolir, surpimir, derrogar, anular, revogar
abominable a. abominable
abort v. abortar, malparir
abound v. abundar, proliferar
about prep. perto
above prep. arriba, riba, ribade
absence n. ausencia, falta
absent a. ausente
absolute a. absoluto -a
absolve v. absolver, perdoar, eximir

absorb v. absorber, sorber

abstain v. absterse, inhibirse

abstemious a. abstemio -a

abstention n. abstención

abstinence n. abstinencia

absurd a. absurdo -a, ilóxico

abundance n. abundancia, profusión, abasto

abundant a. abundante, abondoso, copioso

abuse n. abuso, exceso, atropelo, inxusticia

abuse v. abusar, aproveitase, explotar, violar
(agresión sexual)

abyss n. abismo, precipicio, sima

acacia n. acacia

academy n. academia; escola (centro de estudios
privado)

accede v. acceder, consentir, ceder, transixir

accelerate v. acelerar, apurar, apresurar

accelerator n. acelerador

accent n. acento

accentuate v. acentuar, recalcar, enfatizar, subliñar

accept v. aceptar, admitir, aprovar

access n. acesso, entrada, paso

accessory a. accesorio, complementario,
secundario

accessory n. accesorio, peza, complemento

accident n. accidente, desgracia

acclaim v. aclamar, vitorear

accommodate v. acomodar, axeitar, adecuar

accompany v. acompañar, xuntar

accomplice n. acómplice

accomplish v. realizar, efectuar, levar(se) a cabo

accordance n. acordo, avinza, concerto, convenio, pacto

according a. conforme, acorde, concorde

accordion n. acordeón

accumulate v. acumular, amontoar, amorear(se), amontoar(se), xuntar(se), reunir(se)

accurate a. exacto -a, xusto; puntual, correcto

accusation n. acusación

accuse v. acusar, culpar, inculpar

accused n. acusado -a

accustom v. acostumar

ace n. ás

ache n. dor, mágoa, pena

achieve v. conseguir, acadar, alcanzar, atinxir, lograr, obter

Achilles'
 tendon p. tendón de Aquiles

acid a. & n. acido -a

acknowledge v. recoñecer, coñecer, identificar

acorn n. landra, bellota

acquire v. adquirir, comprar, mercar

acquisition n. adquisición

across adv. través

act v. actuar, portarse, proceder

action n. acción, actuación, feito, movemento

active a. activo -a, espelido, dilixente, agudo, eficaz, rápido

activity n. actividade, acción, movemento

actor n. actor

actress n. actriz

actual a. actual, contempóraneo

acute a. agudo -a, aguzado, afiado

adapt v. adaptar; acomodar(se), amoldar(se), axeitar(se)

adaptation n. adaptación

add v. engadir, sumar, xuntar

adder n. víbora

addition n. adición, amesedura, ampliación, suma

address n. dirección, orientación, camiño

adequate a. adecuado -a, apropiado, axeitado, apto, conveniente

adhere v. adherir, apegar, apelicar, pegar

adhesive a. adhesivo -a

adjacent a. afín

adjective n. adxetivo

adjust v. axustar, acomodar(se), adaptar(se), amoldar(se)

administer v. administrar, gobernar, rexer, dirixir
administration n. administración
admiral n. almirante
admiration n. admiración, exclamación
admire v. admirar, estimar
admit v. admitir
admonish v amoestar, reprender
admonition n. amoestación
adolescence n. adolescencia
adopt v. adoptar, afillar
adore v. adorar, venerar
adorn v. adornar, decorar
adulate v. adular
adult n. adulto -a
adulterate v. adulterar, alterar, falsificar, falsear
adulterer n. adúltero -a
adultery n. adulterio
advance v. avanzar, adiantar
advantage n. vantaxe
adventure n. aventura
adverb n. adverbio
adversary n. adversario-a, inimigo -a
advertise v. anunciar, avisar, comunicar
advertisement n. anuncio, aviso, nova,
    comunicación
advise n. consello, advertencia, recomendación

advise v. aconsellar, consellar, recomendar, suxerir

adviser n. conselleiro -a

aerial a. aéreo-a

affect v. afectar, aparentar, finxir, simular

affection n. afección, afecto

affectionate a. amoroso -a

affirm v. afirmar, asegurar, afianzar, asentar, apoiar

affirmation n. afirmación

afflict v. aflixir(se), apenar(se), acorar(se), magoar(se)

afford v. permitir(se)

afraid a. asustado -a

African a. africano -a

after adv. & prep. despois

afternoon n. serán, tarde

afterwards adv. despois

again adv. outra vez

against prep. Contra

age n. idade

agenda n. axenda

agent n. axente

aggravate v. agravar, empeorar, complicar(se)

aggregate v. agregar(se), sumar(se), axuntar(se), unir(se), incorporar(se)

aggression n. agresión, ataque

agile a. áxil, lixeiro, lizgairo, veloz

agitate v. alborotar; axitar(se), bater, mover(se)

agony n. agonía; fin, decadencia

agree by word of mouth v. apalabrar

agree upon v. acordar

agree v. acordar, convir, decidir

agreeable a. agradable

agreement n. acordo, convenio

agriculture n. agricultura

ahead adv. adiante

aid n. auxilio, axuda

aid v. auxiliar, axudar

aim n. puntería, tino, pulso

aim, v. apuntar, dirixir

air n. ar

airplane n. avión

airport n. aeroporto

alarm n. alarma, alerta, advertencia, aviso

alarm v. alarmar(se), asustar(se), sobresaltar(se), preocupar(se)

album n. album

alcohol n. alcohol, alcol

alcove n. alcoba, cuarto, dormitorio

ale n. cerveja, cervexa

alert v. alertar, advertir, avisar

alien a. estraño -a, estranseiro -a

align v. aliñar

alike a. semellante, parecido, similar
alive a. vivo -a
all a. tódolo -a
allergy n. alerxia
alley n. calello, canellón
alliance n. alianza, unión, coalición
allow v. permitir, consentir, deixar, autorizar
ally n. aliado -a, unido -a
almanac n. almanaque
almond n. amendoa
almost prep. case
alms n. esmola
aloft adv. arriba, riba, riba de
alone a. so (m), soa (f)
aloud adv. voz alta
alphabet n. abecedario, alfabeto
already adv. xa
also adv. tamén
altar n. altar
altar piece n. retablo
alter v. alterar
alteration n. alteración
although conj. ainda que, inda que, anque
altitude n. altitude, altura
altogether adv. xunto -a
aluminum n. aluminio

always adv. sempre
amateur n. afecionado -a
amaze v. asombrar, pasmar, marabillar
ambassador n. embaixador
ambiguous a. ambiguo -a
ambition n. ambición, arela, cobiza
ambitious a. ambicioso-a
ambulance n. ambulancia
American a. americano -a
amid prep. dentro
amiss a. mal
amnesty n. amnistía
among prep. entre
amount n. cantidade
amphibious a. anfibio -a
ample a. amplo -a
amplifier n. amplificador
amplify v. amplificar, ampliar
amputate v. amputar, cortar, mutilar
amulet n. amuleto, fetiche, talismán
amuse v. divertir, entreter
amusement n. diversión
analogy n. analoxía
analysis n. analise, estudo, exame
anarchy n. anarquía, anarquismo, acracia
anatomy n. anatomía

ancestor n. antepasado -a
anchor n. áncora
ancient a. antigo -a, vello -a, vetusco, caduco
and conj. e
anecdote n. anécdota, caso, conto
anemia n. anemia
anesthesia n. anestesia
angel fish n. doncela, xuia
angel n. anxo
anger n. ira, carraxe, furia, furor, cólera, rabia
angle n. ángulo
angler n. pescador -a
angler, fish n. peixe sapo, rabada
angry a. furioso -a, furibundo, carraxento,
    colérico, irado, enfurecido
anguish n. angustia, ansia, ansiedade, inquietude
animal n. animal; bruto, besta
anise n. anís, (pl. aníses)
ankle n. nocello
annexed a. anexo -a
annihilate v. aniquilar, destruir
anniversary n. aniversario
announce v. anunciar
announcement n. aviso
annoy v. amolar, molestar
annoyance n. molestia

annual a. anual
annul v. anular, invalidar
anoint v. unxir, untar
another a. outro -a
answer n. contestación, reposta, réplica
answer v. contestar, responder, dar resposta
ant hill n. formigueiro
ant n. formiga
antelope n. antílope
antenna n. antena
anticipate v. anticipar, adiantar
antiquity n. antigüidade
anus n. ano
anvil n. bigornia
anxiety n. afán, ansia
anxious a. ansioso -a
anybody pr. calquera
apart adv. a parte
apartment n. apartamento, piso
apathy n. apatía, indiferencia, desinterese, abulia
ape n. simio, mono
apex n. ápice, punta
apologize v. excusar
apostle n. apóstolo
apparatus n. aparato, aparello
apparent a. aparente, evidente,

apparition n. aparición
appeal n. apelación
appear v. aparecer, presentarse, surxir, xurdir
appearance n. apariencia, aspecto, cariz, pinta
appendicitis n. apendicite
appendix n. apéndice
appetite n. apetito, anceio, desexo; fame
appetizer n. aperitivo
applaud v. aplaudir, loar, gabar
applause n. aplauso, aprobación
apple n. mazá
apple tree n. maceira
appliance n. aparato, aparello
application n. aplicación
apply v. aplicar, poñer, implantar, fixar
appoint v. nomear, citar
appointment n. cita
appraisal n. avaliación
appreciate v. apreciar, availar, valorar
appreciation n. aprecio, estima, cariño
apprehend v. prender, agarrar
apprentice n. aprendiz
apprenticeship n. aprendizaxe
approach v. aproximar, achegar, acercar(se)
appropriate a. apropiado -a
approve v. aprobar, aceptar

approximate v. aproximar
apricot n. albaricoque
April n. abril
apron n. mandil
apt a. apto -a, idóneo, axeitado, capaz
aptitude n. aptitude, capacidade
aqua vitae n. augardente
aquatic a. acuático -a
Arab n. árabe
arbiter n. árbitro, xuíz
arbitrator n. árbitro
arc n. arco
arch n. arco
archbishop n. arcebispo
archipelago n. arquipélago
architect n. arquitecto -a
architecture n. arquitectura
archive n. arquivo
area n. area, ámbito
argue v. arguir
argument n. argumento
arid a. árido -a
arise v. levantarse, erguerse
aristocracy n. aristocracia, nobreza
arithmetic n. aritmética
ark n. arca

arm n. brazo
arm v. armar
armament n. armamento, armas
armchair n. butaca, cadeira de brasos
armor n. armadura, traxe de guerra
armpit n. axila, sobaco
army n. exército
aroma n. aroma, fragancia, recendo
around adv. & prep. arrededor
arouse v. espertar; incitar, provocar
arrange v. amañar, arranxar, reparar
arrest v. apresar, prender, capturar, coller
arrival n. chegada
arrive v. chegar, aparecer
arrow n. frecha
art n. arte
artery n. arteria
article n. artigo
articulation n. articulación, artello, xunta
artifact n. artefacto
artificial a. artificial; falso, enganoso, ficticio,
    simulado
artisan n. artesán (m), artesa (f)
artist n. artista
as conj. like
ascend v. ascender, subir, ir para arriba

ash n. cinsa
Ash Wednesday p. mércores de cinsas
ashtray n. cinseiro
aside adv. á parte
ask v. preguntar
asleep a. durmido
asparagus n. espárrago
aspect n. aspecto, apariencia, fasquía
asphalt n. asfalto
asphyxiate v. asfixiar, afogar, abafar, atafegar, sufocar
aspiration n. aspiración
aspire v. aspirar
aspirin n. aspirina
ass n. burro -a
assassin n. asasino
assassinate v. asasinar
assassination n. asasinato
assault v. agredir, asaltar
assay n. ensaio
assembly n. asemblea
assent n. asentimento, consentemento
assert v. afirmar, asegurar, afianzar, asentar, apoiar
assertion n. afirmación
assign v. asinar, atribuir
assimilate v. asimilar, absorber

assist v. asistir, concorrer
assistance n. auxilio, asistencia,
assistant n. asistente, axudante, colaborador -a
associate v. asociar, xuntar
association n. asociación
assume v. asumir, aceptar, admitir
assurance n. seguranza, seguridade
assure v. asegurar, afirmar, asentar, fixar
astonish v. asombrar, abraiar, pasmar, marabillar
astray a. perdido, extraviado
astronaut n. astronauta
astute a. astuto -a
astuteness n. astucia, maña, raposería, renartería, zorrería
asylum n. asilo, refugio, ampara, axuda, protección
at prep. in
at present adv. agora
atheism n. ateismo
atheist a. ateo -a
athlete n. atleta
atmosphere n. atmósfera
atom n.átomo
atone v. expiar, pagar
atrium n. adro
attack v agredir, atacar
attain v. alcanzar, coller, pillar

attempt n. intento
attend v. asistir, concorrer
attendance n. asistencia
attendant n. acompañante
attention n. atención
attentive a. atento -a; amable, cortés
attenuate v. atenuar, moderar, minorar, diminuír
attic n. faiado, faio
attitude n. actitude
attorney n. avogado -a; defensor
attract v. atraer, engaiolar, cativar, seducir
attraction n. atracción
attractive a. atractivo -a, xeitoso, feiticeiro, engaiolante, cativador
attribute v. atribuir, imputar
auction n. poxa
audience n. audencia
auditory a. auditivo
augment v. aumentar
august n. agosto
authentic a. auténtico -a
author n. autor -a
authority n. autoridade
authorization n. autorización
authorize v. autorizar
automatic a. automático -a

automobile n. automóbil
autonomy n. autonomía
autumn n. outono
avail v. aproveitar, utilizar, empregar
available a. disponible, libre
avenue n. avenida
average n. medio, metade, centro
aviation n. aviación
aviator n. aviador
avoid v. evitar, impedir
await v. esperar, agardar
award n. premio, recompensa
aware a. consciente
away adv. ausente
awful a. atroz, cruel, terrible
awkward a. torpe; pesado
awl n. punzón, buril
axis n. s. (pl. axes) eixe
axle n. eixe

B

baboon n. mandril, mono africano
baby n. bebé
bachelor n. bacharelato, título da pesoa que xa
    realizou estudios secundarios

bachelor n. single man
back n. espalda
backbone n. espiña dorsal, espiñazo
bacon n. touciño
bacteria n. bacteria
bad a. mal
badge n. emblema, insignia
badly adv. malamente
baffle v. confundir
bag n. bolsa, bulsa, saqueta
bagasse n. bagaño, bagazo
baggage n. equipaxe
bail n. fianza, garantía, depósito
bait n. cebo, carnada, engado, ensenrada
   (para pescar)
bake v. asar; torrar, chamuscar, queimar
baker n. panadeiro, forneiro
balance n. balance (operación contable)
balance n. balance, contrapeso (peza mecánica)
balance v. balancear, abalar, abanear, acanear,
   bambear, mexer
balcony n. balcón, mirador natural
balcony, glass enclosed n. solario
bald a. calvo, pelado (sen pelo), careco; ermo,
   pelado (sen vexetación)
bale n. fardo, vulto, bala, paca

ball n. pelota
balloon n. balón
ballpoint pen n. bolígrafo
banana n. banana, plátano
band (music) n. banda
bandage n. venda, vendaxe
bandit n. bandido, bandoleiro, malefactor,
    atracador, asaltador, ladrón
bang v. golpear, bater, pegar
banish v. desterrar, despatriar, exiliar, deportar
banishment n. desterro
banister n. varanda
bank n. banco, banca (entidad financiera)
banker n. banqueiro
banner n. estandarte, pendón, insignia
banquet n. banquete, festín (comida espléndida)
baptism n. bautismó, bautizo, bauticeiro
baptize v. bautizar, batear
bar (for drinking) n. cantina, taberna
bar n. barra, vara
barbarian a. & n. bárbaro -a
barbarism n. barbaridade, atrocidade,
    bestialidade
barber n. barbeiro -a
barbershop n. barberfa
bare a. espido, nu (m), nua (f)

barefoot a. descalzo -a
bareheaded a. descuberto
bargain n. ganga (cosa boa & barata)
barge n. barcaza
barge v. entrar de súbito
bark n. cortiza, casca grosa do tronco das árbores
bark v. ladrar
barley n. cebada, orxo
barmaid n. camareira no cantina ou taberna
barman n. camareiro no cantina ou taberna
barnacle n. percebe
barometer n. barómetro
baron n. barón
baroness n. baronesa
barrack n. cuartel, lugar onde se aloxan as tropas
    militares
barrel n. barril, barrica, bocoi, pipo, pipote
barren a. esteril, infecundo
barrier n. barreira, atranco, obstáculo
base n. base, alicerse, cimento, fundamento
baseball s. béisbol
basement n. soto
bashful a. timido, apoucado, coibido, coitado
basic a. básico -a, elemental, fundamental
basin (fountain) n. pio (de auga)
basin (river) n. cunca

basis n. base, alicerte, cimento
basket n. cesto
basketball n. baloncesto
Basque a. & n. vasco -a
bass n. róbalo
bat n. morcego
batch n. fornada
bath n. baño
bath tub n. bañeira, baño
bathe v. bañar
bathroom n. cuarto de aseo
bathtub n. bañeira
battalion n. batallón
batter v. mallar, golpear, pegar
battery n. bateria
battle n. batalla
bay n. baia
bayonet n. baioneta
bazaar n. bazar
be able v. ser capaz
be born v. nacer
be v. ser, estar
beach n. praia
beacon n. faro
beak n. pico, peteiro, bico das aves
beam (construction) n. viga, trabe

beam (light) n. raio
bean n. faba
bear n. oso -a
bear v. tolerar, consentir
beard n. barba
bearded a. barbudo -a
bearing n. porte externo dunha pesoa
beast n. besta, bicho, becho, animal
beat v. bater, golpear, pegar, percutir, petar
beautiful a. fermoso -a, belo -a, bonito -a
beauty n. beleza, beldade, bonitura, fermosura
beaver n. castor (mamífero roedor)
because conj. porqué
become v. facerse
bed n. cama, leito
bedroom n. dormitorio, cuarto
bee n.f. abella
beefsteak n. vaca asada
beehive n. colmea
beer n. cerveja, cervexa
beetle n. escaravello
beetroot n. remolacha
before adv. antes
befriend v. favorecer, amparar
beg v. rogar, pregar, pedir, suplicar
beggar n. mendigo, pobre de pedir

begin v. empezar, comenzar, encomezar, principiar
beginner n. principiante
beguile v. engañar, mentir, traicionar
behalf n. favor, patrocinio
behave v. condicirse, comportarse
behavior n. conducta, comportamento
behead v. decapitar, degolar, descabezar
behind adv. detrás, atrás
behold v. mirar, observar
being n. ser, ente
Belgian n. belga
belief n. crenza, idea
believe v. creer
bell n. campá, sino (instrumento)
bellow n. bramido, berro, brúo, voz de touro
bellow v. berrear
bellows n. fol
belly n. barriga, bandullo, ventre
belong v. pertenecer
belongings n.pl. aveños, apeiros, aparellos, trebellos
below a. & prep. baixo -a
belt n. correa, cinto, corda
bench n. banco, banqueta
bend v. torcer, curvar
beneath adv. & prep. debaixo

beneficence n. beneficencia, caridade
benefit n. beneficio, favor
benefit v. beneficiar, favorecer, axudar
benign n. benigno -a, bo, benévolo, indulxente
bent n. torcido, torto
beret n. boina, pucha
berry n. bago, bazo
beside prep. cerca, preto
besides adv. ademais
bet n. aposta, pacto, xugada
betray v. traizoar
betrayal n. traizón, deslealdade, infidelidade, falsidade
better a. mellor, mais bo
between prep. & adv. entre
beverage n. bebida
beware v. precaver, precaverse
bewilder v. abouxar, atordar
beyond adv. fora
bib n. babeiro
bible n.m. Biblia
biceps n. biceps
bicycle n. bicicleta
bidet n. bidé
big a. grande, enorrne
bigness n. grandor, grandura, grandeza

bikini n. bikini
bilingual a. bilingue
bill n. conta; recibo, factura
billiards n. billar
billow n. onda, ola
bin n. recipiente
bind v. atar, amarrar
biography n. biografía
biology n. bioloxía
bird n. paxaro
birth n. nacemento
birthday n. aniversario
biscuit n. biscoito
bit n. anaco, bocado, porción, cacho
bit n. broca, barrena, barreno
bitch s. can (f)
bite v. morder
bitter a. amargo, acedo
bitterness n. amargura, tristura
black a. & n. negro, mouro
blackberry n. amora
blackbird n. merlo, merla
blackboard n. encerado, prancha para escribir
blacken v. ennegrecer, negrexar, negrear
blacksmith n. ferreiro
bladder n. vexiga

blade (plant) n. folla, organo das plantas
blade n. cortador
blame v. culpar, acusar
blanket n. manta da cama, prenda de abrigo
blasphemy n. blasfemia
blast n. raxada, refacho
blaze n. labrarada, laparada
bleak (fish) n. breia, paxel
bleak a. ermo, deserto, despoboado
bleed v. desangrar(se)
bleeding n. hemorraxia
bless v. bendicir, beicer
blessed a. bendito, loado, santiño
blessing n. bendición, beizón
blind a. cego -a, invidente
blindness n. cegueira
blink v. pestanexar, palpebrexar
blinkers n. anteolleiras
bliss n. deleite, agrado
block n. bloque
blockhead n. lerdo
blond a. roxo
blood n. sangue
bloom n. florecemento
bloom v. florecer, churrir
blossom n. gromo, rebento, xermolo

blot n. borrancho, borrón, mancha
blotter n. papel secante
blouse n. blusa
blow n. golpe, choque, impacto
blow v. soprar
blue a. azul
blue blood p. sangue azul
blunt (object) a. romo -a
blunt (person) a. brusco, aspero -a, seco
　(de trato pouco amable)
blunt v. fanar
blush n. rubor, fogaxe, pudor
blush v. ruborizar, ruborizarse
boar n. verrón
board n taboa, taboleiro
boarder n. pensionista
boarding house n. pensión
boarding school n. colexio interno
boat n. buque, barco, navio
boatman, boatwoman n. barqueiro, barqueira
bobbin n. bobina
bodkin n. punzón
body n. corpo
boil v. ferver
boiler n. caldeira, caldeiro
boiling n. ebulición, fervor

bold a. atrevido, audaz
boldness n. atrevemento, audacia
bolster v. animar, alentar
bolt n. ferrolo, picaporte
bolt v. escapar, fuxir
bomb n. bomba
bomb v. bombardear
bomber n. bombardeiro
bondage n. cativerio, catividade
bone marrow n. milo, molo, miola, médula
bone n. óso
bonfire n. fogueira, cacharela
bonnet n. capota
book n. libro
bookcase n. armario para libros
boot n. bota
border n. beira
bottle n. botella
bounce v. brincar, choutar, saltar, pular
bourgeois n. burgueés -a
boxing n. boxeo
brave a. bravo -a, afouto, destemido, valente
bread n. pam, pan
breakfast n. almorzo
breeze n. brisa, nordés
brief a. breve, curto, pequeno

bright a. brillante, coruscante, escintilante, luminoso, radiante
brilliance n. brillo, luz, resplendor
bronchial tube n. branquia
bronchitis n. bronquite
bronze n. bronce
bronze v. broncear
broth n. caldo
brute a. bruto -a
bubble n. burbulla, bolo, goldría, gurgulla
bucket n. balde
buckthorn V. hawthorn
bulb n. bulbo
bullet n. bala, proxetil
bun n. bolo
bundle n. vulto
buoy n. boia
bus n. bus
bustle n. barullo
button n. botón
button up v. abrochar
buttonhole n. ollal, botoeira
buy v. comprar, mercar
buyer n. comprador
buzz n. zunido
by prep. cerca, preto
by-laws n. regulamentos

C

cab. taxi

cabbage n. repolo

cabin n cabana, cabina

cabinet n. gabinete, ministerio (departamento dun governo)

cable n. cable, arame (conductor eléctrico)

cacao n. cacao (árbore)

cactus n. cacto

cage n. gaiola

cake n. pastel

calculate v. calcular

calculation n. calculación

calendar n. calendario

calf n. terneiro, becerro, cuxo

call n. chamada, berro

call v. chamar, convocar, citar, nomear, denominar

calm a. tranquilo -a, apracible, calmo

calm n. tranquilidade, acougo, calma

camel n. camelo

camera (judge's private chamber) n. cámara, cuarto; corpo legislativo

camera (photographic) n. camarota (dun barco), máquina (de cine, TV, fotografía, etc.)

camp n. campo, campiña

camp out v. acampar; pousar, parar, deterse

canal n. canal, canle

cancel v. cancelar, anular, suprimir

cancer n. cáncer (zona do Zodiaco)

cancer n. cancro (tumor maligno)

candid a. cándido -a, candoroso -a, inocente

candidate n. candidato, aspirante

candle n. candea, vela, cirio

candy n. doce, confeito

cane n. caña, canaveira, canivela (talo dalgunhas plantas)

canine tooth n. canino

cannon n. cañón, canón (peza de de artillería)

cannon n. cañon, desfiladero

canoe n. canoa

canon n. canon, regra, precepto

canteen n. cantina, taberna

canvas n. lona

cap n. gorro, pucho

capable a. capaz, capacitado, apto

capacity n. capacidade

cape n. cabo, extremo, punta (xeograf I a)

cape n. capa (prenda de vestir)

capital a. capital, esencial, fundamental, principal

capital n. capital (cidade onde reside o goberno)

capital n. capital (patrimonio)

capsule n. cápsula

captain n. capitán (grao militar)

car n. carro

caravan n. caravana

carrion n. prea

cart n. carro

carton n. cartón

cartoon n. caricatura

cartridge n. cartucho

carve v. esculpir

carving knife n. trinchante

carving n. escultura

case n. caixa, caixón

case n. caso, acontecimento

cash n. diñeiro, moedas

cashier n. caixero

cask n. barril, pipote (un barril de viño)

cast v. tirar, guindar

castanets n. castañola(s)

Castilian a. castelán

cast-iron n. ferro fundido

castle n. castelo

casual a. casual, fortuito

casualty n. victima, ferido

cat n. gato

Catalan n. & a. catalán -a
catalogue n. catálogo
cataract n. catarata, belida (enfermidade ocular)
catch v. coller, agarrar, tomar
cathecism n. catecismo, doctrina
cathedral n. catedral
catholicism n. catolicismo
cattle n. gando, gado
cauldron n. caldeireiro
cauliflower n. coliflor
cause n. causa, motivo
caution n. cautela, coidado, precaución
cautious a. cauteloso, cauto, precavido
cavalcade n. cabalgata
cavalry n. cabaleria
cave n. caverna, cova
cease v. cesar, concluir
cedar n. cedro
ceiling n. teito, tellado
celebrate v. celebrar, festexar
celebrated a. célebre, famoso -a
celery n. apio
cell (convent room) n. cela (cuarto dun convento)
cell (electrical) n. pila eléctrica, batería
cell (jail) n. cela, calabozo (dun cárcere)
cellar n. soto; adega, bodega

cello n. violoncelo
Celtic village n. castro
cement n. cemento
cemetery n. cemiterio, camposanto, necrópole
center n. centro
centimeter n. centímetro
centipede n. ciempiés
central a. central
century n. século, centuria
ceramics n. cerámica
cereal n. cereal
ceremony n. cerimonia, rito
certain a. certo, verdadeiro
certificate n. certificado
certify v. certificar
chain n. cadea, serie, sucesión, restra
chain v. encadear
chair n. cadeira, asento, sela (para montar a cabalo)
chalice n. caliz, copa
chalk n. xiz (pl. xizes)
challenge n. desafío, reto
challenge v. desafiar, segar
chamber n. cámara, cuarto
chamberpot n. bacía
chamois n. rebezo
chamomile n. manzanilla, macela, camomila

champion a. campeón, ganador
champion v. defender, protexer
chance n. azar, acaso, fortuna
chancellor n. chanceller
change n. cambio, alteración
change v. cambiar, permutar
changeable a. variable, cambiable
channel n. canal, canle
chant n. canto, canción, melodía, cantar, cántiga
chaos n. caos, desorde
chapel n. capela; capel (corpo de músicos)
chapter n. capítulo (dun libro)
character n. carácter
charcoal n. carbón; carboncillo (carbon de
    debuxar)
charge n. carga
charity n. caridade
charm n. encanto, feitizo
chart n. carta, mapa
charter n. carta, constitución política
chase n. caza, perseguimento
chase v. perseguir, seguir acosar
chassis n chassis
chastity n. castidade, pureza
chat n. charla, parola, conversa
chat v. charlar, parolar, conversar

chatter n. charla, parrafeo
cheap a. barato -a, económico -a
cheat n. engano, mentira, falsidade
check n. cheque
cheek n. meixela, fazula
cheers inter. saúde
cheese n. queixo
chemical a. químico -a
chemist n. químico -a
cherish v. querer, apreciar
cherry n. cereixa
chest of drawers n. cómoda
chestnut n. beloca
chew v. mascar, mastigar
chick n. pito, pitiño
chicken n. polo
chickpea n. garavanzo
chickweed n. herba paxareira, pampillo
chief n. xefe, xefa
child n.sing. neno, nena
childhood n. nenez, infancia
childish a. infantil
children n.pl. nenos, nenas
chill a. frio
chilly adv. frio
chimney n. cheminea

chimpanzee n. chimpancé
chin n. queixo
china n. porcelana
Chinese a. chinés
chip n. estela, racha, lasca
chisel n. cicel
chivalry n. fidalguía
chloroform n. cloroformo
chocolate n. chocolate
choice n. escollido
choir n. coro
choke v. aforgar, asfixiar
choose n. elixa
choose v. elixir, escoller
chop n. machadazo
chop v. tallar, cortar
chopper n. machada, macheta
chorus n. coro
christen v. bautizar
Christian a. cristiano -a
Christmas n. Nadal
chronicle n. crónica
church n. igrexa
churchyard n. cemiterio, camposanto, necrópole
cider n. cidra
cigar n. xaruto, cigarro

cigarette n. cigarro pito
cinder n cinza
cinema n. cine, cinema
cinnamon n. canela (condimento)
cipher n. cifra, número
circle n. círculo
circuit n circuito
circulate v. circular
circulation n. circulación
circumference n. circunferencia
circumstance n. circumstancia
circus n. circo
cite v. citar, emprazar
citizen n. cidadán, -á
city n. cidade
civilization n. civilización
claim n. reclamación
claim v. reclamar
clam n. ameixa, longueriro
clap n. aplauso, aprobación
clap v. aplaudir, loar, gabar
clarinet n. clarinete
class n. clase, especie
classify v. clasificar, catalogar
classroom n. aula
clatter n. estrondo, bulla

claw n. pouta, gadoupa, garra
clay n. arxila
clean v. limpar
cleave v. fender, abrir
clergy n. clérigo, crego, sacerdote
clergyman n. clero
clerk n. empregado
clever a. habil, destro -a, mañoso -a
client n. cliente
cliff n. farallón, gago, tatexo
climate n. clima, ambiente
climax n. climax
climb n. subida, ascenso
climb v. subir, elevar, ascender, crecer
cling v. aferrarse, afirmarse
clinic n. clínica
clip n. tesoirada
clock n. reloxo
clogs n. zoca
cloister n. claustro
close v. cerrar, pechar
closed a. cerrado
cloth n. tea, tecido, pano
clothe v. vestir
clothing n. roupa, vestimenta, vestido,
    indumentaria

cloud n. nube

cloudy a. nubrado

clown n. pallaso (do circo)

club n. porra, cachaporra

clue n. pista, rastro

cluster n. desorde, barullo

clutch n. embrague

clutch v. embragar

coach n. adestrador

coach n. coche, carruaxe

coal n. carbón

coarse a. rudo, basto, rústico -a

coast n. costa, litoral

coat n. abrigo; abeiradoiro, amparo, refuxio

cobweb n. tea de arana

cock n. galo, capón

cocktail n. cóctel

cocoa n. cacao

cocoon n. botón, abrocho

cod n. bacallao

code n. código

coffee house n. café, cafetería

coffee n. café

coffee pot n. cafeteira

coffin n. ataúde, féretro, cadaleito, caixa

coil n. rolo

coin n. moeda
coincide v. coincidir
cold (illness) n. carraspeira
cold a. frio
collaborate v. colaborar, cooperar
collaboration n. colaboración
collar n. colar, coleira
colleague n. colega, compañeiro
collect v. recoller, coller
collection n. colección, colecta
college n. colexio (centro de ensino)
collide v. chocar, bater
collision n. colisión, choque
colon (anatomy) n. colón
colon (grammar) n. colón
colonel n. coronel
colonize v. colonizar
colony n. colonia
color n. cor
column n. columna
comb n. peite
comb v. peitar(se)
combination n. combinación, mestura
combine v. combinar, mesturar
come v. vir; chegar, presentarse
comedy n. comedia; farxa, finximento

comet n. cometa
comfort n. comodidade
comic a. cómico, gracioso, pándego, divertido -a
comma (grammar) n. coma (signo ortográfico)
command n. comando
command v. comandar
commence v. comenzar, empezar
commend v. recomendar, aconsellar
comment n. comentario
comment v. comentar
commentary n. comentario
commerce n. comercio, tenda, negocio, establecemento
commission n. comisión
committee n. comité, comisión, delegación, representación
communicate v. comunicar
communication n. comunicación
communion n. comunión
communism n. comunismo
compact n. compacto, macizo -a
companion n. compañeiro, colega
companionship n. compañia (acción de acompañar)
company n. compañia (sociedade mercantil)
comparison n. comparanza

compartment n. compartimento

compass n. compás

compassion n. compaixón, compadecemento

competence n. competencia, aptitude

competent a. competente, apto, entendido, experto

competition n. competición, competencia, vivaldade

complaint n. queixa, queixume, laio, lamento; protesta

complement n. complemento

complete a. completo, cheo, atestado; enteiro, integro

complete v. completar, acabar, concluir

complex a. complexo; difícil, complicado

complicate v. complicar(se)

compliment n. cumprimento, afago

comply v. acceder, consentir

compose v. compoñer, compor

composition n. composición, peza, obra

compositor n. compositor

compound a. composto

compound v. compoñer, compor, constituir, integrar

comprehend v. comprender, entender

comprehensive a. exhaustivo, completo

computer n. computador

comrade n. camarada, amigo, compañeiro
conceal v. ocultar, encubrir, agochar
conceit n. presunción
concentrate v. concentrar, centrar, reunir, xuntar
concept n. concepto, idea
concern n. interese, incumbencia
concern v. concernir, incumbir
concert n. concerto
concession n. concesión
conciliate v. conciliar
concious a. consciente
concrete a. concreto
concur v. concorrer, asistir
condemn v. condenar, sentenciar
condition n. condición
condolence n. condolencia, pésame
conductor n. conductor
cone n. cono (corpo xemétrico)
confess v. confesar, comunicar, expresar,
    declarar, revelar
confession n. confesión
confidence n. confidencia
confirm v. confirmar, comprobar
conflagration n. conflagración, incendio
conflict n. conflicto, desacordo
confortable a. confortable, cómodo -a

conforter n. consolado; bufanda
confuse v. confundir, desaconcertar
confusion n. confusión, desorde
congratulate v. congratular, felicitar
congratulation n. congratulación, felicitación
congress n. congreso
conjunction n. conjunción
connect v. conectar
connection n. conexión, contacto
conquer v. conquistar, someter, subxugar
conqueror n. conquistador
conquest n. conquista
conscience n. consciencia, conciencia
consecrate v. consagrar, sacrilizar
consent n. consentimento, permiso, licencia
consent v. consentir, tolerar, permitir
consequence n. consecuencia, resultado
consequent a. consecuente, conseguinte,
   congruente
conserve v. conservar, gardar, manter
consider v. considerar, contemplar
consideration n. consideración, reflexión
consist v. consistir, compoñerse
consolation n. consolación
console v. consolar, confortar, alentar
consonant a. & n. consonante

constellation n. constelación

constipation n. constipación

constitute v. constituir, fundar

consult v. consultar, aconsellarse, consellarse

consumption n. consumo

contagion n. contaxio

contagious a. contaxioso

contain v. conter, ter, encerrar

container n. contido

contaminate v. contaminar

contend v. afirmar, disputar

content a. contento, alegre

contention n. contención

continent n. continente

continuance n. continuación

continue v. continuar, seguir

continuos a. continuo -a, continudo -a

contract n. contrato, pacto

contract v. contratar, axustar

contrary a. contrario -a, oposto -a

contrast v. contrastar

contribute v. contribuir, axudar, coadxuvar, cooperar

contribution n. contribución

control n. control, comprobación, inspección, rexistro; dominio

control v. controlar, comprobar, inspeccionar;
   dominar
controller n. inspector
convene v. convocar, chamar, citar
convent n. convento, moisteiro
conversation n. conversación, conversa, parola,
   palique, parrafeo, coloquio, leria
converse v. conversar, chalar, dialogar
convert v. converter, transformar
convertible n. convertible
convey v. transportar, transmitir
convince v. convencer, persuadir
convoy n. convoi, escolta
cook n cocineiro
cook v. cocinar
cookery n. arte de cocina
cool a. fresco -a; recente, novo
coolness n. frescura, frescor
cooperate v. cooperar, axudar
coordinate v. coordinar
copper n. cobre
copy n. copia
copy v. copiar, reproducir
copyright n. propiedade literaria
coral n. coral (animal mariño)
coral n. coral (música)

cord n. corda
core n. centro, nucleo
coriander n. coandro
cork n. cortiza; casca, tona, pel costra
corn bread n. boroa, broa
corn n. cab, calosidade
corn (plant) n. millo, mainzo
corner n. esquina, aresta
corps n. corpo
corpse n. cadáver, morto, defunto
correct a. correcto -a; cortes, educado -a
correct v. correxir, emendar
correspond v. corresponder; concernir, incumbir
correspondence n. correspondencia
correspondent n. correspondente
corridor n. corredor
corroborate v. corroborar, confirmar
corrugate v. ondular
corrupt v. corromper, descompor, descomponer, estragar, podrecer, apodrentar
corruption n. corrupción
corsair n. corsario, pirata
cortes n. cortes (conxunto formado polo congreso & polo senado)
cost n. custa
cost ?how much does it cost? n. custa; ¿Canto custa?

costume n. disfrace
cot n. berce (cama de nenos)
cottage n. cabana
cotton n. algodón
couch n. sofá, diván
cough n tose
cough v. tusir
council n. xunta, axuntamento
counsel n. consello, advertencia
count v. contar, computar
counter n. mostrador, amosador, expositor
counterfeit n. falso -a
counterpoint n. contrapunta
countess n. condesa
country n. pais, nación
country villa n. pazo
countryman n. paisano, coterraneo -a, concidán
county n. condado
couple n. parella, par; compañeiro -a
courageous a. valeroso -a, valente
course n. curso, fluxo, movemento
court n. corte (conxunto formado polo rei e
    servidores)
courtesy n. cortesía
courtier n. cortesán -a
courtship n. noivado

courtyard n. patio
cousin n. primo -a, curmán
covenant n. convenio, pacto, acordo
cover n. cobertor, colcha, tapa
cover v. cubrir, tapar
covetous a. cobizoso, ambicioso -a, desexoso -a
cow n. vaca
coward a. & n. covarde, apoucado -a, medroso -a
cowshed n. corte, cortello
crab (zodiac sign) n. cáncer (signo do Zodiaco)
crab n. cangrexo, caranguexo (crustáceo)
crack (noise) n. ruxido, estalo, estralo
crack n. abertura, greta
cradle n. berce (cama dos nenos)
craft n. oficio, traballo, profesión
craftsman n. artesán -a
crafty a. astute, listo, cuco
crane (bird) n. grou (ave)
crane n guindastre, guinche
crash n. cheque, colisión
crate n. caixa
crawfish n. langostino
crawl v. gatear, andar a ganchas
crayfish n. langosta
crazy n. tolo -a, louco -a, demente
cream n. crema

crease n. pregamento, dobra
create v. crear, orixinar, producir, fundar
creation n. creación
creature n. criatura
credit n. crédito, prestamo
creditor n. acredor
creed n. credo, creenza, doutrina
creep n. arrastre
creep v. arrastrar, levar, marchar con
creeper n. réptil
crepe n. filloa
crescent a. crecente
crest n. crista, cristo; cima
crew n. tripulación
cricket n. grilo
crime n. crime, delicto
crimson a. carmesí
cripple n. tolleito -a, eivado -a, impedido -a
cripple v. eivar, toller, impedir
criticism n criticismo
criticize v. criticar, censurar, reprobar, condenar
croak n. berro, brado
crocodile n. crocodilo
crook n gancho, garabato, borrancho
crooked a. torcido, torto
crop n. colleita, recolleita

cross n cruz, crucifixo; padecemento, pena
cross v. cruzar, atravesar
crossroad n. encrucillada
crossword n. encrucillado, palabras cruzadas
crouch v. agachar, abaixar
crow n. corvo
crowd n. multitude, xentio
crucifix n. crucifixo
crude a. cru -a; duro -a, rigoroso -a, desapracible
cruel a. cruel, brutal, duro, despiado -a
cruise n. cruceiro (viaxe turístico por mar)
cruise to v. pasear; exhibirse
cruiser n. cruceiro (barco de guerra)
crumb n. miolo, molo, miga
crumble v. migar, esmigallar, esmingallar
crunch v. triturar, esmagar, esmiuzar
crusade n. cruzada (expedición militar)
crush v. machucar, esmagar, triturar
crust n. cortiza; casca; codia, codela
crustaceous n. crustáceo
crutch n. muleta; apoio
cry n. chore, pranto
cry v. chorarñ lamentar, laiar
crystal n. cristal
cub n. cachorro, cadelo (cría do can)
cube n. cubo; hexaedro, tercera potencia

cuckoo n. cuco (ave)
cuff n. puño (dunha prenda de vestir)
culprit n. culpable, causante, responsible
cultivate v. cultivar, traballar a terra
cultivation n. cultivacao, cultivo
culture n. cultura, conñecementos; civilización
cunning n. astuto, liso, cuco
cup n. cunca
cupboard n. armario, despensa
curate n. párroco, crego, sacerdote
cure n. cura, curación
cure v. curar, sandar
curious a. curioso -a; interesante, raro -a
curl n. rizo, rizado,crecho
curl v. rizar(se)
currency n. diñeiro, moedas
current a. corrente, común, normal
current n. corrente, fluxo
curtain n. cortiña
curve n. curva, volta
cushion n. coxín
custard n. crema
custom n. costume, hábito
customs n. alfándega
cut n. corte
cut v. cortar, tallar, rebanar

cycle n. ciclo, etapa, fase, per I odo
cylinder n. cilindro
cymbal n. címbalo, campaiña

D

dad, daddy n. papá
daffodile n. narciso
dagger n. daga, puñal
dahlia n. dalia
dainty a. primoroso -a, habelencioso -a
dairy ri. leitería
daisy n. margarida
dam n. dique, represa
damage n. dano, prexuíso, mal
dame n. dama
damn n. maldito
damn v. maldicir
damp a. húmido -a
damp v. humedecer(se)
dampness n. humidade
dance n. danza
danger n. perigo, risco
dangerous a. perigoso, arriscado -a
dangle v. colgar, pendurar

daphne, flax-leaved n. trobisco, trobisqueira
dare n. reto, desafio
dare v. retar, desafiar
daring a. ousado, arriscado, atrevido, audaz
dark a. moreno -a
darken v. escurecer
darkness n escuridade
darling a. querido -a
darn v. zurcir
dart n. dardo, frecha, saeta
dash n. guión, trazo, raia (signo ortografico)
date (fruit) n. dátil (froita)
date n. cita
date plum n. caqui
daughter n. filha, filla
daughter-in-law n. nora (filla política)
daunt v. atemorizar, amedrar, asustar, espaventar
dauntless a. intrépido -a
dawn n. amencer, amañecer, aclarar, alborecer
day n. dia
daze v. abouxar, aturdir, achourilar
dazzle v. cegar, asombrar
dead a. morto -a, morrido -a
deaden v. amortecer, atenuar
deadly adv. mortal, letal
deaf n. xordo

deafening n. enxordecedor, abouxador
deafness n. xordeira, xordén
deal n. negocio, quefacer, asunto
deal v. negociar, comerciar, traficar
dealer n. traficante
dean n. decano
dear a. querido -a; amado -a
death n. morte, felacemento
deathless n. inmortal, inmorredoiro
debate n. debate, discusión
debauch n. libertinaxe
debt n. débeda
debtor n. debedor
debut n. debut, presentación
decade n. decade
decadence n. decadencia, decaemento
decant v. decantar
decay v. decaer, debilitarse, esmorecer, ir a menos
decease n. falecemento, morte, pasamento
deceit n. engano, calote, mentira
deceitful a. enganoso
deceive v. enganar, mentir, falsear
December n. decembro, mes do Nadal
decency n. decencia
decent a. decente, honesto, puduroso -a
deception n. decepción, desengano, desilución

decide v. decidir, convir, resolver, acordar
decided a. decidido, acordado, resolto
decimal a. decimal
decimate v. dezmar, decimar
decision n. decisión, acordo
decisive a. decisivo, definitivo
deck n. cuberta, sollado (dun barco)
declaration n. declaración
declare v. declarar
decline n. declinación, pendente (do terreo)
decline v. declinar
decorate v. decorar, adornar
decoration n. decoración, ornamentación
decoy n. maquinación, argallada
decrease n. diminución, mingua
decrease v. diminuir, minguar, apoucar
decree n. decreto, resolución
decry v. vituperar, censurar, reprender
dedicate v. dedicar, destinar, ofrecer, brindar
dedication n. dedicación
deduce v. deducir, derivar, inferir
deduction n. dedución
deed n. feito, acto
deem v. xulgar, considerar
deep a. profundo, fondo
deer n. cervo, veado

defamation n. difamación, calumnia
defamatory a. infamatorio, infamante
defame v. difamar, desacreditar, impefecci o n
default v. faltar, fallar
defeat n. derrota, fracaso, revés
defeat v. derrotar, vencer
defect n. defecto, imperfección, deficiencia
defend v. defender, protexer, gardar
defendant n. acusado
defender n. defensor
defense n. defensa
defer v. diferir, defer, retardar, atrasar
define v. definir, delimitar, determinar, precisar,
    explicar
definition n. definición
definitive a. definitivo
deflate v. desinchar
defy v. desafiar, retar
degree n. grao (dun ángulo); xerarquía
delay n. demora, retraso, tardanza
delay v. demorar, atrasar, retardar
deliberate a. deliberado -a, intencionado -a
deliberate v. reflexionar, pensar, meditar
delicacy n. delicadeza
delicate a. delicado, fráxil
delight n. delicia, pracer, deleite

deliver v. entregar
delivery n. entrega
delta (Greek letter) n. delta (letra grega)
delta n. delta (desembocadura dun rio)
deluge n. inundación, asolagamento
demand n. demanda, petición, pedimento
demand v. demandar, pedir, solicitar
democracy n. democracia
demolish v. demoler, derrubar, derruir
demon n. demo, diaño, diablo, diabro, demoño
demonstrate v. demostrar, probar, evidenciar
demonstration n. demonstración
den n. cubil, tobo, tobeira, gorida
dense a. denso -a, mesto, espeso, concentrado, basto
density n. densidade
dent n. aboladura
dent v. abolar(se)
dentist n. dentista, odontólogo
denude v. denudar
denunciation n. denuncia
deny v. negar, desmentir
depart v. sair, partir, marchar
department n. departamento
depend v. depender
dependent n. dependente

depict v. representar

depot n. depósito, almacenamento

depress v. deprimir, abater, desanimar, desmoralizar

depression n. depresión, abatemento

deprive v. privar, desposuir

depth n. profundidade, fondura

deputy n. deputado (parlamentario)

derange v. desarranxar

derision n. irrisión, escarnio, escarbecemento

derive v. derivar

derrick n. guindastre, guinche

descend v. descender, baixar

descent n. descenso, baixada

describe v. describir, trazar

description n. descrición

desert a. deserto -a, desértico -a, despoboado -a

desert v. desamparar, abandonar

deserve v. merecer

deserving a. meritorio -a

design n. deseño, esbozo, boceto

designate v. designar

designer n. deseñador -a

desirable a. desexable

desire n. desexo, devezo, degoro, agoada, ansia, anhelo

desire v. desexar, querer
desist v. desistir, renunciar
desk n. escritorio; pupitre
desolate a. abatido -a, afixido -a
despair n. desesperación, desespero
despair v. desesperar
despicable a. vil, malvado -a
despise v. desprezar
dessert n. postre, sobremesa
destiny n. destino; sorte, fado, fortuna
destroy v. destruir
destroyer n. destructor
destruction n. destrucción, estrago, desfeita
detach v. separar, apartar
detain v. deter; arrestar, prender
detect v. descubir, destapar
detection n. deteción
detective n. detective
deter v. disaudir
determination n. determinación
determine v. determinar, decidir, resolver
determined a. determinado -a, definido -a
detest v. detestar, aborrecer
detriment n. detrimento, dano
develop v. desenvolver, crecer, prosperar
development n. desenvolvemento, progreso

deviate v. desviar
deviation n. desviación, desvio
device n. dispositivo
devil n. diabo, diabro, demo, demonia, diaño, deño
devilish a. diabólico
devise v. inventar
devoted a. devoto -a
devour v. devorar, tragar, engullir
devout a. piadoso -a; devoto -a
dew n. rosada
diabetes n. diabete
diagnosis n. diagnóstico
diagonal a. diagonal
dial n. dial (dos receptores radioteléfonicos)
dialect n. dialecto
dialogue n. dialogo, conversa, charla
diameter n. diámetro
diamond n. diamante
diary n. diario
dice n. dados
dictate v. dictar
dictation n. dictado
dictator n. dictador, autócrata
dictionary n. diccionario
die n. dado
die v. morrer, fallecer

dieresis n. diérese
differ v. disentir, discrepar
difference n. diferencia
different a. diferente, distinto -a
difficult a. difícil
difficulty n. dificultade
diffuse v. difundir
dig v. escabar, cavar
digest v. dixerir
digestion n. dixestión
dignify v. dignificar, ennobrecer
dignity n. dignidade
dike n. dique
dilate v. dilatar
diligent n. dilixente, asiduo -a
dill n. herba agulleira
dim a. tenue, débil, opaco -a
dimension n. dimensión
diminish v. disminuir, minguar, apoucar, afrouxar, decrecer
dimness n. opacidade
dine v. cear, comer
dining room n. comedor
dinner n. comida
dip n. caida
dip v. afundir(se)
diplomacy n. diplomacia

direct a. dereito -a

direct v. dirixir, conducir, orientar, guiar

direction n. dirección, orientación, camiño, rumbo

director n. director -a

directory n. directorio

dirt n. suciedade, lixo, inmundicia, porcallada

dirty a. sucio -a, lixado -a

dirty v. emporcar(se), manchar(se)

disagree v. disentir, discrepar

disagreement n. discrepancia, desacordo, diverxencia

disappear v. desaparecer, marchar, esvaerse, ausentarse

disappoint v. desilusionar

disappointment n. desilución, desengano

disaster n. desastre, desgracia

discharge n. descarga

discharge v. descargar; desabafar, desafogar

disciple n. discipulo -a, alumno -a

discipline n. disciplina

discount n. desconto

discourse n. discurso, alocución

discover v. descubrir, destapar, atopar, achar

discovery n. descubrimento

discreet a. discreto -a, asisado, axuizado, cordo, sensato

discriminate v. discriminar

discuss v. discutir, debater

discussion n. discusión, controversia, polémica

disease n. enfermidade, doenza, mal

disgrace n. desgracia

disguise n. disfrace, traxe de máscara

disguise v. disfrazar, finxir

disgust n. disgusto, pesar, mágoa, descontento, fastío, tedio

disgust v. disgustar, desagradar, despracer; magoar

disgusting a. repugnante, aborrecible

dish n. prato

dishonest a. fraudulento

dishonesty n. fraude, fraudulencia, defraudación, dolo, engano

disk n. disco

dislike n. antipatia, animadversión

dismay n. consternación, digusto, desconsolo, pena

dismiss v. despedir, desempregar

disobey v. desobedecer

display v. despregar, desdobrar

displease v. desagradar, disgustar

dispose v. dispoñer, dispor

dispute v. disputar, cismar, tirapuxar, barallar, latricar, rifar

disregard n. descoido, desleixo, abandono

disregard v. descoidar, desatender, abandonar
distance n. distancia, treito, tirada
distant a. lonxe, distante
distaste n. desagrado, disgusto
distill v. destilar
distinct a. distinto, diferente
distinction n. distinción, distingo
distinguish v. distinguir, sobreancear
distort v. deformar, alterar, desfigurar
distract v. distraer, entreter, enredar, divertir
distress n. dor, pena
distribute v. distribuir, repartir
distribution n. distribución
district n. distrito
distrust n. desconfianza, receo
distrust v. desconfiar, sospeitar
disturb v. molestar, perturbar
ditch n. foxo, gabia
dive n. mergullo, submersión
dive v. mergullar
diver (bird) n. corvo marino (paxaro)
diver n. mergullador
diverge v. diverxer
diverse a. diverso -a, distinto, diferente
diversify v. diversificar
divide v. dividir, partir, repartir

divine a. divino -a; sublime, excelso, perfecto

division n. división; discordia desacordo, desunión

divorce n. divorcio, desacordo

divorce v. divorciar, descasar

dizziness n. mareo, desmaio

dizzy a. vertixinoso -a

dock n peirao

doctor n. doutor

dodge v. esquivar, eludir

dog fish, dog shark n. cazón

dog n. can, cadela

doll n. moneca (f), moneco (m)

dollar n. dolar

dolphin n. delfín

domain n. dominio

dome n. cúpula, cuberta; casca

dominate v. dominar

domination n. dominación

dominion n. dominio, territorio, ámbito

donkey n. burro, asno

doom n. sino, fado, destino

door n. porta, entrada

doorway n. entrada, portal

dory (fish) n. rapante (peixe)

dose n. dose, ración, porción, medida

dot n. punto

double n. dobre, duplo

double v. dobrar, duplicar

doubt n. dúbida

doubt v. dubidar

doubtful a. dubidoso, incerto

dove n. pombo, pomba

down adv. abaixo

doze v. durmiñar

dozen n. ducia

draft n. xiro (forma de envio por correo)

drag v. arrastrar, levar

dragon n. dragón

dragonfly n. cabalino de demo, libélula, libeliña

drain n. desaugadoiro

drain v. desaugar, verter, afluir, desembocar

drama n. drama, teatro, dramaturxia (xénero literario)

draw debuxar

drawing n. debuxo

drawing pin n. chincheta, tachola

drawing room n. salón

dread n. terror, pavor

dread v. temer, recear, sospeitar

dream n. soño, fantasía, imaxinación
dream v. soñar, fantasiar
dreary a. lúgubre, triste, funesto -a
dress n. vestidura, vestido
dressmaker n. modista
drift n. corriente, garete
drill n. barreno, (barrena grande)
drill v. tradear, furar, perforar
drink n. bebiba
drink v. beber, engulir
drive n. paseo
drive v. pasear
driver n. conductor
drizzle n. chuvisca, babuña, chuviñada
drizzle v. chuviscar, chuviñar, babuñar
drop n. gota, pinga
drop v. gotear, gotexar, pingar
drove n. rebano, fato, grea (de animais)
drown v. afogar, asfixiar(se)
drug n. droga; estupefaciente, narcótico
drum n. tambor
drunk n. borracho, bébedo, ebrio, embriagado -a
dry a. seco-a, enxoito -a, murcho, mucio
duchess n. duquesa
duck n. pato, parrulo

duckling n. parruliño

due a. debido -a, necesario -a, conveniente, obrigado

duke n. duque

dull a. obtuso -a, torpe, lento

dumb a. lerdo -a

dummy a. simulado -a, finxido -a

dung a. esterco, estrume, cuito

dunghill n. esterqueira

during prep. durante

dusk n. crepúsculo

dusky a. escuro -a; pardo -a, moreno -a

dust n. po, lixo, chisco

duster n. gardapó

dustman n. vertedeiro de lixo

dusty a. poirento, cheo de po

duty n. deber, obriga, obrigación

dwarf n. anano -a, gnomo

dwell v. habitar, residir, vivir, morar, ocupar, poboar

dwelling n. morada, domicilio, vivenda, casa

dye n. tinxidura

dye v. tinguir, tinxir, colorar

dying a. moribundo -a, agonizante

dynamic a. dinámico -a, movido -a, vivo -a

E

each a. cada
eager a. impaciente, inquedo -a
eagerness n. ansia, anhelo
eagle n. aguia, aiga
ear n. orella
ear wax n. cerume
earl n. conde
earldom n. condado
early adv. temperán -a, temporán -a, de cedo
earn v. gañar, ganar
earnest a. grave, serio -a
earnings n. ganancia, gaño
earring n. arel, ariño
earth n. terra (o noso planeta); chan, piso
earthquake n. terremoto, sismo, tremor de terra
ease n. facilidade
easel n. cabalete
easily adv. facilmente, doadamente
easiness n. facilidade, habelencia, xeito
East n. oriente, saliente, nacente, leste
Easter n. Pascua de Resurrección
easy a. fácil, doado, facedeiro
easy chair n. butaca
eat v. comer, alimentarse

eatable a. comestible, comedeiro
ebony n. ébano
eccentric a. excéntrico -a
echo n. eco
eclipse n. eclipse
economy n economía
edge n. borde, beira
edify v. edificar, construir, erexir
edit v. editar, publicar
edition n. edición
editor n. editor
educate v. educar
education n. educación
eel n. anguía
effect n. efecto, resultado
efficacious a. eficaz
efficacy n. eficacia, eficiencia
effort n. esforzo, traballo
effusive a. efusivo -a, afectuoso-a
egg n. ovo
eggplant n. berenxena
eight n. oito
eighteen n. dezaoito
eighth a. oitavo -a
eighty n. oitenta
either a. caiquera

elastic a. elástico -a
elbow n. cóbado
elder (tree) n. sabugueiro, sabugo, bieiteiro
elder a. comparativo mais vello, mais ancián
eldest a. superlativo: mais vello, mais ancián
elect v. elexir, escoller
election n. elección
electric a. eléctrico -a
electric fan n. abano eléctrico
electrician n. electricista
electricity n. electricidade
elegant a. elegante, distinguido -a
elementary a. elemental, fundamental, básico, primordial
elephant n. elefante
elevator n. ascensor
eleven n. once
eleventh a. décimo primeiro
eliminate v. eliminar, excluir
ellipse n. elipse
elm n. olmo, olmeiro
elongate v. alongar, estirar
else a. outro -a
elude v. eludir, esquivar
embark v. embarcar, involucrar, meter, envolver
embarrass v. embarazar, atrancar, estorbar

embassy n. embaixada
embers n.pl. rescaldos, brasas, ascuas
emblem n. emblema, insignia
embody v. encarnar, personificar
embrace v. abrazar, cinguir, apreixar
embroider v. bordar, recamar
embryo n. embrión
emerald n. esmeralda
emerge v. xurdir, aparecer, emerxer
emergency n. emerxencia, emerción
emery n. esmeril
emigration n. emigración
emit v. emitir, irradiar, producir, radiar
emotion n. emoción
emperor n. emperador
empire n. imperio
employ v. empregar, usar, utilizar, facer uso de
employee n. empregado -a
employer n. patrón -ona, amo -a, xefe
employment n emprego, oficio
empower v. facultar, autorizar
empress n. emperatriz
empty a. beliero, baldeiro
enable v. permitir, autorizar
enamel n. esmalte
enclose v. cercar, cerrar, rodear, choer

enclosure n. cercado, cerrado
encounter n. encontro, reunión
encourage v. animar, alentar
encyclopedia n. enciclopedia
end n. fin, rebate, acabamento, final
end v. terminar, acabar, concluir
endeavor n. esforzo, sacrificio
ending n. fin, conclusión, remate, termo, fin
endless a. interminable, inacabable
endorse v. endorsar
endow v. dotar, proveer
endowment n. dotación
endurance n. resistencia, paciencia
endure v. perdurar, persistir
enemy n. inimigo -a, adversario -a
energetic a. enérxico -a
energy n. enerxia, forza, vigor, poder
enervate v. debilitar, esmorecer, devecer,
    degorar, decaer
engagement n. compromiso, obriga
engine n. máquina, motor
engineer n. enxeñeiro -a
English n. inglés
engrave v. imprimir
engraving n. gravado
enjoin v. impoñer, impor

enjoy v. gozar, disfrutar

enjoyment n. gozo, pracer

enlarge v. alongar, estirar

enlighten v. alumar, alumear, iluminar

enlist v. enganchar, alistar, recrutar (xente para o exército)

enliven v. animar, alegrar

enmity n. inimizade, hostilidade

enormous a. enorme, immenso -a

enough a. & adv. suficiente, ahondo, bastante

enrage v. enfurecer, alporizar

enrich v. enriquecer

ensemble n. conxunto, grupo

entangle v. enmarañar

enter v. entrar, penetrar

enterprise n. empresa, iniciativa

entertain v. entreter, distraer

entertaining n. entretemento

enthusiasm n. entusiasmo, fervor

entire a. enteiro -a, completo -a,

entrance n. entrada, acceso, paso

entreat v. suplicar, implorar, pregar

entrust v. confiar

entry n. entrada, acceso

envelop v. envolver

envelope n. sobre

envenom v. envelenar, intoxicar
enviable a. envexable
envious a. envexoso, cobizoso
environment n ambiente
environs n.pl. arredores
envy n. envexa
envy v. envexar
epidemic n. epidemia, andazo
epoch n. época, tempo
equal a. igual, idéntico
equality n. igualdade
equator n. ecuador
equilibrium n. equilibro
equip v. equipar
equipment n. equipo, grupo
equity n. equidade, igualdade, identidade
equivocal a. equívoco -a, ambiguo -a
era n. era, época
erase v. borrar, eliminar, suprimir
eraser n. borrador
erect v. erexir, construir, fabricar, erguer
ermine n. armiño
err v. errar, equivocarse, confundirse, enganarse,
    trabucarse
errand n. recado, mandado
error n. error, equivocación

escalator n. escaleira mecánica

escape v. escapar, fuxir, liscar

escort n. escolta

escort v. escoltar

essay n. ensaio

essence n. esencia

essential a. esencial, principal

establish v. establecer

establishment n. establecemento

estate n. patrimonio, herdanza

estimate n. estimación, estima, aprecio

estuary n. estuario, esteiro

eternal a. eterno -a

ether n. éter

ethics n.pl. ética, moral

evaluate v. availar, taxar, valorar

eve n. véspera

even (calm) a. sereno -a

even a. chan, plano

even adv. ainda, inda

evening n. tarde, serán

event n. acontecemento, suceso, feito, caso, sucedido

ever adv. sempre

evermore adv. eterno, sin fin

every pr. cada

evidence n. evidencia, convicción, seguridade

evil a. malvado -a, canalla, maligno, maldito, perverso, malandrín, malfeitor

evoke v. evocar, lembrar, recordar

ewe n. ovella

exact a. exacto -a, xusto, correcto

exaggerate v. esaxerar, aumentar, inchar

exaggeration n. esaxeración

examination n. exame, proba, exercicio

examine v. examinar, observar, mirar

example n. exemplo, modelo

excavator n. escavador

exceed v. exceder, sobrepasar

exceeding a. excedente

excellent a. excelente, óptimo, magnífico, admirable

except v. exceptuar, excluir

exception n. excepción

excess n. exceso, excedente

exchange n. cambio, alteración

exchange v. cambiar, trocar, permutar

excite v. excitar, activar, estimular, incitar, aguilloar

excitement n. excitación

exclaim v. exclamar, berrar

exclamation n. exclamación

exclude v. excluír, eliminar

excuse n. escusa, desculpa

excuse v. escusar, desculpar(se)

execute v. executar; axustizar (a un condenado)

executor n. executor

exercise n. exercicio; práctica

exert v. exercitar, exercer

exhaust n. escape

exhaust, v. escapar, fuxir, liscar

exhibit v. exhibir, espoñer

exile n. exilio, desterro

exist v. existir, ser haber

existence n. existencia, vida

expand v. estender, estirar

expansion n. expansión

expatriate v. expatriar(se)

expect v. esperar, agardar

expectation n. expectativa, espera

expel v. expulsar

expense n. expensas, costas

expensive a. caro -a

experience n. experiencia, práctica

expert n. experto -a, entendido -a

explain v. explicar, ensinar, expoñer

explanation n. explicación

explode v. estoupar, estourar, rebentar

explore v. explorar, examina, tantear
explorer n. explorador -a
explosion n. explosión, estoupido, estalo
expose v. expoñer
expound v. expoñer, presentar
express a. expreso -a
extend n. extensión
extend v. estender, estirar
external a. externo -a
extinguish v. extinguir, apagar
extract n. extracto
extract v. extractar, tirar, sacar, quitar
extraordinary a. extraordinario -a
extreme a. extremo -a
eye n. ollo
eyebrow n. cella, sobrecella
eyelash n. pestana, perfeba
eyelid n. pálpebra
eyetooth n. dente canino

F

fa (musical note) n. cuarta nota da escala musical
fable n. fábula, relato, narración, conto
fabric n. tecido, tea, pano

fabrication n. fábrica, manufactura
face n. cara, face, rostro
facilitate v. facilitar
facility n. facilidad
fact n. feito
factory n. fábrica
faculty n. facultade, capacidade; facultade
    (universitaria)
fail v. fallar, errar
failure n. fracaso, fallo
faint a. tenue, sútil
faint n. desmaio, dada, esmorecemento
faint v. desmaiar, abaterse
fair a. fermoso - a, belo -a, bonito -a
fair n. feira, mercado
fairy n. fada
faith n. fe, confianza
faithful a. fiel, leal
faithfulness n. fidelidade, lealtade
Fall (season) n. outoño (estación do ano)
fall n. caida, tombo, zoupada
fall v. caer, afundirse, derrubarse, esborrallarse,
    desprenderse
falling n. falla (defecto)
false a. falso; hipócrita, finxido
falsehood n. falsidade

falsify v. falsificar, falsear, adulterar
fame n. fama, celebridade, popularidade
family n. familia, linaxe
famine n. fame
famous a. famoso -a, afamado -a, célebre
fan n. abano, abanico
fancy n. extravagante
far adv. lonxe
farewell inter. adeus, abur; despedida
farm n. leira, eido, herdade, terreo, predio
farm v. cultivar, traballar (a terra)
fascination n. fascinación
fashion n. moda
fast a. rápido, lixeiro, veloz
fast n. xaxún
fast v. xaxuar
fasting n. xaxún
fat a. & n. gordo -a; groso -a
fatality n. fatalidade
father n. pai, proxenitor
father-in-law n. sogro
fatherland n. patria
fatty a. graxendo, lardudo
fault n. falta, fallo
faultless a. impecable
faun n. fauno

favor n. favor, axuda, mercé
favorite a. & n. favorito -a.
fear n. medo, temor, pavor
fear v. temer, recear, sospeitar, supoñer,
   estanguecer
fearless a. intrépido, audaz
feast n. banquete, festín
feather n. pluma, pena
February n. febreiro
fecundity n. fecundidade
fee n. honorario, honorífico
feed n. comida, alimento
feed v. alimentar
feel n. sensación
feel v. sentir, percibir
felicitate v. felicitar, cumprimentar
felicity n. felicidade
fellow n. compañeiro
female n. femia
feminine a. femenino -a
fence n. cerca, cercado
fennel n. fionllo, fiuncho
fermentation n. fermentación
fern n. fento, felgo, fieito, fieta, fenta, folgueira
ferret n. furón
ferry n. balsa (artefacto para navegar)

ferryboat n. barca
fervent a. fervente, vehemente
fetters n.pl. broche(s)
fever n. febre, quentura
fib n. embuste, mentira
fibber a. mentiroso -a, mentirán, troleiro,
    enganoso, falso
fiction n. ficción, finximento, simulación, engano,
    apariencia, invención
fiddle n. violin
fiddler n violinista
field n. campo, campiña
fierce a. feroz, fero, bravo -a
fifteen n. quince
fifteenth a. décimo quinto -a
fifth a. quinto -a
fiftieth a. quincuaxésimo -a
fifty n. cincuenta
fig n. figo
fight v. combater, loitar
figure n. figura, forma
file n. ficheiro, rexistro, arquivo
file n. lima
file v. limar, pulir
filigree n. filigrana
fill v. encher

filling n. enchedura
film n. pelicula; membrana
filthy a. sucio, cotroso, ensuciado, emporcado,
    enzoufado, manchado, lixado
financial a. financeiro -a
find v. encontrar, atopar, achar, localizar
fine a. fino -a; esvelto -a
fine n. multa, sanción
finger n. dedo (apéndice das mans)
fingerprint n. impresión dactilar
finish v. terminar, rematar, acabar
fir n. abeto
fire (weapon) v. disparar, tirar
fire n. lume, incendio, fogueira, fogo
fire v. despedir, desempregar
firm a. firme, decidido, fixo, seguro
firm n. firma, sinatura; marca comercial
first a. & n. primeiro
fish n. peixe
fisherman n. pescador
fishing n. pesca
fist n. puño (man pechada)
fit a. apto, propio
fit v. adaptar(se), acomodar(se)
fitness n. aptitude, boa saúde
five a. & n. cinco

fix n. apuro, dificultade
fix v. amañar, reparar, arranxar
fixed a. amañado -a
flag n. bandeira
flame n. chama, lapa
flamingo n. flamengo (ave)
flannel n. flanela
flap n. aba (sombreiro)
flash n. relampo, alustro, lostrego relustro
flask n. frasco
flat a. chan, plano, liso
flat n. chan, plano, lazo
flatter v. adular, afagar
flattery n. adulación, afago
flavor n. sabor, gusto
flavorless n. insipido, insulso
flaw n. tacha, falta, defecto, erro
flea n. pulga
flee v. fuxir, liscar
fleece n. vélaro; golden fleece, vélaro de ouro
fleece v. tosquiar, rapar
fleet n flota
flesh n. carne
flex v. dobrar, torcer
flight n. voo, voudura
flipper n. aleta; gardalama (dos automóbiles)

float n. flotador
float v. flotar
flock n. rebaño (conxunto de gando; figurado:
    conxuncto de feis católicos)
flock v. congregar(se), xunrtar(se), reunir(se)
flood n. inundación, asolgamento
flood v. inundar(se), asolagar(se)
floor n. chan
florist n. florista, floreiro
flounder (fish) n. solla (peixe)
flour n. farina
flourish v. prosperar, mellorar, progresar
flow n. fluxo
flow v. fluir
flower n. flor
flute n. frauta
flutter v. bater (bate-las ás)
fly n. voo, voadura
fly v. voar
flying fish n. peixe voador
flying gurnad (fish) n. escacho, miñato (peixe)
foam n. escuma, espuma
foam v. escumar, espumar
focus v. enfocar
foe n .inimigo, adversario
fog n. borraxeira, brétama, neboa

foggy a. nebuloso, neboento, bretemoso
fold n. dobra, dobrez
fold v. dobrar, pregar
foliage n. follaxe
folk n. xente
follow v. seguir, perseguir, suceder
follower n. seguidor, partidario, adepto, discipulo
following a. seguinte
fond a. afectuoso, afable, cariñoso -a
food n. comida, alimento
fool a. & n. parvo, bobo, babeco
foolish a. tonto, impredente
foot n. pé
football n. futbol, balompé
footwear n. calzado
for prep. para
forbid v. prohibir, privar, vedar
force n. forza, poder, potencia
force v. forzar
forceful a. enérxico -a
ford n. vao
ford v. vadear, atravesar
fore n. anterior, precedente
forearm n. antebrazo
forecast n. prognóstico, vaticinio, predicción

forefinger n. dedo indice
forehead n. testa, frente
foreign n. forasteiro, foráneo -a
foreigner n. extranxeiro, estraño
foreman n. encargado
forerunner n. precursor
foresee v. prever, presupoñer, presupor, adiviñar
foresight n. previción, cautela
forest n. bosque, fraga, monte
foretell v. predecir, profetizar, presaxiar
forever adv. sempre
foreword n. prefacio, prólogo
forge n. fragua, forxa
forge v. forxar, fraguar
forget v. esquecer
forgive v. perdoar, absolver
forgiveness n. perdón, indulto, indulxencia
fork n. garfo, trinchante
form n. forma; feitío, apariencia, aspecto
form v. formar, crear
former a. antigo, vello
formula n. formula, receita
forsake v. abandonar, deixar
fort n. forte, fortaleza, baluarte, bastión
forth adv. adiante
forthcoming a. vindeiro, futuro

forthwith adv. immediatamente, de contado, axiña, de seguida

fortieth a. cuadraxésimo

fortify v. fortificar, fortalecer, reforzar

fortnight n. quincena (periodo de quince dias)

fortress n. fortaleza, baluarte, bastión, forte

fortune n. fortuna

forty a. & n. corenta

forward adv. dianteiro, atacante

foster v. fomentar, estimular

found v. fundar, crear, instituir

foundation n. fundación, fundanza

founder n. fundador

fountain n. fonte; causa, orixin, procedencia

fourteenth a. décimocuarto

fourth a. cuarto

fowl n. ave

fox n. raposo

fox shark n. melga (peixe)

foxglove n. croqué, éstalote, herba de San Xoan, alcroque

fraction n. fracción

fragile a. fráxil, feble, débil

frame n. marco, armazón

frame v. enmarcar, encadrar

frantic a. frenético -a

fraud n. fraude, engano

free a. libre; ceibo, ceibe, solto (que non está preso)

freedom n. liberdade

freeze v. conxelar, xear

French a. francés -a

French bean n. feixón, faiba

frequency n. frecuencia

frequent a. frecuente, repetido

frequently adv. frecuentemente

fresh a. fresco -a; recente, novo

Friday n. venves, sexta feira

fried a. frito, fritido

fried egg n. ovo frito, ovo fritido

friend n. amigo -a; compañeiro, camarada

friendly adv. amigablemente

friendship n. amizade

fright n. susto, sobresalto

frighten v. asustar, meter ou poner medo

frightful a. espantoso -a, horroroso -a

frock n. sotana (vestidura talar negra dos cregos)

frog n. ra

frolicsome a. argalleiro

from prep. desde

frond n. fronde, folla, remaxe

front n. fronte, frontiscipio, fachada

frontier n. fronteira, raia; límite, linde, estrema,
    liña divisoria

frontispiece n. frontispicio
frost n. xeada, carazo, carouzo
frown n. cello, entrecello
fruit n. froita
frustrate to v. frustar, impedir, evitar
fry v. fritir, frixir
frying pan n. tixola,sartaña
fuel n. combustible
fugitive a. fuxitivo -a, fuxido -a
full a. cheo -a, repleto -a
fun n. diversión, entretemento
function n. función, traballo, actividade
function v. funcionar, actuar
fund n. fondo; capital caudal
fundamental a. fundamental
funeral a. funeral, funerario
funeral n. funeral, honras fúnebres
fungus n. fungo
funny a. cómico, gracioso -a
fur n. pelt, leather
furious a. furioso -a, furibundo -a
furnace n. forno
furnish v. subministrar, abastecer, fornecer, prover
furniture n. moble
furrow n. suco, rego
further adv. mais lonxe

furze n. toxo, xesta
fuselage n. fuselaxe
fusion n. fusión
future n. futuro, porvir

G

gabardine n. gabardina
gabble v. parola, larctar, tarabelear
gabbler a. falador, paroleiro, leriante; charlatán
gag n. mordaza
gaiety n. alegria, euforia
gain v. gañar, ganar
galaxy n. galaxia
gall (anatomy) n. fel, bile
gall n. descaro, atrevemento
gallant a. gallardo, valeroso, valente
galleon n. galeón, galera
gallery n. galeria, sala; corredor; mina (camino subterráneo)
galley n. cociña (dun barco)
gallon n. galón
gallop n. galope
gallop v. galopar
gallows n. patibulo, cadafalso

game n. xogo; xoga, xógara, artello
gang n. cuadrilla, grupo
gap n. abertura, apertura
garage n. garaxe
garden n. xardin
gardener n. xardineiro -a
gargoyle n. gárgola
garlic n. allo
garment n. peza (dun vestido ou calzado)
garter n. liga
gas n gas
gassy a. gasoso -a
gate n. portal, entrada
gather v. reunir(se)
gauge n. medida, mesura
gauge v. medir, graduar, calibrar
gay a. alegre, festivo -a, ledo, xubiloso, contento
gazelle n. gacela
gem n. xema, pedra preciosa
general a. xeral (pl. gerais)
general n. xeneral (do exército)
generate v. xerar, producir
generation n. xeración (pl. xeracións)
generous a. xerenoso -a, magnanimo -a
genet n. xineta, rabisaco

genial a. xenial; magnífico, extraordinario, excelente, fabuloso, pasmoso

genius n. xenio; intelixencia, talento, habilidade

gentle n. xentil, cortés

gentleman n. xentilhome, cabaleiro, señor

geography n. xeografía

geranium n. xeranio

germ n. xerme

German a. alemán -a

Germany n. Álemaña

germinate v. xerminar, xermolar

gesture n. ademán, aceno, xesto

gesture v. xesticular, acenar, cenar

get v. conseguir, lograr, obter

ghastly a. espantoso, terrible, horroroso

ghost n. fantasma, pantasma, espectro

giant a. xigante, colosal, enorme, inmenso

giant n. xigante, ogro, titán

giddiness n. vértixe, mareo

gift n. regalo, obsequio, presente, agasallo

gild v. dourar

gill n. garnelas, gala, galadas, galaxas

gilt a. dourado -a

gilt head (fish) n. salema (peixe)

gin n. xenebra

giraffe n. xirafa

girdle n. faixa
girl n. nena, nenina, rapaza
give v. dar, ceder
giver n. donatario, dador, doante
glacier n. glaciar
glad a. contento -a, alegre
glamor n. encanto, feitizo
glance v. ollar, mirar, fitar
gland n. glándula
glare n. resplandor
glare v. resplandecer
glass n. vidro
glasses n.pl. anteollos, gafas
glimpse n. escintileo, reflexo, viso
glimpse v. abiscar, entrever
globe n. globo
gloom n. melancolia
gloomy a. melancólico
glory n. gloria, ceo; sono, fama, éxito
glove n. guante, luva
glow n. resplandor, claror
glow v. resplandecer, brillar
glue n. cola, pegamento
glue v. encolar, colar, apegar
go v. ir; estenderse, chegar; marchar, funcionar,
    dirixirse, conducir

goal n. meta, chegada; obxetivo, fin

goal n. meta, porteria (no xogo de fútbol)

goaler n. carcereiro

goat n. cabra, chiba

God n. deus, divinidade

godchild n. afillado -a

goddaughter n. afillada

Goddess n. deusa

godfather n. padriño

godless n. ateo, ateísta

godlike a. divino -a

godmother n. madriña

godson n. afillado

gold n. ouro

golden a. dourado -a

goldfinch n. xilgaro, pintasilgo, picardo

good a. bo (m), boa (f)

good-bye inter. adeus, abur

goodness n. bondade, amabilidade, benevolencia, benignidade, corialidade

goods & chattels n.pl. aveños

goose n. (pl. geese) ganso

gorilla n. gorila

gorse n. toxo

gospel n. evanxeo

gossip n. chisme, chisma, chistófano, chilindrada

gout n. gota (enfermidade)

govern v. gobernar, dirixir, conducir, administrar, rexer, guiar; mandar

governess n. institutriz

government n. goberno

governor n. gobernador

gown n. toga, traxe, talar de cerimonia

grace n. gracia, garbo

graceful a. garboso -a, garrido -a, gallardo -a, elegante

gracious a. benigno -a, benévolo -a, indulxente

grade n. grao, nivel

gradual a. gradual, progresivo -a

graduate v. graduar, graduar(se), diplomar(se)

graft n. enxerto

graft v. enxertar, enxerir

grain n. gran, semente

gram n. gramo (abreviatura é gr.)

grammar n. gramática

grand a. gran, grande

grandchildren n. pl. netos

granddaughter n. neta

grandfather n. avó

grandma (familiar) n. avoa

grandmother n. avoa

grandson n. neto

grandstand n. tribuna

granite n. granito

grant n. subvención

grant v. outorgar, conceder, consentir

grape n. uva, bago

grasp v. arragar, aferrar

grass n. herba

grasshopper n. saltón

grateful a. agradecido

gratify v. satisfacer; saldar, pagar aboar, liquidar, indemnizar

gratitude n. gratitude, agradecemento

grave a. grave, serio, importante

grave n. sepultura, sepulcro, tumba

gravestone n. lápida

graveyard n. cemiterio, camposanto, necrópole

gravity n. gravidade

grease n. graxa

grease v. engraxar

great a. gran, grande

great-grandfather n. bisavó

great-grandmother n. bisavoa

greatness n. grandeza, grandor

Greek a. grego -a

green a. verde

greet v. saudar; cumprimentar

grenade n. granada (bomba de mano)
grey a. gris, cincento
greyhound n. galgo
grief n. pesar, pena, tristeza, pesadumbre
grievance n. agravio, afronta, aldrexe
grill n. grella
grimace n. aceno, xesto, ceno
grind n. moenda, moedura
grind v. moer, triturar
grip v. agarrar, aferrar, asir
groan n. xemido, laio, salouco, salaio, saluco
groan v. xemer, laiar, saloucar, salaiar, salucar,
    queixarse
grocer n. tendeiro
groceries n.pl. comestibles, alimentos, víveres
ground n. chan, terra
groundwork n. traballo fundamental ou básico
group n. grupo, conxunto
group v. agroupar, reunir(se)
grouse n. galiñola, galiña de rio
grow n. crecemento, medra
grow v. crecer, medrar
growl n. gruñido
growl v. gruñir, griñir, gruñir
grown-up a. adulto -a
growth n. crecemento, medra

guarantee n. garantíá, seguridade
guard n. garda, vixilancia, vixía
guard v. gardar, protexer, defender
guardian angel n. anxo de guarda
guess n. conxectura, suposición
guess v. conxecturar
guest n. hospede
guide n. guia, guieiro
guide v. guiar, conducir
guild n. gremio, confraría
guilt n. culpa
guilty a. culpable
guinea n. guinea
guitar n. guitarra
gulf n. golfo, enseada
gull n. gaivota
gum (anatomy) n. enxiva
gum n. goma
gun n. arma (de fogo)
gunman n. pistoleiro
gunpowder n. pólvora (mestura explosiva)
gust n. raxada, refacho
gut n. tripa
gutter n. canle, cano (das augas)
gymnasium n. ximmasio
gypsy n. xitano -a

H

habit n. custome, hábito
habituate v. habituarse, acostumarse, afacerse
haggard a. desencaixado -a
hail (greeting) n. saúdo, salutación
hail (weather) n. sarabia
hail v. sarabiar
hair dressing n. perruquería, barbería
hair n. pelo, cabelo
hair-brained a. tarabelo -a
hairdresser n perruqueiro -a
hake n. pescada, pixota
half a metade
hall n. vestíbulo, entrada
hallow v. consagrar, sacrilizar
halloween n. véspera de dia de Tódolos Santos
halt n. alto (orde)
halt v. deter, parar
ham n. xamón, pernil
hammer n. martelo (ferramenta)
hammer n. martelo (un dos osículos do oido)
hammock n. hamaca
hamper n. canasta, cesta
hamper v. obstaculizar, atrancar, cangar, estorbar
hand n. man (pl. mans)

handful n. mangado
handicap n. desvantaxe
handicraft n. oficio, traballo, arte mecánica
handkerchief n. pano, pano de man, pano do nariz
handle n. asa, mango, agarradeira
handle v. manexar, manipular
handrail n. pasamans (varanda) da escaleira
handshake n. apretón de mans
handsome a. guapo, ben parecido
handy a. destro, hábil, experto, áxil
hang v. colgar
hangar n. hangar
hanger n. percha, colgadoiro
hank n. madeixa
happen v. ocorrer, acontecer, suceder, pasar
happiness n. felicidade
happy a. feliz, afortunado -a
harass v. acousar, abusar
harassment n. acoso
harbor n. porto
hard a. duro -a
harden v. endurecer
hardness n. dureza
hardship(s) n. privacions, penurias
hardy n. resistente, duro, forte
hare n. lebre

harm n. daño, prexuiso, mal
harmful a. dañino, danoso, malo
harmless a. inofensivo -a, inocuo -a
harmony n. harmonía, concordia
harness n. arnés, arreos, aparello (das cabalerias)
harp n. arpa
harpoon n. arpón
harry v. pillar, saquear, roubar
harsh a. aspero -a, duro -a
harvest n. colleita, recolleita
harvest v. recolleitar, recoller
haste n. presa, urxencia, apurp
hasty a. apresurado, apurado
hat n. sombreiro, chapeu
hatch n. niñada, niada, rolada
hatch v. incubar
hatchet n. anciño, angazo
hate n. odio, xenreira, zuna,
hateful a. aborrecible, abominable, detestable
hatter n. sombrereiro
haughty a. soberbio, orgulloso -a, vaidoso -a
haul n. tirón
haul v. tirar, guindar
haunt v. frecuentar
have v. ter, posuir
haven n. abrigo, amparo, refuxio, abra

havoc n. estrago, destrozo, destrucción

hawk n. falcón

hawthorn n. espiño

hay n feo, forraxe

haystack n. palleiro

hazard n. azar

hazel n. castaño

hazelnut n. abelá

he pr. sing. el

head n. cabeza

heading n. titulo

headline n. titular

headmaster n. director de colexio

headmistress n. directora de colexio

headquarters n. cuarte xeneral

heady a. impetuoso -a, brioso -a, enérxico

heal v. curar, sandar

healing n. cura, curación

health n. sáude

healthy a. saudable, san (m), sa (f)

heap n. montón, morea, monte

heap v. amontonar, amorear, congregar

hear v. oir, ouvir

hearer n. oínte

hearing n. audición

heart n. corazón

hearth n. lar, lareira, fogar
hearty a. cordial, afectuoso -a
heat n. calor
heat v. quentar
heater n. quentador
heathen n. pagán -a
heathenism n. paganismo, paganía
heather n. breixo, uz, urce, torga, tergueira
heating n. calefacción
heave v. lanzar, abalanzar, botar
heaven n. ceo
heavenly a. celestial
heavy a. pesado -a
hedge n. sebe, bardado, cerrume, zarrume
hedgehog n. ourizo
heed n. atención
heel n. tacón
height n. altura, elevación
heinous a. atroz, horroroso -a
heinousness n. atrocidade, crueldade
    barbaridade, animalada
heir n. herdeiro
heir v. herdar
heirdom n. hedanza, herdo
heiress n. herdeira
helicopter n. helicóptero

hell n. inferno
hellebore n. veratro
hello inter. boas, ola
helm n. temón
helmet n. casco
help n. axuda, auxilio
help v. axudar, prestar axuda
helper n. axudante
helpful a. útil, apto -a
helpless a. impotente, incapaz
helve n. mango, agarradoira
hem n. beira, borda, orela, ourela
hen n. galiña, pita
hepatic a. hepático
her pr. la
herald n. heraldo, mensaxeiro, progoeiro
herb n. herba
here adv. aquí
heresy n. herexía
heretic a. herético -a
heritage n. herdanza
hermetic a. hermético -a
hermit n. ermitán (m), ermitá (f), anacoreta
hermitage n. ermida
hero n. heroe
heroic a. heroico -a

heroine n. heroina
heron n. garza
herring n. arenque
hers pr. seu (m), sua (f)
herself pr. ela mesma
hesitate v. vacilar
hesitation n. indecisión, vacilación
hew v. tronzar, cortar, abater
hewer n. cortador
hide & seek (to play) v. (children's game) pandar
hide n. coiro, pel
hide v. esconder(se), ocultar(se)
hideous a. horroroso -a, horrendo -a
high a. alto -a, elevado -a
highness n. alteza
highway n. estrada
hike n. camiñada, andada
hike v. caminar, andar
hiker n. excursionista
hill n. monte, outeiro
hilly a. montuoso -a
hilt n. empunadura
him pr. el
himself pr. el mesmo
hind a. posterior
hinder v. estorbar, impedir, obstaculizar

hindrance n. impedimento, atranco
hinge n. bisagra
hint n. insinuación, suxerencia
hint v. insinuar, suxerir
hip n. cadeira
hippopotamus n. hipopótamo
hire n. alugamento, alugueiro, arrendo,
   arrendamento
hire v. alugar, arrendar
his pr. su (m.), sua (f.)
hiss n. asubio
hiss v. asubiar, zoar, zumbar, pitar
history n. historia
hit n. golpe
hit v. golpear, bater, pegar
hive n. colmea, abelleira, enxame
hoard v. acumular, xuntar
hoarse a. rouco -a
hobby n. pasatempo, entretemento, diversión
hoe n. legón, aixadón
hoist n. cabria, guindastre
hoist v. alzar, levantar, erguer
hold v. agarrar, aferrar
hole n. buraco, burato, furaco
holiness n. santidade
hollow a. oco, baleiro, baldeiro

holly n. acevo, acevro, acibro, xardón
holy a. santo -a
holy day n. dia festivo
Holy Ghost n. Espiritu Santo
Holy Week n. Semana Santa
Holy Writ n. Biblia
home n. lar, lareira, fogar
homeland n. terra natal
homesickness n. nostalxia, señardade
hometown n. cidade ou pobo natal
homework n. tarea escolar
honor n. honor, honra, dignidade
hook n. gancho
hook v. enganchar, agarrar
hoop n. aro, anel, argola
hop v. saltar, brincar
hope n. esperanza
hopeless a. desesperado
horizon n. horizonte
horn n. corno
hornet n. abáboro, abázcaro, tártaro
horrible a. horrible, arrepiante, espantoso -a
horrid a. arrepiante, espantoso -a
horse n. cabalo
horseman n. xinete
horsepower n. cabalo de forza

horseshoe n. ferradura
hose n. mangueira, manga
hospital n. hospital
Host (church liturgy) n. Hostia
host n. anfitrión, hóspede
hostage n. refén
hostess n. anfitriona
hot a. quente
hotel n. hotel
hound n. sabuxo (can de caza)
hour n. hora
house n. casa
household a. caseiro -a
housekeeper n. ama de chaves
hovel n. choza, choupana
how adv. como
howl n. ouveo, ouleo
howl v. ouvear, aulear
hug n. abrazo, aperta, apreixo
hug to, v. abrazar, cinguir, apreixar
human n. humano -a
humane a. huminitario -a caritativo -a
humankind n. humanidade
humble a. humilde
humor n. humor
hump n. xiba, corcova, carrumba, lomba

hundred a. & n. cen
hundredth a. & n. centésimo
hunger n. fame
hungry a. famento, esfameado, famélico
hunt n. caza
hunt v. cazar
hunter n. cazador -a
hurl v. lanzar, abalanzar, guindar, botar
hurrah inter. hurra
hurricane n. furacán, vendaval
hurry n. urxenxia, apuro
hurry v. apurar, acelerar, adiantar apresurar
hurt n. ferida, lesión
hurt v. ferir, lastimar
husband n. home, marido, esposo
hush inter. silencio!
hut n. cabana, choza
hyacinth n. xacinto
hymn n. himno
hyphen n. raia (signo ortográfico)

I

I pr eu
Iberian a. ibérico -a, íbero -a

ice cream n. xeado
ice n. xeo
iceberg n. témpano
iconoclast a. & n. inoclasta
icy a. conxelado -a
idea n. idea, opinión, crenza, plan
ideal a. ideal
identical a. idéntico -a, igual
identify, to. v. identificar, recoñer
idiocy n. idiotez, idiocia
idiom n. idioma, lingua
idiot a. idiota, aparvado -a
idle v. vagar, vaguear, deambular
idleness n. ociosidade, folganza
idol n. ídolo, icono
idolater n. idálatra
idolatry n. idolatría
idyll n. idilio
if conj. si
ignite v. acender, prender
ignition n. ignición, combustión
ignoble a. innobre, mesquiño, abxeto, vil
ignorance n. ignorancia
ignorant a. ignorante, inculto
ignore v. ignorar, descoñecer
ill a. enfermo, doente

illegal a ilegal
illiterate a. analfabeto
illness n enfermidade, doenza, mal
illuminate v iluminar, alumar, alumear, dar luz
illumination n. iluminación
illusion n. ilusión, aparencia
illustrate v. ilustrar, instruir, ensinar, aprender, educar
illustration n. ilustración
image n. imaxe
imagine v. imaxinar
imitate v. imitar, arremedar
imitation n. imitación, emulación
immense a. inmenso -a; inmensurable, inconmemsurable, enorme
immoral a. inmoral, indecoroso -a
immortal a. inmortal, inmorredoiro -a
immovable a. inmóbil, quieto, quedo
impasse n. rua cega, camiño sen saida
impeach v. acusar, denunciar
impeccable a. impecable, perecto -a
impel v. impeler, apuxar
implore v. implorar, pedir, rogar, suplicar
imply v. implicar, envolver, enredar, comprometer
impolite a. descortés

import n. importación
import v. importar; interesar
importance n. importancia, interese, relevancia, valor
important a. importancia
impose v. impoñer, impor
imposing a. impoñente, impresioniante
impossible a. imposible, impracticable, inviable, irrealizable
impress n. impresión, tiraxe, tirada (acción e resultado de imprimir)
imprint v. imprimir, imprentar
imprison v. encarcerar, encadear, prender
improper a. impropio -a
improve v. mellorar; progresar, prosperar; recuperarse
improvement n. mellora, melloramento
improvise v. improvisar, repentizar
impulse n. impulso
impute v. imputar
in prep. dentro
inability n. incapadade
inaugurate v. inagurar
inauguration n. inauguración
incentive n. incentivo, acicate, aliciente, estímulo
inch n. polgada (medida inglesa = 2,54 cm.)

inclination n. inclinación
incline v. inclinar, ladear, torcer
include v. incluir, introducir, meter
including a. incluido -a
income n. ingreso, entrada
incompetence n. incompetencia, ineptitude
increase n. aumento
increase v. aumentar, acrecentar, incrementar
incubate v. incubar
indefatigable a. infatigable, incansable
indented a. dentado -a, arpado -a
independent a. independente
index n. índice, catálogo
indicate v. indicar, sinalar
indicator n. indicador
indifferent a. indiferente
indignation n. indignación
induce v. inducir, estimular, impulsar, empuxar
indulge v. compracer, satisfacer
indulgence n. consentimento
industrious a. industrioso -a, emprendedor -a
industry n. industria, destreza, habilidade
infancy n. infancia, nenez
infantry n. infantería
infect v infectar, contaxiar
infection n. infección

inferior n. inferior
influence v. influir
inform v. informar
information n. información
infringe v. infrinxir, quebrantar
ingenious a. inxenuo -a
inhabit v. habitar, vivir, morar
inhabitant n. habitante
inhale v. inhalar, aspirar
inherit v. herdar
inheritance n. herdanza, herdo
iniquity n. iniquidade, maldade, crueldade
initial a. inicial
initial v. asinar, firmar
initiate v. iniciar
initiation n. iniciación
inject v. inxectar
injection n. inxeción
injured a. ferido -a
injury n. ferida
ink n. tinta
inkstand n. tinteiro
inn n. pousada, fonda, hospedería, aloxamento
inner a. interno -a, interior
innocent a. inocente, inxenuo
inoculate v. inocular

inquire v. preguntar, inquirir
inquiry n. pregunta
insanity n. loucura, demencia
insect n. insecto
insert n. inserción
insert v. inserir, meter
inside a. dentro
insight n. perspicacia, agudez, sagacidade
insist v. insistir, porfiar, persistir
insistence n. insistencia, temía, porfía
insomnia n. insomnio, desvelo
inspect v. inspeccionar
inspection n. inspección, exame, recoñecimento
inspector n. inspector
inspiration n. inspiración
inspire v. inspirar, alentar; aspirar, respirar
install v. instalar, montar
installation n. instalación
instance n. instancia
instant n. instante, intre, momento
instep n. empena, peito, do pé
instinct n. instinto
institute n. instituto
instruct v. instruir, educar, ensinar
instruction n. instrucción, ensinanza, ensino
instrument n. instrumento, utensilio, aparello

insulate v. illar
insulation n. illamento
insult n. insulto, aldraxe
insult v. insultar, ofender, aldrexar
insurance n. seguro
insure v. asegurar
intelligence n. intelixencia
intend v. intentar, tentar
intense a. intenso -a, forte
interest n. interese
interesting a. interesante
interior a. interior, interno -a
interpreter n. intérprete
interrupt v. interromper
interruption n. interrupcción, corte
interval n. intervalo
intervene v. intervir
intervention n. intervención
interview v. entrevistar
interview, n. entrevista
intestine n. intestino, tripa
intimate a. íntimo
into prep. cara a, en dirección a
introduce v. introducir, meter
introduction n. introdución
intruder a. intruso -a

invade v. invadir
invader n. invasor
invent v. inventar
invention n. invención, invento
inversion n. investimento
investigate v. investigar
invitation n. invitación, convite
invite v. invitar, convidar
involve v. enredar, enmarañar
iris n. flor de lis
iron n. ferro
irony n. ironía
irrigate v. irrigar, regar
irrigation n. irrigación, rega
Islam n. Islam, islamismo
island n. illa
islander n. illeiro
isolate v. illar, afastar
issue n. cuestión, asunto
issue v. distribuir, repartir
isthmus n. istmo
it pr. neutro lo, la
Italian n. italiano -a
italics n.pl. letra cursiva, letra itálica
itch n. prurito
item n. artigo

its pr. neutral seu
itself pr. neutro mesmo
ivory n. marfil, amalfi
ivy n. hedra, hedreira

J

jab n. cotobelada
jabber n. algarabía, algareo
jabberer a. faladeiro, falador, paraleiro, falangueiro
jack (fish) n. lucio (peixe)
jack (up) v. alzar, levantar, levantar con un gato
jack fish n. xurelo, chicharra, xurela
jack n. gato (instrumento mecanico)
jackal n chacal
jackdaw n. choia
jacket n. chaqueta
jade n xade
jag n puga
jagged a dentado - a, serrado -a
jail n. cárcere
jail n. cárcere; cadea, prisón, presidio
jailer n. carcereiro
jam n marmelada

jam v. atacar(se), obstruir(se)
January n. xaneiro
Japanese a & n xaponés -a
jar n. tarro
jargon n. xerga, argot
jasmine n. xasmin
jasper n xaste
jaundice n. ictericia
jaundiced a. icérico -a
javelin n. xavalina, pica
jaw n. mandíbula, queixada, maxila
jay n gajo (paxaro)
jealous a. celoso -a
jealousy n. celo
jeer n. mofa, burla
jeer v. mofarse, burlarse
jelly fish n. medusa, augumar
jelly n. xelea
jerk n. tirón
jerk v. sacudir, tirar
jersey n. xerxi
jest n. broma, chiste, burla
jest v. chancear, chacotear
Jesuit n. Xesuíta
jet n. jet (avión a reacción)
jetty n. peirao, embarcadoiro

Jew n. xudeu
jewel n. xoia, alfaia
jeweller n .xoieiro
jewellery n. xoieria
Jewess n. xudia
Jewish n. xudaico -a
job n. traballo, labor, ocupación
jobber n. detallista, minorista
jockey n. jockey
jocund a. alegre, ledo, contento -a
jog n. trote
jog v. trotar
join v, unir, xuntar
joint n. xuntura, xunta, unión
joke n. chiste, conto, gracia
joke v. chancear, chacotear
joker n. bromista, argallán
jolly a. alegre, ledo, xuliboso, contento -a
jolt n. sacudida, golpe, abalo,
jota (dance) n. jota (baile popular en Aragón,
    Valencia e Navarra)
journal n. diario, xornal, periódico
journalist n. periodista, xornalista
journey n. viaxe
journey v. viaxar
jowl n. queixada

joy n. gozo, pracer
jubilee n xubileo
judge n. xuis
judge v. xulgar
judgement n. xuizo
judicious a. xuisozo
jug n. xerro, cántaro
juggle n. xogo de mans
juggle v. facer xogo de mans
juggler n. malabarista
jugular a & n. xugular
juice n. zume
July n. xullo
jumble v. revolver, desordenar
jump n. salto, brinco
jump v. saltar, brincar
jumper n. saltador
junction n. xuntura, unión, conexión
June n. junio
jungle n. xungla, selva
junior a. menor
juniper n. xenebreiro
jurist n. xurista
jury n. xurado
just a. xusto -a
justice n. xustiza

justification n. xustificacíon
justify v. xustificar
jut v. sainte, saliente
juvenile n. xuvenil

K

kangaroo n. canguro
karate n. kárate
keel n. quilla, carena
keen a. agudo, aguzado afiado
keeness n. agudeza, perspicacia
keep v. manter, conservar
keeper n. gardián, vixiante
kennel n. canceira; fato, manda (de cans)
kerb (curb) n. bordo
kerchief n. pano de man, pano de nariz
kernel n. gran
kettle n. cafeteira
key n. chave
keyboard n. tecla
keyholder n. chaveiro
keyhole n. ollo (de pechadura)
khaki n. caqui
kick n. patada, couce

kick v. patear, patexar

kid n. cabrito, cabuxo, chivo

kidnap v. secuestrar, raptar

kidnapper n. secuestrador, raptor

kidnapping n. secuestro, rapto

kidney n. ril

kill v. matar, quita-la vida (causa-la morte)

killer n. matador, matachín, matón, sangrador

kilogram n. quilogramo

kilometer n. quilómetro

kind a. benigno -a, bo (m), boa (f)

kindergarten n. xardín de infancia, gardería

kindle v. acender, prender

kindliness n. bondade, amabilidade

kindly a. bondadoso -a, bo, boa

kindness n. bondade, cariño, afecto

kindred a. achegado -a; próximo -a, arrimado -a

kindred n. parentesco, parentela

king n. rei, monarca

kingdom n. reinado

kingfisher n. picapeixe, paxaro pescador, rei da auga

kinglike a. real

kingship n. maxestade

kiosk n. quiosco

kiss n. bisco, beixo, ósculo

kiss v. bicar, beixar

kit n. equipo (conxunto de útiles)

kitchen n. cuciña; gastronomía (arte culinaria)

kite (bird) n. miñato (ave de rapiña diurna)

kite n. papaventos (xoguete)

kitten n. gatiño, miquiño

knave n. falsario, falso, impostor, tramposo

knavery n. trampa, engano, argallada

knead v. amasar, padexar

knee n. xeonllo

knife n. coitelo

knight n. cabaleiro

knight (chess) n. cabalo (de xadrez)

knit v. tecer

knob n. protuberancia, saínte

knock n. porrada, mocada, estacazo, pancada

knock v. apegar, golpear, bater

knot (nautical) n. nó (velocidade marítima)

knot n. nó, unión, ligame, vínculo

knot v. anoar, atar

know v. conecer, saber

knowing n. coñecemento

knowledge n. sabedoria, sabenza

knuckle n. coteno, cotelo, cotomelo, noca

knurled a. nodoso -a

L

la (musical note) n. sexta nota da escala musical
label n. rótula, cartel, letreiro, inscripción, etiqueta
label v. rotular, pintar
labor n. labor, traballo, tarefa
labor v. traballar con ardor
laboratory n. laboratorio
laborer n. obreiro, traballador
laborious a. laborioso
labyrinth n. labirinto, dédalo
lace n. encaixe
lace v. adornar con encaixes
lack n. carencia, falta, falla
lack v. carecer
lackey n. lacaio, criado, servente
laconic a. lacónico -a, breve, conciso -a
laconism n. laconismo, concesión
lacquer n. laca
lad n. mozo, rapaz
ladder n. escaleira
laddle n. cullerón, garfela
lady n. dama, señora, dona
lag v. atrasar, demorar, tardar
lagoon n. lagoa

lair n. cubil, tobo, tobeira, gorida
lake n. lago
lamb n. ano, cordeiro
lame a. & n. coxo -a
lame v. eivar, empioucar
lameness n. coxeira, coxén
lament n. lamento, queixume, queixa
lament v. lamentar, queixar(se), doer(se)
lamp n. lámpada
lance n. lanza
lancer n. lanceiro
lancet n. lanceta
land n. terra, terreo
land v. desembarcar
landholder n. terratenente
landlady n. dona, propietaria, posuidora
landlord n. dono, propietario, posuidor
landscape n. paixase, panorama, vista
lane n. camiño, via, vieiro, verea
language n. linguaxe, fala, lingua
languid a. lánguido -a, débil
languish v. languidecer
lantern n. lanterna
lap n. faldra, saia, aba
lapel n. solapa, lapela
lapidary n. lapidario

lapse n. lapso
lapse v. transcorrer, pasar
larboard n. babor
lard n. manteiga
larder n. despensa
large a. grande, enorme
lark n. laverca, cotovia, calandra
larynx n. larinxe
lash v. azoutar, bourar, bater, zorregar, zurrar
lass n. chica, moza, rapaza
lassitude n. lasitude, debilidade
last a. último -a
last v. durar
latch n. picaporte, picador
late adv. tardio, tardeiro, tardego, serodio
lately adv últimamente, recentemente
lathe n. torno
lather n. enxaboadura
lather v. enxaboar
Latin n. latín
latitude n. latitude
latrine n. latrina, retrete
latter a. posterior; moderno -a, novo -a
laugh n. risa, riso
laugh v. rir
laughter n. risa

launch n. lanzamento
launch v. lanzar, botar
laundress n. lavandeira
laundry n. lavadoiro
laurel n. laureiro
lavatory n. lavatorio
lavender n. lavanda, cor violeta
lavish a. pródigo -a
lavish v. prodigar
law n. lei, regra, norma
lawful a. legal
lawfulness n. legalidade
lawn n. céspede, panasco, relva
lawsuit n. preito, xuíso
lawyer n. avogado, defensor
laxatíve a. laxativo, laxante
lay v. poñer, pór
layer n. capa, estrato
laze (away) v. malgastar, delapidar
laziness n. preguiza, galbana, nugalla
lazy a. preguiceiro, preguizoso
lead n. chumbo
lead v. guiar, conducir
leader n. xefe, xefa, caudillo
leadership n. liderato
leaf n. folla

league n. liga. alianza
leak n. goteira, pingueira, abeira
leak v. gotear, gotexar, pingar
lean a. delgado -a, fraco -a
lean v. recostar(se)
leap frog (children's game) n. araña, panda
(xogo infantil)
leap n. salto, brinco
leap to v. saltar, brincar
leap year n. ano bisesto
learn v aprender
learning n. erudicción
lease n. arrendo, arrendamento
lease v. arrendar, alugar
least a. menor, inferior, mais pequeno
leather n. coiro, pel, curtida
leave v. sair
leaves n.pl. follas
lecture n. conferencia
lecture v. dar conferencias
lecturer n. conferenciante
ledge n. andel, aldazeiro
left a. esquerdo -a
leg n. perna
legal a legal, lícito
legality n. legalidade

legend n. lenda
legion n. lexión
legislation n. lexislación
legitimate a. lexitimo -a
legitimate v. lexitimar, legalizar
leisure n. ocio, falgfanza
lemon n. limón
lend v. prestar, emprestar
lending n. préstamo, emprésito
length n. lonxitude, largura
lengthen v. alongar, estirar
lens n. lente
Lent n. coresma
lentil n. lentella
leopard n. leopardo
leper hospital n. lazareto (hospital para leprosos)
leper n. leproso -a lázaro
leprosy n. lepra
lesion n. lesión, contusión, dano, ferida
less adv. menor, inferior
lesser a. menor, mais pequeno
lesson n. lección
lest conj. por medo de que
let (to rent) v. arrendar, alugar
let v. permitir, deixar
letter (alphabet) n. letra, grafemo

letter n. carta, epístola
lettered a. letrado -a, douto -a, culto -a, instruido -a
lettuce n. leituga
levant n. levante, leste, nacente
level a. chan, plano, liso
level n. nivel
level v. nivelar
lever n. panca
levity n. frivolidade
liability n. risco
liable a. responsable
liaison n. enlace, unión
liar n. mentireiro -a
libel n. calumnia
libel v. calumniar, difamar
liberality n. liberalidade, largueza, xenerosidade
liberate v. liberar
liberty n. liberdade
librarian n. bibliotecario -a
licence n. permiso, licencia, autorización
licenciate n. licendiado -a; sabido, pedante
licit a. lícito -a, lexítimo -a, legal
lid n. tapa
lie n. mentira, embuste, trola
lie v. mentir
lieutenant colonel n. tenente coronel

lieutenant general n. tenente xeneral
lieutenant n. tenente
life n. vida
life time n. curso de vida
lifeboat n. lancha de salvamento
lifeless a. exámine, morto -a
lift a. alzamento, levantamento
lift v. alzar, levantar, erguir
light a. livian -a, lixeiro -a
light n. luz
light v. acender, prender
lighten v. alixeirar, aliviar
lighter n. acendedor, chisqueiro
lighthouse n. faro
lighting n. iluminación
lightly adv. lixeiramente, levemente
lightning n. relampo, alustro, lóstrego, relustro
like a. igual, parecido -a, semellante
like v. gustar, agradar
likely adv. verosimilmente
likeness n. seme
likewise adv. tamén, igualmente
lilac n. lila
limb n. membro, extremidade
limber a. áxil, flexible
lime (fruit) n. lima (froita)

lime juice n. zumo de lima
lime n. cal
lime tree n. limeira
limit n. límite
limp n. coixera, coxén
limp v. coxear, trenquear, ranquear
linden tree n. tileiro
line p. liña
line v. aliñar
linen n. liño, lenzo, tea, pano, roupa branca
liner n. vapor (barco a vapor)
link n. vencello, vínculo
link v. vincular
lion n. león
lioness n. leoa, leona
lip n. labio, beizo
liqueur p. licor
liquid a. &. p. liquido -a
liquidate v. liquidar
liquor n. licor
list n. lista
list v. enumerar
listener n. ointe
litany n. ladaina
literary a. literario -a
literature n. literatura

litter (stretcher)n. liteira

litter n. camada, cria

little a. pequeno -a; pouco -a

live a. vivido -a

live v. vivir, existir

lively a. vivo -a, vivaz

liver n. fígado

living room n. cuarto de estar denhua casa

lizard n. lagarto

llama n. llama (mamífero da America andina meridional)

load n. carga

load v. cargar

loaf n. molete (de pan)

loaf v. folgazanear

loan n. préstamo

loan v. prestar, emprestar

lobby n. vestíbulo, entrada

lobster n. langosta

lock n. pechadura

lock v. cerrar, pechar

locomotive n. locomotora

locust n. langosta (insecto)

lodge n. loxa (masónica)

lodge v. aloxar, albergar, acomodar

lodger n. hóspede

loft n. faiado
lofty a. elevado -a, alto -a
log n. tronco (talo leñoso dunha árbore)
logic a. lóxica
lone a. so (m), soa (f)
loneliness n. soidade
long n. longo -a
longitude n. lonxitude, longura
look n. mirada, mira, ollada
look v. mirar, ollar, observar
looking glass n. espello
loom n. tecedora (maquina para tecer)
loom v. asomar, aparecer
loop n. ollal; buraco, burato
loose a. solto -a
loose v. soltar, ceibar, libertar
loosen v. desatar, desencadear
looseness n. soltura, desenvoltura
lord n. señor
Lord's prayer n. Pai Noso
lose v. perder, extraviar
loss n. perda, escape, fuga
lost a. perdido -a, extraviado -a
lote n. lote, conxunto
loud a. rexo -a, forte
loud speaker n. altofalante

lounge chair p. sofá

lounge n. folganza

lout n. basto, rudo

loutish a. groseiro -a, tosco -a, basto -a

love n. amor, cariño, estima

love v. amar, querer

lovely a. encantador -a, fermoso -a

lover n. amante, querido -a,

low a. baixo -a; debaixo -a

loyalty n. lealdade, fidelidade

luck n. sorte, fortuna, ventura

luckly adv. afortunadamente, por sorte, por
  fortuna

lucky a. afortunado -a, venturoso -a, felix, deitoso -a

luggage n. equipaxe

lump n. terrón (de azucre)

lunch n. comida

lunch v. comer, alimentar(se)

lung n. pulmón

lute n. laúde

luxuriant a. frondoso -a; exhuberante

luxurious a. luxoso -a

luxury n. luxo, ostestación, adorno

lye n. lixivia

lynx n. lobo cerval, lince

lyre p. lira (instrumento musicical)

M

macaroni n. macarrón
mace n. maza
macerate v. macerar, mazar, abrandar
machine n. máquina
machinery n. maquinaria
mackerel n. xarda
mackintosh n. impermeable
mad a. tolo -a; louco -a, demente
madam n. señora
magazine n. revista (publicación periódica)
magic n. maxia (arte marabillosa)
magical a. máxico -a
magician n. mago, prestidixitador, ilusionista
magisterio n. maxisterio
magistrate n. maxistrado
magnanimity n. magnanimidade, xenerosidade
magnanimous a. magnánimo -a, xeneroso -a
magnet n. imán
magnetism n. magnetismo
magnificence n. magnificencia, grandiosidade, solemnidade
magnificent a. magnífico -a, esplendido -a, suntuoso -a
magnify v. magnificar; exaltar, enxalzar, glorificar
magpie n. pega

maid n. criada, serventa
maiden n. doncela
mail box n. buzón
mail n. correo
main a. principal, esencial, fundamental
mainland n. continente, terra firma
maintain v. manter, conservar
maintenance n. mantemento
maize n. milo, mainzo
majestic a. maxestuoso a
majesty n. maxestade
majority a. maioria
make v. facer, realizar
maker n. facedor
male n. macho
malignant a. maligno, pernicioso
mallet n. mazo
mallow n. malva
mammal a. mamífero
mammoth n. mastodonte
man like n. viril, masculino
man n. home, humano
manacle n. grillón
manage v. maneixar, dirixir, controlar
management n. maneixo
manager n. xerente

mandolin n. mandolina
mane n. crina, croma, melena (de león)
maneuver n. manobra
manger n. presebe
mango n. mango (froita)
manhood n. virilidade, masculinidade
manifold n. tubo múltiple
manipulate v. manipular, manexar
mankind n. humanidade, o xénero humano
mannequin n. manequí
manner n. maneira, modo
manor n. casa, casa grande, casa fidalga
mansion n. mansión, pazo
mantis, praying n. parraguesa, santiña
mantle n. manto, capa
manufacture n. manufactura; fábrica
manure n. esterco, estrume, cuito, argueiro
manuscript n. manuscrito
many a. moito, en cantidade
map n. mapa
marble n. mármore
March n. marzo
mare n. egua, besta
margin n. marxe, beira
marine a. marino -a
mariner n. marinero -a

marionette n. marioneta, monicreque, títere

mark n. marca

mark v. marcar, sinalar, indicar

market n. mercado

market v. vender

marmalade n. marmelada, confitura de froitas

maroon n. castaño -a

marquis n. marqués

marquise n. marquesa

marriage n. matrimonio, casamento

married n. casado -a

marrow n. miolo, miola, mola, médula

marry v. casar, desposar

marsh n. lamazal, tremedal, braña, boedo

marshal n. mariscal

marshy a. pantanoso -a, palustre, lacemento -a

marten n. marta, martuxa (mamífero carcinero)

martyr n. mártir

martyrdom n. martirio, suplicio, tormento, padecemento

martyrize v. martirizar, atormentar, torturar, facer sufrir

marvel n. marabilla, prodixio, portento

marvelous a. marabilloso -a, portentoso -a, abraiante, asombroso -a

masculine a. masculino, varonil, viril

mash n. mestura
mash v. mesturar
mask n. máscara, caranta, caruta, careta
mask v. enmascarar, encaretar, disfrazar
mason n. albanel (pl. albaneis)
mass n. misa
massage n. masaxe, noticia, comunicación
massif n. masa (de vexetación)
massive a. masivo -a
mast n. mastro, paso, hasta
master n. mestre; profesor
master v. dominar
mastery n. dominio
mastiff n. mastín
mat n. esteira
match (sports) n. partido (deporte)
match n. misto, fósforo
match v. emparellar
maté (bush) n. mate, herba mate
mate n. cónsuxe, consorte
mate v. casar(se); desposar
material a. material, físico, corp o reo
material n. material, materia
mathematics n. matématica
matron n. matrona, comadroa
matter n. materia, asunto, cuestión

mattock n. aixadón, sacho grande

mattress n. colchón

mature a maduro -a, maderecido -a

mature v. madurar, madurecer

matureness n. madurez, madureza

maximum a. máximo -a

may be adv. quizais, quizabes, quizá, se cadra

may fly n. efémera (insecto)

May n. maio

mayonnaise n. maluesa

mayor a. maior, mor, mais grande

mayor n. alcalde (m); alcaldesa (f)

maze n. labirinto, dádelo

maze v. enredar

me pr. me, a min

meadow n. prado

meagre a. escaso -a, mesquiño, taca n o-a

meal n. comida, alimento

mean a. mesquiño -a

mean n. medio, metade

mean v. significar, demotar

meander v. serpear

meaning n. significado, relevante

meanness n. mezquindade, ruindade

means n.pl. medios, recusos

meantime adv. namentres, mentres, mentres
   tanto, entrementres, en tanto

measure n. medida, medición
measure v. medir
meat n. carne
mechanic n. mecánico
medal n. medalla
medical a. médico -a
medicine n. medicina; menciña, medicamento
medley n. mestura
meek a. submiso -a, obediente, dócil
meekness n. mansedume
meet n. encontro, xuntanza, reunión
meet v. encontrar, atopar, achar, localizar
meeting n. reunión, xuntanza
melic n. mélica (planta)
mellow a. maduro -a, madurecido -a
melon n. melón
melt v. derreter, fundir(se), disolver(se)
melting n. derretemento
member n. membro, extremidade, apéndice
membrane n. membrana
memoir n. memoria (literaria)
memorize v. memorizar
memory n. memoria (facultade de lembrar)
menace v. amenazar
mend n. remendo, mendo
mend v. remendar, mender

mention n. mención, referencia, alusión

mention v. mencionar, nomear, amentar, facer mención

menu n. menú

merchandise n. mercancia, mercadoría

merchandise v. comerciar, negociar, traficar

merchant n. negociante

merciful a. misericordioso -a, compasivo -a, piadoso -a

merciless a. desapladado -a, cruel

mercy n. misericordia, compaixón, piedade

merely adv. simplemente, sinxelmente

merit n. mérito, merecemento

merry a. alegre, ledo -a, xubiloso -a, gozoso -a

merry-go-round n. currusel, cabaliños

mesh n. malla

mesh v. enredar, enlear(se), enmarañarse

message n. menxase, noticia, comunicación

messenger n. mensaxeiro, recadeiro

Messiah n. Mesias, salvador

metal n. metal

metamorphosis n. metamorfose

meter n. metro

method n. métode, procedemento, sistema

methodical a. metódico -a, sistemático -a

microscope n. microscopio

mid a. medio -a
midday n. mediodia, as doce
middle a. medio -a
Middle Age n. idade media
middle aged a. idade media
midget n. anano, gnomo
midnight n. media noite
midwife n. parteira, comadroa, matrona
might n. poderio, poder, forza
mighty a. poderoso -a
migrate v. emigrar, migar
mild a. suave, brando
mile n. milla (medida inglesa equivalente a 1.609 metros)
milestone n. marco
militant a. militante
military a. & n. militar
milk n. leite
milk v. muxir, munguir
mill n. muiño
mill v. moer, triturar
miller n. muiñeiro
millimeter n. milímetro
million n. millón
mind n. mente, intelecto
mind v. decidirse, resolverse

mindful a. atento, dilixente

mindless a irreflexiblo -a

mine (warfare) n. mina (artefacto bélico)

mine n. mina (extracción de minerais)

mine pr. meu (m), miña (f)

miner n. mineiro

mingle v. mesturar, revolver

minimum a. mínimo -a

mining n. minería

minister n. ministro

ministry n. ministerio, mester, misión

minor a. menor, inferior

minority a. minoría; minoridade (idade anterior a madurez)

minstrel n. xograr (artista ambulante)

mint n. menta, hortelá, cecimbre

mint v. amodear, bater (facer moedas)

minus a. negativo -a

minute (time) n. minuto (sesaxésima parte da hora e do grao)

minute a. miudo -a (moi pequeno)

minx n. marta, martuxa

miracle n. milagre

miraculous a. milagroso -a

mirage n. espellismo, ilusión óptica

mire n. lama, lodo

mirror n. espello
mirth n alegria, animación, rebouxa, troula,
  esmorga
misadventure n. desenventura, desgracia
mischief n. travesura, trasnada, trasgada,
  facatrualda
misdeed n. delicto, facatrualda
misdoer n. malfeitor, delicuente, criminal
miser a. avaro -a, avarento -a, avaricioso -a
misery n. miseria, lacería
misfortune n. desventura, desgracia, sorte adversa
mislay v. extraviar, perder
Miss n. señorita
miss v. fallar, errar
missile n. proxectil
mission n. misión, comisión, encargo
mist n. borraxeira, brétama, fuscallo
mistake n. error, erro
mistaken a. erróneo, inexacto
mister n. señor
mistress n. amante, querida
mistrust n. receo, desconfianza
misunderstanding n. equivocación,
  malentendido -a
mitigate v. mitigar, moderar, atenuar
mixed a. mixto -a, mesturado -a

mixer n. mesturbador
mixture n. mestura
moan n. xemido, laio, saouco, saliao
moan v. xemer, laiar, saloucar, salaiar
moat n. foso, foxo
mockery n. burla, mofia, escarnio
mode n. modo, forma, maneira
model n. modelo, muestra, exemplar
model v. modelar
modification n modificación, alteración
modify v. modificar, alterar, cambiar
moist a. húmido -a
moisten v humedecer, humectar
moisture n. humidade, humén
mold n. molde
mold v. moldear
moment n. momento, intre, instante
monarch n. monarca, rei, soberano
monarchy n. monarquía, reino
monastery n. moistero, convento, cenobio
Monday n. luns, segunda feira
money n moeda
money, hush n. prezo de silencio (dunha persoa)
monitor n. monitor, adestrador
monk n. monxe, frade, freire, cenobita
monkey n. mono, macaco, mico

monotony n. monotonía, aburrimento
monsoon n. monzón
monster n. monstro
monstrous a. monstruoso -a
month n. mes
mood n. estado de ánimo
moon n. lua, satélite
moonlight n. luar; luarada, lueiro
Moor n. mouro, árabe, musulmán
moor n. páramo, ermo, gándara
moor v. amarrar (unha embarcación)
mop v. fregar
moraine (geology) n. morea
moral n. moral, moralidade
morale n. ánimo, espírutu, alento
more adv. mais
moreover adv. ademais
morning n. mañá; mañá (tempo futuro)
morsel n. bocado, trabadela
mortar n. masa, argamasa
mortar n. morteiro (peza de artillería)
mortar n. morteiro, machucador
mortgage n. hipoteca
mosque n. mesquita (templo árabe)
mosquito n. mosquito
most a. sumo grao, máximo

moth n. traza, cousa, carruncho
mother n. nai, mai, madre
mother-in-law n. sogra
motion n. movimento
motivate v. motivar
motivation n. motivación, estímulo
motive n. motivo, causa, razón
motorcycle n. motocicleta
mount (geography) n. monte, montaña
mount n. montura, cabalgadura, sela
mount v. montar, cabalgar, solapar
mountain n. montaña
mourn v. lamentar; queixarse, doerse, laiarse
mourning bride n. viuva de xardín
mourning n. lamento, lamentación, queixume, queixa, laio
mouse n. rato
mouth n. boca
mouthpiece n. boquilla
move n. movimento, axitación
move v. mover, desprezar
movie n película, filme
moving a. movedizo -a
much a. moito -a
mud n. barro, arxila; lama, lodo
mudguard n. gardalama, paralama

muffle v. amortecer, atenuar, minorar, moderar
muffler n. silenciador
mullet n. muxo (peixe marino)
multiplication n. multiplicación
multiply v. multiplicar, incrementar, aumentar
municipality n. municipalidade
muraena (fish) n. murea (peixe)
murder n. asasinato, homicidio
murderer n. asasino, homicida
muscle n. músculo
muscular a. musculoso, muscular
museum n. museo
mushroom n. fungo
music n. música
musician n. músico
mussel n. mexillón
must n. obrigación, obriga, deber
mustache n. bigote
mustard n. mostaza
musteline n. mustélido
mute n. mudo -a, silencioso -a, calado -a
mutiny n. motin, amotinamento
mutton n. carne de carneiro
mutual a. mutuo -a, recíproco -a
muzzle n. fociño
my a. meu (m), mina (f)

myrrh n. mirra
myself pr. eu mesmo
mystery n. misterio, enigma
myth n. mito

N

nacre n. nácara
nag n. faco (cabalo ruín)
nag v. rosnar, roñar, refungar
nail (anatomy) n. una, unlla
nail (hardware) n. cravo, punta
nail v. cravar, espetar, chantar
naked a. espido -a, despido -a, nu (m), nua (f)
name n. nome
name v. nomear, chamar, citar, mencionar
nameless a. anónimo -a
nap n.sesta
nap v. durmir a sesta
nape n. caluga, brouca
napkin n. pano de mesa
narcissist a. narcisista
narcissus n. narciso
narrate v. narrar, relatar
narration n. narración, conto, historia, relato

narrow a. estreito -a, angosto -a
narrowness n. estreiteza, estreitura
nasty a. desagradable
nation n. nación
nationality n. nacionalidade, cidadanía
native n. nativo -a, natal; aborixe, indíxena, natural
nature n. natureza
naught adv. nada, ren
naughtiness n. travesura, trasnada, trasgada
naughty a. & n. pícaro, pillo, pillabán, malicioso
nave n. nave (espacio entre muros, arcadas, etc.)
navel n. embigo, embigueira, cordón umbilical
navigate v. navegar, voar (un avión, globo, etc.)
navigation n. navegación
Navigator n. navegante, nauta
navy n. mariña de guerra
nay adv. non
near adv. cerca, preto
nearly adv. case
neat a. pulcro, limpio -a, aseado -a
neatness n. pulcritude
necessary a necesario -a, inevitable, indispensable
necessity n. necesidade
neck n. colo, pescozo
necklace n. colar, coleira

necktie n. gravata
need n. necesidade
need v. necesitar, precisar
needle n. agulla
needless a. superfluo -a, inútil, innecesario -a
negative a. negativo -a
neglect n. descoido, desleixo, abandono
neglect v. descoidar, desatender, abandonar
neigh n. rincho
neigh,to v. rinchar
neighbor n. veciño, próximo, lindante, limitrófe
neighborhood n. veciñanza; arrededores
neither art. ningún (m), ningha (f)
nephew n. sobrino
nerve n. nervio
nervous a. nervioso -a
nest n. niño
net a. neto, líquido -a
network n. malla, rede
neuter a. neutro -a
neutral a. neutro, neutral, impartial
neutrality n. neutralidade
neutron n. neutrón
never adv. nunca, xamais
nevermore adv. nunca mais
nevertheless adv. sen embargo, non obstante

new a. novo -a, recente, moderno -a, nacente

news n.pl. noticia(s), nova

newspaper n. periódico, xornal

next a. próximo -a, contiguo -a

nice a. simpático -a, gracioso -a, agradable

nickel n. niquel (metal); moeda de cinco
    centavos nos Estados Unidos

nickname n. sobrenome, alcume, alcuño

niece n. sobriña

niggardly a. aforrón -a, amarrado -a, mesquiño -a

night n. noite

nightingale n. reiseñor, rousinol

nightly a. nocturno

nightmare n. pesadelo (soño desagradable)

nil adv. nada, cero

nimble a. áxil, lixeiro

nine n. & a. nove

nineteen n. & a. dezanove

nineteenth a. & n. dezanoveno -a

ninety n. & a. noventa

ninth a. & n. noveno -a, nono -a

nip n. belisco, mordiscada.

no adv. no, ninguno -a

nobility n. nobreza, aristocracia; honradez,
    honestidade

noble a. & n. nobre, aristócrata, fidalgo; honrado,
    honesto

nobody pr. ninguén, ningunha persoa
noise n. ruido, barullo, confusión, desorde
noisy a. ruidoso -a, estrondoso -a
nomad n. & a. nómada
nominate v. nomear, designar, elixir
nomination n. nomeamento, designación
none pr. nada, ren
nonsense n. desatino, despropósito, insensatez
noon n. mediodia, as doce
noose n. nó corredío
nor conj. tampouco non
normal a. normal, corrente, común
normally adv. normalmente
Norse a. & n. escandinavo -a
North n. norte, setentrión
nose n. nariz
nostrils n.pl ventas (orificios de nariz)
not adv. non
note n. nota, apuntamento
note v. anotar, apuntar, inscribir
notebook n. caderno
noted a. coñecido -a, afamado -a, célebre
notice n. noticia
notification n. notificación
notify v. notificar, comunicar
notion n. noción, idea

notoriety n. notoriedade
notwithstanding adv. sen embargo, non obstante
noun n. substantivo, nome
nourish v. alimentar, nutrir, manter, soster,
    sustentar, dar alimento
nourishing a. nutritivo -a, alimenticio -a
nourishment n. alimento, alimentación
novel n. novela
novelty n. novidade
November n. novembro
novice a. & n. novicio -a, novato -a
now adv. agora, arestora
nowadays adv. hoxe en dia
noxious a. nocivo -a, dañino -a, prexudicial
nozzle n. tobeira
nuance n. matiz, ton
nucleus n. núcleo, carozo, corazón de certas
    froitas
nude a. espido -a, despido -a
nudity n. nudismo
nuisance n. molestia, fastio, disgusto
null a. nulo -a, anulado -a
nullify v. anular, invalidar
number n. número
number v. numerar, contar, enumerar
numerous a. numeroso -a, abundante, copioso -a

nun n. monxa, freira

nurse n. enfermeiro -a

nut (hardware) n. porca, rosca

nut n. noz, cuncho, concho, croucho (fruto da nogueira)

nutcracker n. crebanoces, quebranoces, escachanoces

nutritive a. nutritivo -a; alimenticio -a

nymph n. ninfa (divinidade campestre), crisálida

O

o art.sing., os pl., the

ó contracción da prep a. & art. o (tamén se pode escribir ao)

O en maiscula, abreviatura de Oeste, punto cardinal

oak n. carballo

oar n. remo

oasis n.(sing.), **oases** (pl.) oasis (no deserto)

oat n. cebada, orxo

oath n. xuramento; blasfemia, maldición

obdurate a. obstinado -a, obsecado -a, teimoso, teimudo, testán

obedience n. obedencia, submisión

obedient n. obediente

obelisk n. obelisco
obey v. obedecer, acatar, cumprir, respectar
object n. obxecto
object v. obxetar
objection n. obxección
obligation n. obrigación, obriga
oblige v. obrigar, forzar, compeler; mandar
obliging a. compracente, servicial
obliterate v. borrar, eliminar, suprimir
oblivion n. esquecemento
oblivious a. esquecedizo -a
oblong a. alongado -a, oblongo -a
obscure n. escuro -a
obscurity n. escuridade
observance n. observancia, cumprimento
observation n. observación
observe v. observar, mirar, examina
obstacle n. obstáculo, estorbo
obstinacy n. obstinación, teimosía
obstinate a. obstinado -a, teimonoso -a
obstruct v. obstruir, atascar
obstruction n. obstrucción, atranco
obtain v. obter, conseguir, ga n ar, lograr
obtainable a. accesible, alcanzable
obtuse a. obtuso -a, mocho, remo (sen punta)
obvious a. evidente, ostensible

occasion n. ocasión, momento

occasional a. ocasisonal, casual

occult a. oculto -a, acochado -a

occupancy n. tenencia

occupation n. ocupación; colocación, entrego, traballo

occupy v. ocupar, posuir; habitar

occur v. ocorrer, acontecer, suceder

occurrence n. ocorrencia, circumstancia

ocean n. océano

oceanography n. oceanografía

ocelot n. ocelote

o'clock adv. abreviatura de tempo, 12 o'clock

October n. outubro

octopus n. polbo

oculist n. oculista, oftalmólogo

odd a. impar; incomparable, singular, único

oddity n. rareza, excentricidade

odds n.pl. probabilidades

odor n. olor, cheiro

odorless a. inodoro (que non tene odor)

odorous a. oloroso -a, odorante, aromático -a

of prep. de

off a. apartado, alejado, separado

off adv. lejos, a distancia, fóra

offend v. ofender, maltratar, aldraxar

offense n. ofensa, afronta, aldraxe, agravio

offensive a. ofensivo -a, inxurioso -a, aldraxante

offer v. ofrecer, brindar, presentar

office n. oficina, despacho

official a. oficial, formal

officiate v. oficiar, celebrar

offset n. compensación, indemnización

offset v. compezar, indemnizar

offspring n. rebento, brote, gromo, abrocho, xermolo

often adv. a miúdo

ogre n. ogro, monstro

oil n. aceite

oily a. aceitoso -a

ointment n. pomada, crema, unguento

old a. vello -a, ancia (f), ancian (m)

old-fashioned a. antigo -a, antigo -a, anticuado -a

oldness n. vellez, senectude, ancianidade

oligarchy n. oligarquía

olive n. oliva

olive oil n. aceite de oliva

olympiad n. olimpiada, xogos olímpicos

omelet n. tortilla

omen n. presaxio, algoro, presentimento

omission n. omisión, elusión

omit v. omitir, deixar, pasar, pasar por alto

on prep. en, sobre, rima de

once adv. unha vez

one a. un (m), unha (f)

onion n. cebola

only adv. únicamente, soamente

onset n. comenzo, inicio, principio, encomenzo, empezo

onslaught n. acometida, embate, ataque

onward a. para adelante

ooze v. zumegar

opacity n. opacidade

opaque a. opaco -a

open a. abierto -a; descuberto -a

open v. abrir, desatrancar

opening n. abertura, apertura

opera n. opera

operate v. operar, actuar, obrar

operation n. operación

operator n. operador -a

opine v. opinar, pensar, coidar, crer

opinion n. opinón

opponent a. opoñente, rival

opportunity n. oportunidade

oppose v. opor, opoñer

opposite a. oposto -a

opposition n. oposición
oppress v. oprimir, apertar
oppression n. opresión
oppressive a. opresivo -a
opprobrium n. oprobio, deshonra, vergonza,
    ignominia
optician n. óptico
optimist n. optimista
option n. opción, posibilidade, alternativa
opulence n. opulencia, abundancia, riqueza
or conj. ou
oral a .oral
orange a. laranxa, alaranxado -a
orange n. laranxa
oration n. oración, pregaria, rogo
orator n. orador
oratory n. oratorio (lugar para rezar),
    composición musical sagrada
orbit n. órbita, ámbito, campo
orchard n. horta
orchestra n. orquestra
orchid n. orquídea
order n. orde
order v. ordenar, mandar
orderly adv. ordenadamente
ordinary a. ordinario -a

ore n. mineral, mena
organ n.órgano
organization n. organizáción
organize v. organizar
origin n. orixe
originally n. orixinariamente, orixinalmente
oriol, oriole n. ouriolo, vichelocrego, nicola (ave)
ornament n. ornamento, ornato
orphan a. & n. orfo -a
orthography n. ortografía
oscillate v. oscilar, abalar, abanear, bambear
osier basket (to catch fish) n. nasa
ostracism n ostracismo
ostrich n. aveztruz
other a. outro -a
otherwise adv. de outro modo
ought v. deber, estar obrigado
ounce (animal) n. onza (mamifero carcicero)
ounce (weight measure) n. onza (medida de peso)
our a. noso, nosa
ours pr. nosos, nosas
ourselves pr. nós mesmos
out adv. externo, exterior
outcast a. paria
outcome n. resultado, consecuencia
outdoor n. aire libre

outer a. exterior

outside n. fóra

outskirts n.pl. arredores, contornia, periferia, rodeada, alfoz

outstanding a. sobresaliente

oval a. oval, ovalado -a,

oval n óvolo

oven n. forno

over adv. por riba

over prep. sobre

overalls n.pl. gardapó

overcast n. encapotado, anubado, anubrado, nubento, nuboso

overlook v. omitir, deixar, pasar por alto

overtake v. alcanzar, adiantarse, sobresair

overtime adv. horas extras

overwhelm v. pesar, oprimir

owe v. deber ter débedas

owl n. curuxa

owl, little n. moucho

own a. propio -a; exclusivo, particular, de seu

own v. posuír, ter

ownership n. propiedade, dominio, posesión

ox n., **oxen** (pl.) n. boi, touro

oxygen n. osíxeno

oyster n. ostra

P

pace n. paso, marcha
pace v. medir os pasos
pacific a. pacífico -a, tranquilo -a, sosegado -a
pack n. vulto, fardo
pack v. empacar, empaquetar, enfardar, enfardelar
page n. páxina
pageant n. espectáculo
pail n. balde, caldeiro
pain n. dor, dolor, dó, coita, mágoa, pena, pesar, aflicción
pain v. doer
painful a. doloroso -a
painstaking a. esmerado -a, meticuloso -a
paint n. pintura
paint v. pintar, colorar, debuxar
painting n. pintura, cadro (obra pintada)
pair n. par, paralla (conxunto de duas unidades)
pair v. emparellar
pajamas n.pl. pixama(s)
pal n. camarada, amigo, compañeiro
palace n. pazo, palacio
palate n. padal, ceo de boca
palatial a. señorial, señoril

pale a. pálido -a, descorado -a, descolorido -a
paleness n. palidez
palette n. paleta (de pintor, utensilio do abanel)
pall n. pano mortuorio
pall of smoke n. capa de nube de fume
palm (anatomy) n. palma (da man)
palm n. palma (planta de familia da palmeira)
palsy n. parálise
paltry a. fútil, insignicante
pamper v. aloumiñar, acariciar, consentir
pamphlet n. folleto
pan n. cazola, cazolo
panel n. panel
paneled a. & n. con panales
pannier n. canasto
pant v. arquexar, alasar
pantry n. despensa
pants n.pl. pantalon(es)
papacy n. pontificado
paper n. papel (sustancia feira de fibras vexetais)
paprika n. pemento
parable n. parabola (narración simbólica)
parabola n. parabola (xeometría)
parachute n. paracaídas
paradise n. paraiso, edén
paragraph n. parágrafo

parallel a. parelelo -a
paralysis n. parálise
paralytic n. & a. paralítico -a
paralyze v. paralizar, entumecer
parasite a. parásito -a; inútil
parasite n. parásito
parcel n. lote, parcela, terreo
parcel out v. parcelar, repartir, distribuir
parch v. resecar(se),secar
parched a. reseco -a, moi seco
parchment n. pergamiño, pergumeo
pardon n. perdón, indulto
pardon v. perdoar, absolver
parents n.pl. pai e nai
parish n. parroquia, freguesía
park n. parque, xardín
park v. aparcar, estacionar
parliament n. parlamento
parliamentary a. parlamentario -a
parrot n. loro, papagaio
parse v. analizar (gramatica)
parsley n. perexil
parson n. cura, crego, sacerdote
part n. parte, fracción, anaco
part v. partir, repartir
partake v. comer, beber

partial a. parcial
participle n. participio
particle n. partícula
particular a. particular, característico -a
partner n. socio, camarada, compa n eiro -a
partridge n. perdiz
parturient n. parturiente
parturition n. parto
party n. partido (político)
pass n. paso (xeografía); salvoconducto
pass v. pasar
passage n. pasaxe
passenger n. pasaxeiro -a, viaxeiro -a
passer-by n. transeunte
passion n. paixón
passionate a. apaixonado -a
passport n. pasaporte
past n. pasado
paste n. pasta
paste v. empastar
pastime n. pasatempo, entretemento, diversión
pastry n. pasteles, doces
pasty a. pálido -a
patch n. remendo, mendo
patch v. remendar, mendar
path n. camiño, vía, vieiro, verea, carreiro

pathetic a. patético -a
patience n. paciencia, calma
patient n. paciente, enfermo -a, doente
patriot a. & n. patriota
patrol n. patrulla, partida, cuadrilla
patrol v. patrullar
patron n. patrón (m); amo, señor, xefe
pattern n. modelo, patrón, protótipo
paunch n. panza, barriga; bandullo, calleiro
   (ventre dos animais)
pause n. pausa, parada, interrupción
pave v. pavimentar
pavement n. pavimento
pavilion n. pavillón
paw n. pouta, gadoupa, garra
pawn (chess) n. peón (peza do xedrez)
pawn n. empeño
pawn v. empeñar, hipotecar
pawnbroker n. prestamista
pay v. pagar
payment n. pago, paga, pegamento
pea n. chícaro, ervello, ervella
peace n. paz, tranquilidade, acougo, calma,
   repouso, sosego, quietude
peach n. melocotón, pexego
peacock n. pavón, pavo real

peak n. cume, cima, pico

peanut n. cacauete

pear n. pera

pearl n. perla

peasant n. campesino, labrego, labrador

pebble n. seixo, callau, coio, pelouro, canto

pedal n. pedal

peel n. pel, pela, pelica, tona, monda (cuberta exterior dalgunhas froitas)

peel v. pelar, estoanar, montar (quita-la pel á froita)

peer n. par, igual, semellante

pelvis n. pelve

pen (writing utensil) n. pluma (utensilio para escribir)

pen in v. encerrar

pen n. curral

penalty n. castigo, pena, sanción

pencil n. lapis

pendulum n. péndulo

penguin n. pingüín (pl. pingüíns)

penicillin n. penicilina

penknife n. canivete

penny n. penique

peony n. peonia

people n. xente

pepper n. pementa
perceive v. percibir
perch (fish) n. perca (peixe)
perch n. percha, colgadoiro
perch v. colocar (en alto)
perfect a. perfecto -a
perform v. executar, realizar, practicar
performance n. execución, intrerpretación
perfume n. perfume, aroma, fragancia, recendo
perfume v. perfumar, aromatizar
perhaps adv. quizais, quizabes, quizá, se cadra
peril n. perigo, risco
period n. período
periscope n. periscopio
perish v. deteriorar, estragar
periwinkle n. pervinca
permanence n. permanencia
permanent a. permanente
permission n. permiso, autorización,
    consentimento
permit n. permiso, licencia
permit v. permitir, consentir
permute v. permutar, cambiar, trocar
perpendicular a. perpendicular
persecution n. persecución, perseguimento
persist v. persistir

person n. pesoa
perspective n. perspectiva
perspicacious a. perspicaz, agudo, sagaz, vivo
perspire v. transpirar, suar
persuade v. persuadir, convencer
persuasion n. persuación
perturb v. perturbar, alterar
peruse v. examinar, mirar con atención
pester v. molestar, importunar, amolar
pet a. favorito -a, predilecto -a
pet n. animal doméstico de casa
pet v. mimar, acariciar
petal n. pétalo
petrel n. petrel, alma negra (ave mariña)
petroleum n. petróleo
petticoat n. enagua, biso
petty a. insignificante, frívolo
phantom n. fantasma, pantasma, espectro,
espíritu
pharmacy n. farmacia, botica
pharynx n. farinxe
pheasant n. faisán
phenomenon n. sing. (phenomena, pl),
fenómeno, apariencia
phlegm n. flegma
phone n. abreviatura de teléfono

photography n. fotografía, foto
phrase n. frase, expresión
physical a. físico, material
physician n. médico -a
physicist n. físico
physics n.pl. física
physiognomy n. fisionomía
piano n. piano
pick n. pico (ferramenta)
pick v. escoller, elixir, seleccionar
pickerel (fish) n. sollo (peixe)
picket n estaca
pickle n. escabeche
picnic n. picnic (comida á campo, merenda campestre)
picture n. cadro, pintura
picture v. pintar, debuxar
picturesque a. pintoresco
pie n. pastel
piece n. peza, anaco, cacho
pierce v. taladrar, penetrar
pig n. cerdo, porco -a, marr a n -a, cocho
pigeon n. pomba
pigsty n. cortello (corte de porcos)
pile (electricity) n. pila (electrica), batería
pile (mound) n. morea, montóa

pile (water fountain) n. pia (recipiente para
   conter auga)
pile v. amorear, amontoar, acumular, xuntar
pilgrim n. peregrino -a, romeiro -a, viaxeiro -a
pill n. pílula, comprimido
pillar n. piar, columna, pilastra
pillow n. almofada, cabeceira, cabeceiro, cabezal
pilot n. piloto
pilot v. pilotar, conducir, guiar
pin n. alfinete
pincers n.pl. tenaces
pinch n. helisco, beliscadura
pinch v. beliscar, rebeliscar, peniscar
pine n. piñeiro
pine v. languidecer, esmorecer
pineapple n. ananás
pinion n. piñón (roda dunha engranaxe)
pink a. rosado -a
pint n. pinta (medida de líquidos)
pioneer n. pioneiro
pious a. piadoso -a; pio, devoto -a, relixioso -a
pipe n. pipa
piper n. frautista, gaiteiro
pipette n. pipeta
pirate n. pirata, corsario (ladrón do mar)
pirate v. piratear, saquear (no mar)

pistol n. pistola
piston n. pistón, émbolo
pit (fruit) n. carbuña, croia, cola, caguna, caroa
pit n. focha, fochanca, burato, foca
pitcher n. botador en beisbol
pith n. tegumento, medula, miolo (dos osos)
pity n. piedade, compaxión
place n. lugar, espacio, sitio
place v. colocar, situar
plague n. praga
plain a. chan, plano -a, liso -a
plaint n. querela, preito
plait n. pregamento, dobra
plait v. trenzar, pregar, dobrar
plan n. proxecto, plano
plan v. proxectar, preparar
planet n. planeta
plank n. táboa; taboleoiro
plant n. planta
plant v. plantar, sementar
plaster v. enxesar
plate n. prato
plateau n. meseta, mesa
platform n. plataforma
platinum n. platino
play hide & seek (children's game) v. pandar

play n. xogo

play v. xogar, divertirese, entreterse

plea n. peitición, pedido, pedimento

plead v. alegar, aducir, aportar

pleasant a. grato -a, agradable, pracenteiro -a

please inter. por favor

please v. agradar, compracer

pleasure n. pracer, gusto, gozo, alegría

plenty n. abundancia, profusión

pliers n.pl. alicates

plot (of land) n. parcela, terreo

plot n. trama, maquinación, intriga

plot v. conspirar, confabularse, conxurarse

plotter n. conspirador -a

plover (bird) n. píldora (ave)

plow n. arado

plow v. arar, labrar

pluck n. valor, coraxe

pluck v. arrincar, arrancar

plucky a. valente, decidido -a, ousado -a

plug n. tapón, tampón

plum n. cirola, ameixa

plum tree n. ciroleira, ameixera

plumber n. tratante de chumbo

plume n. pluma, penucha

plump a. gordecho, gordeiro

plunge n. mergullo, submersión
plunge v. zambullir
plural a. & n. plural
pocket n. peto
pod n. vaiña
poem n. poema
poet n. poeta (m)
poetess n. poeta (f)
poetry n. poesía
point n. punto
point to v. sinalar
pointer n. indicador
poison n. pezoña, veleno
pole n. pao, hasta
pole n. polo (xeografía)
police n. policía
policy n. política
polish n. púlido, puido
polish v. pulir, puir
polite a. cortés, amable
politeness n. cortesía, amabilidade, afabilidade,
    cordialidade, bo trato
political a. político -a
politics n. política (arte de gobernar)
poll n. votación
poll v. votar

pond n. charca, poza
pontiff n. pontífice; Romano pontífice (o Papa)
pony n. cabaliño
pool n. piscina
poop n. popa
poor a. pobre; humilde, modesto
popcorn n. floco de millo
pope n. Papa
poplar tree n. chopo (árbore)
population n. poboación
porcelain n. porcelana
porch n. pórtico
pore n. poro
porgy n. prago (peixe)
pork n. came de porco
porter n. porteiro -a
portfolio n. carteira (de ministro)
portrait n. retrato
position n. posición, situación, localización
position v. colocar, situar(se), acomodar(se), poñer(se)
positive a. positivo -a
possess v. posuir, ter
possession n. posesíón
possessive a. posesivo -a
possible a. posible

post (employment) n. posto, cargo, oficio
post n. poste, esteo, pao
post office n. correos, oficina postal
postage n. franqueo
postcard n. tarxeta postal
posterity n. posteridade
postman (m) n. carteiro
postmark n. cuño
postpone v. pospoñer, pospor, postergar
postwoman (f) n. carteira
pot n. ola, pota, cazola
potato n. pataca, baloca
pottery n. olería, cerámica
pouch n. bolsa, bulsa
poultice n. emplasto
poultry n. aves de curral
pound n. libra (medida de peso)
pound n. moeda de distintos paises
pound v. machucar, esmagar
pour v. verter, botar, deitar
powder n. po, lixo
power n. poder, capacidade
powerful a. poderoso -a
practical a. práctico -a
practice n. práctica
practice v. practicar; realizar, efetuar, facer, leva
a cabo

prairie n. pradería
praise n. eloxio, gabanza, loanza
praise v. eloxiar, gabar, loar, exalzar
praiseworthy a. loable, encomiable, gabable
prawn n. gamba
pray v. rezar, pregar, orar
prayer n. oración, pregaria
preach v. predicar
preacher n. predicador
precocious a. precoz, prematuro, temperán -a
predict v. predecir, profetizar, presaxiar, prognos-
    ticar, vaticinar, adiviñar
prediction n. predicción
preface n. prefacio, prólogo
prefer v. preferir
pregnant a. embarazada
prejudice n. prexuízo, xuício previo
preparation n. preparación
prepare v. preparar
preposition n. preposición
present a. presente
present v. presentar, amostar
preserve n. conserva
preserve v. preserver, conservar
president n. presidente -a
press n. prensa

press release n. comunicado
press v. apertar, apresionar
pressure n. presión
prestige n. prestixio
pretty a. bonito -a, belo -a, fermoso -a
prevailing a. predominante, preponderante
prevent v. previr
prevention n. prevención
previous a. previo -a
price n. prezo
prick n. picada, aguilloada
prick v. punzar, picar
pride n. orgullo
priest n. cura, crego, sacerdote
prime a. primo, primeiro
prince n. príncipe
princess n. princesa
principle n. principio, fundamento
print v. imprimir, imprentar
printer n. impresor -a
printing n. imprenta
prison n. cárcere, prisión (pl. prisións)
prisoner n. prisoneiro -a, preso -a
privacy n. intimidade
private a. privado -a
private n. soldado raso

privilege n. privilexio, vantaxe
prize n. premio, recompensa
probability n. probabilidade, posibilidade
probable a. probable, verosímil
procedure n. procedemento
proceeding n. procedemento
process n. proceso, desenvolvemento
produce v. producir, xerar, dar
product n. producto
profess v. profesar
profession n. profesión
professor n. profesor -a
profile n. perfil, contorno, silueta
profit n. proveito, beneficio, utilidade, ganancia
profit v. aproveitar
profound a. profundo -a, hondo -a
program n. programa
program v. programar
progress n. progreso
progress v. progresar, avanzar, adiantar
prohibit v. prohibir, privar, vedar
prohibition n. prohibición
project n. proxecto
project v. proxectar, lanzar, emitir
projector n. proxector
promenade n. paseo

promise n. promesa
promise v. prometer
pronoun n. pronome
proof (alcoholic) a. graduación de alcool das
  bebidas alcólicas
proof n. proba
propaganda n. propaganda, publicidade
propel v. impulsar, apuxar, impeler
propeller n. hélice
proper a. propio -a
property n. propiedade, dominio, posesión
prophecy n. profecía, predicción, presaxio
proposal n. proposta, proposición
propose v. propoñer, propor
propriety n. decoro, dignidade, recato
prorogue v. prorogar, alongar, prolongar
prose n. prosa
prospective a. presunto -a
prosper v .prosperar, mellorar, progresar
prosperous a. próspero -a
protect v. protexer, defender, preservar
protection n. protección
protest n. protesta
protest v. protestar
protractor n. transportador (utensilio de
  debuxo)

proud a. orgulloso -a, fechendoso -a, soberbio -a
prove v. investigar, indagar
proverb n. proverbio, aforismo, refrán
provide v. prover
province n. provincia
prow n. proa
prudent a. prudente, sensato -a, discreto -a
prune n. cirola, ameixa
prune v. podar
psychology n. psicoloxía
pub n. taberna, cantina
public a. público -a
publication n. publicación
publish v. publicar
publisher n. editor
pudding n. pudín (pl. pudins)
puff n. sopro
pull n. tirón
pull v. tirar, guindar
pulls n. pulso
pulpit n. púlpito
pulse n. pulso
pulse v. latexar, palpitar, bater
pump n. bomba
pump v. bombear
pumpkin n. calabaza, cabaza

punch (beverage) n. ponche (bebida)
punch (fist) n. puñazo, puñada
punch (hardware) n. punzón (ferramenta con punta)
punch v. golpear, bater, pegar, percutir
punctuate v. puntuar
punish v. castigar, punir, penalizar
punishment n. castigo, pena, sanción
pupil n. alumno -a, discípulo, estudiante, colexial
pupil (eye) n. pupíla do ollo
puppet n. títere, monicreque, monocaco
puppy n. cachorro, cadela
purchase n. compra
purchase v. comprar
purchaser n. comprador
pure a. puro -a, recto -a, honrado -a
purgative n. purgante, laxante
purgatory n. purgatorio
purge n. purga
purge v. purgar
purification n. purificatión
purify v. purificar
purity n. pureza, inocencia
purple a. purpúreo -a
purpose n. propósito
pursue v. perseguir, seguir

push n. empuxón, abalón
push v. empuxar, empurrar
puss, pussy V. kitten
puzzle n. enigma
pyramid n. pirámide
python n. pitón (serpe)

Q

quack n. grallo (dalgunhas aves)
quadrate a. cadrado -a
quadrille n. cuadrilla, grupo, banda
quail n. paspallás
quail v. tremer, entaguecer (ter medo)
quaint a. curioso-a, orixinal
quake n. tremor
Quaker n. cuáquero
qualification n. calificación
qualify v. cualificar, xulgar
quality n. calidade
quantity n. cantidade
quarantine n. corentena
quarrel n. rifa, liorta, pelexa
quarrel v. rifar, contender, disputar, pelexar
quarry n. cantería

quarter a. cuarto -a
quarter n. cuartel
quarterly adv. trimestral
quash v. anular, invalidar
quay n. peirao, porto
queasiness n. nausea
queasy n. nauseabundo -a, noxeno -a
queen n. raina
queer a. raro -a, estraño -a
quell v. reprimir, conter
quench v. saciar, satisfacer
query n. pregunta
query v. preguntar
quest n. busca, procura
question n. pregunta
queue n. cola, fila, ringleira
quick a. rápido -a
quicken v. acelerar
quicksilver n. mercurio
quiet a. calado -a, silencioso -a
quilt n. colcha, sobrecama, cobertor, cubertor
quince n. marmeleiro
quit v. renunciar, abandonar
quite adv. completamente
quotation marks n.pl. comiñas
quotation n. cita, referencia

quote (price) n. cota
quote n. cita, referencia
quote v. citar
quotidian a. cotidian -a, habitual
quotient n. cociente

R

rabbit n. coello, coenllo
rabble n. chusma
rabid a. rabioso -a, doente, danado (que padece a rabia)
rabies n. rabia, hidrofofía
race (competition) n. carreira (acción de correr)
race (ethnology) n. raza
race v. correr
racetrack n. hipódromo
rack (torture instrument) n. cabalo de tortura
rack n. estante, andel
rack v. torturar
racket (sports) n. raqueta (pa empregada en deportes como tenis)
racket n. trampa, estafa
radiate v. radiar, irradiar
radiator n. radiador

radio n. radio
radium n. radio (elemento metálico)
radius n. radio
raffle n. rifa
raffle v. rifar
raft n. balsa (artefacto para navegar)
rafter n. viga
rag n. trapo
rage n. rabia, ira
ragged a. farrapento -a
raging a. rabioso -a, furioso -a
ragman n. trapeiro, farrapeiro
raid n. incursión
raid v. atacar, asaltar
rail n. riel, carril
railing n. varanda
railway n. ferrocarril, ferrovía, vía férrea, camiño de ferro, tren
rain n. chuvia, choiva
rain v. chover
rainbow n. arco de vella, arco iris
rainfall n. precipitación (de auga)
rainy a. chuviñoso, chuvioso
raise v. levantar, alzar, elevar
raisin n. uva seca
rake n. angazo, ancino (aveño de labranza)

rake v. angazar, anciñar
rally n. reunión, xuntanza
rally v. reunir(se), xuntar(se)
ram n. carneiro
ramble v. vagar, deambular
ramification n. ramificación
ramp n. rample, pendente
rampart n. terraplén´, recheo
rancor n. rencor, resentimento
rancorous a. rancoroso -a
random a. ó azar
range n. alcance
ranger n. gardabosques
rank n. rango, clase,categoría, xerarquía
rank v. clasificar, ordenar
ransom n. rescate (prezo pagado por unha liberación)
ransom v. rescatar, liberar
rapacity n. rapacidade, rapina
rapid a. rápido -a, lexeiro -a, veloz
rapine n. rapina
rapt a. absorto -a, consumido -a, pasmado -a
rarity n. rareza; obxeto raro, curioso
rash a. erupción (lesións cutánea)
rashness n. temeridade, imprudencia
rat n. rata

rate n. taxa, índice, porcentaxe

rather adv. máis ben

ratification n. ratificación

ratify v. ratificar

ration n. ración, porción

ration v. racionar

rational a. racional, lóxico -a, razoable

rattle n. cascabel, axóúrere, axouro

rattle snake n. serpe de crótalo, serpe de cascabel

ravage v. arrasar, desvastar, destruir

rave v. delirar, desvariar

ravege n. estrago, destrozo, destructión

raven n. corvo, gralla

ravenous a. famento -a, esfameado -a, famélico

ravine n. barranco, barranca, covo, abismo

ravish v. violar, abusar sexualmente

raw a. cru (m), crua (f)

ray n. raio

raze v. arrasar, destruir

razor n. navalla barbeira

reach n. alcance

reach v. alcanzar

react v. reaccionar

reaction n. reacción

read v. ler

reader n. lector
reading n. lectura
ready a. listo -a, disposto, preparado
real a. real, verdadeiro -a
reality n. realidade, verdade, certeza
realize v. realizar, efectuar
realm n. reino, ámbito, campo
ream n. resma (de papel)
reap v. segar, recolleitar, recoller
reaper n. segador, seitureiro
reaping n. sega, seitura, ceifa
reappear v. reaparecer
rear a. posterior
rear admiral n. contraalmirante
reason n. razón
reason v. razoar
reassurance n. reaseguranza
rebate n. rebaixa
rebate v. rebaixar
rebel n. rebelde, insurrecto
rebel v. rebelarse, sublevarse, alzarse
rebellion n. rebelión, revolta, sublevaci o n
rebound n. rebote
rebound v. rebotar
rebuff n. desaire
rebuff v. desairar

rebut v. refutar, rebatir
recall v. recordar, lembrar ternamente
receipt n. recibo
receive v. recibir, percibir, levar
receiver n. & a. receptor
reception n. recepción
receptionist n. recepcionista
recipe n. receita, formula
reciprocity n. reciprocidade
recite v. recitar, declamar
reckon v. calcular
reclaim v. reclamar
reclamation n. reclamación
recline v. reclinar
recognition n. recoñecimento
recognize v. recoñecer, coñocer
recoil n. retroceso
recoil v. retroceder, recuar
recollect v. recordar, lembrar
recollection n. recolección
recommend v. recomendar
recommendation n. recomendación
recompense n. recompensa, comnpensación
recompense v. recompesar
reconcile v. reconciliar(se), amigar(se)
reconciliation n. reconciliación

reconnoiter v. explorar (militar)
record n. rexistro, disco
record player n. tocadiscos
record v. rexistrar
recorder n. rexistrador
recount v. referir, contar, relatar
recourse n. recurso
recover v. recobrar, recuperar
recovery n. reclamación
recreation n. recreo
recruit n. recruta
rectangle n. rectángulo
rectification n. rectificación
recuperate v. recuperar, recobrar
recurrence n. repetición
red a. roxo -a
redden v. arrubiar
reddish a. avermellado -a, encarnado -a, arrubiado -a
redeem v. redimir
redeemer n. redentor
redness n. roibén (pl. roibens)
redoubtable a. temible, témero
redress n. reparación
redress v. reparar, compoñer
reduce v. reducir

reduction n. reducción
reed n. cana
reef n. arrecife
reek v. feder, apestar
reel n. carrete
refer v. referir, aludir
referee n. árbitro
reference n. referencia
refine v. refina, purificar
refinement n. refinamento, elegancia, perfección
refinery n. refinería
refit v. reparar; arranxar
reflect v. reflectir
reflector n. reflector
reform v. reformar
reformation n. reforma
refresh v. refrescar
refreshment n. refresco, refrixerio
refrigerator n. refrixerador, frigorífico
refuge n. rebuxio, abrigo, abeiro
refund n. refundición
refund v. refundir
refuse n. lixo, desperdicio, inmundicia
refuse v. refusar; denegar, negar
regal a. rexio, real, maxestuoso -a
regard n. respecto, consideración

regarding prep. con respecto a
regards n. recordos, saúdos
regenerate v. rexenear
regeneration n. rexeneració´n
regime n. réxime; maneira de vivir
region n. rexión, territorio
register n. rexistro
register v. rexistrar
regret n. remordemento, remoso, pesar
regret v. lamentar; queixarse, doerse
regrettable a. lamentable, penoso, deplorable
regular a. regular, metódico -a, ordenado -a
regulate v. regular, axustar
regulation n. regulamento
rehearsal n. ensaio, práctica
rehearse v. ensaiar, practicar
reign n. reinado
reign v. reinar
rein n. renda
rein v. refrear
reindeer n. reno
reinforce v. reforzar
reject v. rexeitar, refugar, rechazar
rejection n. rexeitamento, rechazo
rejoice v. alegrar, divertir(se), animar(se)
relapse n. recaída

relate v. relatar, contar, expor, expoñer, narrar
relation n. relato, narración
relationship n. parentesco, parentela; afinidade
relative a. relativo -a
relative n. parente, familiar
relax v. descansar
release n. liberacion
release v. liberar, soltar
reliable a. seguro -a, firme de carácter
reliance n. confianza, seguranza, certeza
relic n. reliquia; vestixio
relief n. alivio, conforto
relieve v. socorrer, auxiliar, axudar
religion n. relixión, fé
religious a. relixioso -a
relish n. condimento; adobo, aliño
rely v. depender (de)
remain v. permanecer
remainder n. residuo, resto, sobrante
remake v. refacer, reconstruir
remark n. observación, nota, comentario
remark v. observar, notar
remedy n. remedio
remedy v. remediar
remember v. recordar, lembrar (ter de mente)
remembrance n. rocordo, lembranza

remind v. recordar, lembrar, acordar
reminder n. advertencia
remit v. remitir, enviar, mandar
remittance n. remesa, remisión, envio
remnant n. resto, residuo, sobrante
remonstrate v. protestar, queixarse
remora (fish) n. remora (peixe)
remorse n. remordemento, remorso, pesar
remove v. remover, remexer, apartar, quitar
remunerate v. remunerar, pagar, retribuir
rend v. esgazar, rachar, rasgar
render v. deterrer, fundir
renew v. renovar, reemprender(se)
renewal n. renovo, gromo, robento
renounce v. renunciar
renovation n. renovación
renown n. renome, fama
rent n. alugamento, alugeiro, arrendo
rent v. alugar, arrendar
reorganize v. reorganizar
repair n. reparo, reparación
repair v. reparar, compoñer
repeal v. revogar, abolir, abrogar, anular
repeat v. repetir, imitar, remedar
repel v. repeler, repudiar
repellent a. repulsivo -a, repugnante, repelente

repent v. arrepentirse
replace v. substituir
reply v. contestar, responder
report n. informe
report v. informar
reporter n. reporteiro
repose v. repousar, quedar tranquilo ou inactivo
reprehend v. reprender, amoestar
represent v. representar
representative a. representativo -a
representative n. representante
repress v. represar
repression n. represión (pl. represións)
reprieve n. suspensión, indulto
reprisal n. represalia, vinganza
reproach n. reproche, censura, recriminación
reproach v. reprochar, censurar, recriminar
reproduce v. reproducir
reproduction n. reprodución
reprove v. reprobar, censurar, desprobar
reptile a. & n. réptil
republic n. república
repudiate v. repudiar, rexeitar
repulsion n. repulsión, aversión
reputable a. acreditado -a
request n. rogo, súplica

request v. rogar, pregar, pedir, suplicar
require v. requerir, pedir
requirement n. requisito; formalidade, esixencia legal ou administrativa
rescue n. rescate
rescue v. rescatar, recobrar, recuperar
research v. investigar
resemblance n. semellanza
resemble v. semellar; asemellarse
resent v. resentir(se)
resentment n. resentimento
reserve n. reserva
reserve v. reservar
reservoir n. embalse (de auga)
reside v. residir, vivir
residence n. residencia; vivenda ou casa luxosa
residue n. residuo, resto, sobrante
resign v. resignar, renunciar
resignation n. resignación, paciencia; renuncia
resin n. resina, mástique
resist v. resistir
resistance n. resistencia, oposición
resolution n. resolución, solución
resolve v. resolver, solucionar
resort n. recurso
resort v. recorrer, acudir

respect n. respecto
respect v. respectar
respite n. tregua, pousa
respond v. responder, contestar
response n. reposta
responsible a. responsable, culpable
rest (arithmetic) n. resto, residuo, sobrante
rest n. descanso, repouso
rest v. descansar, repousar
restful a. tranquilo -a, apacible
restless a. desasosegado -a, intranquilo -a, inquedo -a
restore v. restaurar, restituir
restrain v. reprimir, conter
restrict v. restrinxir, limitar
result n. resultado
result v. resultar
resume v. resumir; abreviar, reducir
resurrection n. resurrección, renacemento
retail n. pormenor
retain v. reter
retard v. retardar, aprazar
retire v. xubilar, retirar
retouch n. retoque
retouch v. retocar
retract v. retractar

retribution n. retribución
return n. regreso, volta, retorno
return v. regresar, volver, retornar
reveal n. revelar
revelation n. revelación
revelry n. xolda, foliada, esmorga, chola
revenge n. vinganza, desquite
revenge v. vingar, vingarse, desquitarse
revenue n. ingreso(s)
revere v. reverenciar, adorar, venerar
reverie n. sono, ilusión, fantasía
reverse n. reverso, revés
review n. repaso, revisión
revise v. revisar, repasar, reexaminar
revival n. renacemento, renovación, reanimación
revive v. revivir, resucitar, rexurdir
revocation n. revogación, anulación
revoke v. revogar, abolir, invalidar
revolt v. rebelarse, sublevarse
revolve v. resolver, solucionar
revolver (fire arm) n. revólver (arma do fogo)
revolving a. xiratorio -a, rotatorio -a
revue n. revista (espectáculo teatral)
reward n. recompensa, premio
reward v. premiar, recompensar, galardoar
rhinoceros n. rinoceronte

rhyme n. rima
rhythm n. ritmo
rib n. costela
ribbon n. cinta, tira, faixa
rib-grass n. platain, correola
rice n. arroz
rich a. rico -a
richness n. riqueza, abundancia
rickets n. raquitismo
rickety a. raquítico -a
riddle n. adiviña, enigma
ride n. paseo
ride to v. pasear
rider n. pasaxeiro
ridge n. crista, cima (dun monte)
ridicule n. ridículo
ridicule v. ridiculizar
rifle n. rifle, carabina
right a. dereito -a, recto -a
right v. endereitar
righteous a. xusto -a, equitativo -a
righteousness n. rectitude, honradez
rigid a. rixido -a, teso -a, erguido -a
rigidity n. rixidez, dureza, inflexibilidade
rind n. casca, tona
ring n. anel (pl. aneis)

rinse v. enxaguar
riot n. motín, disturbio
riot v. amotinar(se), rebelar(se)
rip n. rachón, racho, rachadura
rip v. engazar, rachar, esguizar
ripe n. maduro -a
ripen v. madurar, madurecer
rise n. subida, ascenso
rise v. subir, elevar
risk n. risco, perigo
risky a. arriscado -a
rite n. rito
rival n. rival, adversario, competidor
rival v. rivalizar, competir
rivalry n. rivalidade, competencia
river n. rio
rivet n. remache
rivet v. remachar
road n. estrada
roar n. ruxido, bramido
roar v. ruxir, bramar, bruar
roast n. asado
roast v. asar
rob v. roubar, furtar
robber n. ladrón -a

robbery n. roubo

robe n. túnica, manto

robin n. paparrubio, poporroibo, pisco

rocket. n. foguete

rocking chair n. cadeira mexedora

rocky a. rochoso -a, penedoso -a

rod n. vara, pao

rogue n. falsario, tramposo

roguery n. picardía, malicia

role n. rol, parte de obra teatral que representa
cada actor

roll n. bolo

roll v. rodar, xirar

roller n. rodo, rolo, rodete

romance n. romance; aventura amorosa
pasaxeira; enredo, lío

rood n. cruz, crucifixo

roof n. teito; tallado

rook n. roca, rocha

rook (chess) n. torre (peza de xogo do xadrez)

rookie a. novoto -a, principiante, inexperto -a

room n. cuarto

rooster n. galo

root n. raiz

rope n. lazo, corda

rose n. rosa
rosebush n. roseira
rosemary n. romeu
rot n. putrefacción
rot v. podrecer
rotary a. rotario -a
rotten a. putefracto -a, podre
rough a. áspero -a, esgrevio -a
round a. redondo -a
roundabout a. tortuoso -a
rouse v. espertar, incitar, provocar
rout n. desbandada, derrota
rout v. derrotar, vencer
route n. ruta, rota, camino
rove v. vagar, vaguear, vagabundear
row n. fileira, ringleira, fila
row v. remar, vogar
royal a. real (relativo a realeza)
royal jelly p. xelea real
royalty n. realeza
rub n. fricción, friccionamento
rub out v. borrar
rubber n. caucho
rubbish n. lixo, desperdicio
ruby n. rubí

rucksack n. mochila
rude a. rudo -a
rug n. alfombra
ruin n. ruina, restos, vestixios
ruin v. arruinar, destruir
rule n. regra
rule v. mandar, ordeñar, imponer
rum n. ron
rumble n. reoxar, atronar
ruminant a. & n. rumiante
run n. corrida, carreira
run v. correr
rung n. banzo, chanzo, paso
runner n. corredor
rupture n. rompemento, rompedura, rotura
rush n. ímpeto, brio, enerxía
rush v. precipitar(se)
rust (chemistry) n. ferruxe (óxido de ferro)
rust (parasite) n. ferruxe (fungo parásito
  dos cerais)
rust v. oxidar, enfurrarse
rut n. celo, raxeira, xaneira (excitación sexual)
ruthless a. despiadado -a, cruel
ruthlessness n. crueldade
rye n. centeo

S

saber n. sabre
sable n. marta zibelina, sable
sabot n. zoca
sack n. saco
sack v. ensacar, saquetear
sacred a. sagrado -a, sacro -a
sacredness n. sagrado
sacrifice n. sacrificio, immolación
sacrifice v. sacrificar, immolar
sad a. triste, apenado -a
sadden v. entristecer
saddle bag n. alforxa
saddle n. sela (para montar a cabalo)
saddle v. enselar
sadness n. tristeza, tristura
safe n. seguro -a
safeguard n. salvagarda
safety n. seguridade, seguranza, certeza
safety pin n. imperdible, prendedor
safety razor n. máquina de afeitar
saffron n. azafrán
sagacious a. sagaz, perspicaz
sage (botany) n. salvia, sarxa, xarxa (planta
   medicinal)

sage n. sabio -a, douto -a, erudito -a

sail n. vela (do barco)

sail v. navegar, singrar (o barco)

sailing ship n. barco ou buque de vela

sailor n. mariñeiro

Saint James n. Santiago

saint n. santo -a

sake n. motivo

salable a. vendible

salad n. ensalada

salamander n. pintega, salmántiga, pinchora

salary n. salario, paga

sale n. venta

sale v. vender

sallow a. amarelado -a

sally n. incursión (pl. incursións)

salmon n. salmón (peixe)

saloon n. salón

salsa (music) n. salsa (música)

salsa n. salsa (condimento)

salt n. sal

salt v. salgar

salutation n. salutación, saúde, saudación

salute v. saludar

salvage n. salvamento

salvage v. salvar; rescatar

salvation n. salvación
salve n. ungüento
salver n. bandexa, prato
same a. mesmo -a, igual
sample n. mostra
sample v. probar
sanctify v. santificar
sanctuary n. santuario
sand n. area
sandal n. sandalía
sandwich n. sandwich
sane a. cordo -a, sensato -a
sanity n. cordura, sensatez
sap n. zume (dos vexetais)
sap v. extraer o zume
sapphire n. zafiro
sardine n. sardiña
sash n. faixa
sateen n. satén
satellite n. satélite
satiate v. saciar, satisfacer
satisfaction n. satisfacción
satisfy v. satisfacer
Saturday n. sábado
sauce n. salsa
saucepan n. cazola

saucer n. prato
saucer, flying n. prato voador
sauciness n. descaro, insolencia
saucy a. descarado -a, insolente
sausage n. salchicha
savage n. salvaxe
save v. salvar, librar
saving n. sabina (árbore)
Savior a. & n. Salvador
savor n. sabor, gusto
savory a. salgado -a, sabroso -a
saw p. serra (ferramenta)
saw v. serrar
sawdust p. serraduras
saxophone n. saxofón
say v. dicir
saying n. dito, dita
scab n. bostela, carapola
scab v. boicotear unha folga
scabbard n. funda (dunha arma)
scaffold n. cadafalso
scald n. escalda, escaldadura
scald v. escaldar(se)
scale (instrumentation)n. escala (graduación dun instrumento de medida)
scale n. escama (membrana da pel)

scale v. escalar

scallop n. venera, concha (de peregrino), concha de vieira

scan v. escudriñar, pescudar

scandal n. escándalo

scanty n. escaso -a, insuficiente

scar n. cicatriz

scarce a. escaso -a

scarf n. bufanda

scarlet a. escarlata

scarlet fever n. escarlatina

scatter v. esparexer(se)

scavenger n. animal que se alimenta de prea

scene n. escena

scenery n. escenario

scent n. aroma, fragancia

scepter n. cetro, bastón de mando

schedule n. horario

schedule v. programar

scheme n. proxecto, plano

scholar n. escolar

school mate n. colega de escola ou colexio

school n. escola

schooner n. goleta

science n. ciencia

scientific a. & n. científico -a

scintilla n. chispa
scintillate v. escintillar
scissors n.pl. tesoira
scope n. alcance, magnitude
scorch v. chamuscar, queimar
score (musical) n. partitura (música)
score n. amósega, marca, risco
scorn n. desdén, desapego, indiferencia
scorn v. desbotar, menopreciar, desprezar
scorpion n. escorpión, alacrán
scoundrel n. pícaro, pillo
scour v. refregar, fregar
scourer n. estropallo
scout n. explorador
scout v. explorar
scrap n. chisco, migalla, miga, petisco
scrape v. raspar, riscar
scratch v. rabunñar, esgañudar, gaduñar, garduñar
scream v. berrar, gritar, vocear, vociferar
screech n. berro, grito, alarido,chio
screech v. berrar, gritar, chiar
screen n. pantalla
screen v. proxectar
screw n. parafuso
screw v. aparafusar
screwdriver n. desparafusador

scribe n. amanuense, escribente, copista
scrimp v. escatimar
scrub n. maleza, mato
scrub v. fregar, estregar
scruple n. escrúpulo
scrutiny n. escrutinio
sculpt v. esculpir
sculpture n. escultura
scum n. borra, pouso; chusma, xentella
scythe n. gadaña
sea bream (fish) n. chopa (peixe)
sea n. mar
sea wall n. dique maritimo
seaboard n. costa litoral
seagull n. gaivota
seal (animal) n. foca (animal)
seal n. selo, cuño
seal v. selar, cerrar
seam (mining) n. veta, filón, vea (nunha mina)
seam n. costura, xuntura
search n. busca
search v. buscar
seasickness n. mareo
seasonable a. propio con estación (verán, etc.)
seat n. asento, cadeira
seaweed n. alga, argaso

secede v. separar(se)
seclude v. illar, apartar
seclusion n. illamento
second n. segundo
second v. secundar
secret n. secreto, oculto
secretary n. secretario -a
section n. sección, corte
secular a. secular
secure a. seguro -a, protexido a
sedate a. sosegado -a
seduce v. seducir, tentar
seducer n. seductor
see v. ver, mirar
See, Holy n. Santa Sede
seed n. semente
seed v. sementar
seek v. buscar, investigar, procurar
seem v. parecer
seeming n. aparente
seer n. adiviño -a
seesaw n. balancín
segment n. segmento
seize v. agarrar, aferrar, asir
seldom adv. rara vez
select v. selecionar, escoller, elixir

selection n. selección
self a. mesmo, propio -a
sell v. vender
seller n. vendedor -a
semicolon n. punto e coma (;)
senate n. senado
senator p. senador
send v. enviar, mandar, remitir
sender n. remitente
senior a. & n. maior, mais vello, de mais edade
sensation n. sensación
sense n. sentido
senseless a. insensible
sensitive a. sensitivo -a
sentence n. sentencia (decisión xudicial)
sentence n. sentencia (gramática), aforismo
sentinel n. sentinela, vixia, garda
sentry v. sentinel
separate v. separar
separation n. separación
September n. setembro
septic a. escéptico -a, incredulo -a
sepulcher n. sepulcro, sepultura, nicho
sequel n. consecuencia
sequent a. consecuente
seraph n. serafín (anxo celestial)

serenade n. serenada
serf n. servo -a
sergeant n. sarxento
series n.pl. serie(s)
serious a. serio -a
sermon n. sermón
serpent n. serpe, serpente
servant n. servente
serve v. servir
service n. servicio
servitude n. servidume
session n. sesión
set a. rixido -a, inflexible
set forth v. expoñer, explicar
set on v. azurrar
set out v. set forth, to
settle down v. asentarse, instalarse, establecerse
settle p. colocar(se), situart(se)
settlement n. establecemento
seven a. sete
seventeen a. dezasete
seventeenth a. decimo sétimo
several a. varios -as, diversos -as
severe a. severo -a, estricto -a
sew v. coser
sewer n. cloaca, sumidoiro

sewing machine n. máquina de coser
sewing n. costura, cosedura
sex n. sexo, sexualidade
shabby n. raido -a
shackle n. grillón, ferros
shade n. sombra
shadow n. sombra
shady a. sombreado -a, sombrio -a
shaft n. agarradoira; eixe (mecánica)
shaggy a. láudo -a, peludo-a
shake v. sacudir, bater con violencia
shallow a. superficial, pouco profundo
sham n. fraude, engano
shame n. vergonza, vergoña
shameless a. desvergonzado -a, desvergoñado -a
shank n. zanca
shanty n. choza, choupana, cabana
shape n. forma
shape v. formar
shapeless p. informe, fato de forma
shapely a. proporcionado -a, harmonioso -a,
    equilibrado -a
share n. porción, participación
share v. compartir, repartir
shareholder n. accionista
shark n. tiburón, quenlla**

sharp a. afilado -a

sharpen v. afiar, aguzar

shave v. afeitar(se)

shaving brush p. brocha (utensilho para afeitarse)

shawl n. mantón

she pr. ela

sheaf n. (sing.), **sheaves** (pl.) gavela

shear v. tosquiar, rapar

shearer n. tosquiador

sheep dog n. can pastor

sheep n. ovella

sheer a. escarpado -a, espinado -a

sheet p. folla (lámina de papel)

shelf n. (sing.), **shelves** (pl.) estante

shell (artillery) n. proxectil (artillería)

shell n. casca

shepherd (m), n. pastor

shepherdess (f), n. pastora

sheriff n. sherif, xerife

shield n. escudo

shield v. escudar, amparar

shift n. cambio

shift v. cambiar

shilling n. xelín (moeda)

shine v. brillar, escintilar

ship p. barco, buque, navío, embarcación

ship v. embarcar
ship worm n. broma (molusco)
shirk v. eludir, esquivar
shock p. choque, commoción violenta
shock v. sorprender
shoe n. zapato (calzado)
shoemaker n. zapateiro
shoot n. renovo, xermolo
shoot v. disparar, tirar (unha arma de fogo)
shooter n. disparador
shop n. tenda, comercio
shop v. ir de compras
shopkeeper n. tendeiro -a
shore n. praia; ribeira do mar ou dun gran rio
short a. corto -a
short circuit n. corto circuito
shortage n. escaseza, falta, insuficiencia
shorten v. acurtar, recortar
shove n. empuxón
shove v. empuxar, apuxar
shovel n. pa
show n. espectáculo, actuación
show v. exhibir, lucir, ostentar
shower (rain) n. chuvasco
shower n. ducha
shower v. regar

showman n. empresario
shrew (mouse) n. muscaraña, muraño
shrewd a. perspicaz, sagaz
shrub n. arbusto
shut v. cerrar, zarrar
shutter n. poxigo, postigo
shuttle (textile machinery) n. lanzadeira
shuttle n. transporte rápido entre dos sitios
sick a. enfermo -a, doente
sicken v. enfermar
sickness n. enfermidade, mal, doenza
side n. lado, costado
sidewalk n. beirarrúa
sieve n. cribo, peneira, sirgo
sieve v. peneirar, cribar
sigh n. suspiro
sigh v. suspirar
sight (vision) n. vista, visión
sight n. mira (de fusil)
sightless a. cego -a, invidente
sign language n. grafema mudo
sign n. sinal, indicio
sign v. firmar, asinar
signal n. sinal, signo
signature n. firma, sinatura
significance n. significación

signify v. significar, denotar, designar
silence n. silencio
silence v. silenciar, calar
silent a. silencioso -a
silently adv. silenciosamente
silk n. seda
sill n. repisa, estante
silver n. prata
silversmith n. prateiro, ourive, xoieiro
similar a. similar, semellante, parecido
simmer v. ferver a lume baixo
simple a. simple
simplify v. simplificar
sin n. pecado
sin v. pecar
since prep. desde
sincere a. sincero -a
sincerely adv. sinceramente
sincerity n. sinceridade, franqueza; autencidade
sinew n. tendón
sinewy a. vigoroso -a
sinful a. pecaminoso -a
sing v. cantar
singer n. cantador -a
singing n. canción, cántiga
single a. único, só

sinister a. sinestro -a

sink n. vertedeiro

sink v. afundir, mergullar, submerxer

sinner n. pecador -a

sip n. sorbo, pingo

sip v. sorber, chapar

Sir n. sir, título inglés

sister n. irmá

sister-in-law n. cuñada

sit down strike n. folga de brazos caidos

sit v. sentar

site n. sitio, lugar, parte

situation n. situación, colocación, circumstancia, conxuntura

six a. seis

sixteen a. desaseis

sixteenth a. décimo sexto

sixth a. sexto

size n. tamaño, grandor, grandura

skate n. patinaxe, patín

skate v. patinar (con patíns)

skater n. patinador -a

skeleton n. esqueleto; armazón, estructura

sketch n. bosquexo, esbozo

sketch v. bosquezar, esbozar

ski n. esquí

ski v. esquiar
skid v. patinar, esvarar
skier n. esquiador
skill n. habilidade, destreza
skillful a. destro, hábil
skim v. desnatar
skin n. pel, pelico, coiro (dun animal)
skip n. brinco, chimpo, souto, salto
skip v. brincar, choutar, saltar, brincar
skipper (navy) n. capitán dun barco
skipper n. brincador, saltador
skirt n. faldra, saia
skull n. cranio
sky n. ceo
slack a. frouxo -a, preguiceriro -a
slam n. portazo
slam v. cerrar dun portazo
slang n. argot, xerga
slap p. labazada, bofetada, lampazo
slash n. coitelada, navallada
slash v. acoitelar, anavallar
slate n. encerado (prancha para escribir)
slate n. lousa
slaughter n. matanza, masacre
slaughter v. matar
slave n. escravo -a, servo

slavery n. escravitude; sometemento, opresión, tiranía

slavish a. servil (pl. servís)

slay v. matar

sled n. zorra (vehículo para andar pola neve ou pola xelo)

sledge, v. sled

sleep v. durmir

sleeper n. dormente, que dorme

slender a. esvelto -a, lanzal

slice n. tallada

slice v. tallar, cortar

slide v. esbarar

slim a. delgado -a, fraco -a

sling n. bebida de whisky ou ron, auga con azucre e limón

sling v. lanzar, botar

slip (feminine apparel) n. biso (prenda fmenina)

slip n. escorregada, escorregón, esvarón

slipper n. zapatilla, pantunfla, alpargata

slobber n. baba, babuxa

slobber v. babexar, babear

slogan n. lema, emblema

slope p. inclinación

sloppy n. descoidado

sloth n. preguiza, galbana

slothful a. preguiceiro -a, preguizoso -a

slow a. lento -a, tardo -a

slowness n. lentitude, tardanza

sluggish a. preguiceiro -a

sluice n. esclusa (represa pa facilita-la navegación)

slum n. arrabalde, alfoz (pl. alfoces)

smack n. labazada, bofetada

smack v. zoupar, bater, losquear

small a. pequeno -a, baixo, breve, curto

smart a. listo -a, agudo -a, perspicaz

smash n. choque, tropezón

smash v. quebrar, crebar, romper

smell v. choirar, ulir

smile n. sorriso

smile v. sorrir

smith n. ferreiro

smithy n. fragua, forxa

smog n. fume (smoke) mais brétame (fog)

smoke n. fume

smoke v. fumar

smooth a. liso -a, chan. laso

smother v. afogar, asfixiar(se)

smuggler n. contrabandista

smuggling n. contrabando

snack n. porción, chisca

snail ´n. caracol (de terra)

snake n. serpe, serpente

snapshot n. instantánea (fotografía)

snare (for game) n. buíz (rede para cazar páxaros)

snare n. trampa, celada, emboscada

snare v. emboscar

snarl n. gruñido

snarl v. gruñir, griñir, refungar, roñar, rosmar

sneeze n. espirro, esbirro

sneeze v. espirrar, esbirrar

snob n. & a. (latín: sine nobilitate, sen nobreza)

snooze n. sesta; soneca

snore v. roncar; bramar, ruxir, bruar

snort v. refolgar, bufar, fungar

snout n. fociño, morro

snow fall n. nevada, neverada

snow flake n. folerpa de neve

snow n. neve

snow v. nevar

so adv. asi, deste xeito

soak n. remollo

soak v. remollar

soap n. xabón

soap v. exaboar

soapwort n. xaoeira, herba xaboeira

soar v. remontar(se), elevar(se) (as aves ou avións)

sob n. salouco, saliaio

sob v. saloucar, salucar

social a. social

socket (anatomy) n. cunca (dos ollos)

socket (electricity) n. enchufe (eléctrico)

soda n. soda

sofa n. sofá

soft a. brando -a

softness n. brandura

soil n. chan, terra, solo

soldier n. soldado -a

sole ((fish) n. linguado (peixe)

sole a. só -a, único -a

sole (anatomy) n. planta (parte do pé)

solid a. sólido -a, firme, fixo, estable, macizo, consistente

solid n. sólido

solidly v. solidificar(se)

solution (remedy) n. solución, remedio

solution n. solución (acción de disolver)

solve v. resolver, solucionar

solvent a. solvente

somber a. sombrio -a

some a. algún (m) algunha (f)

somebody pr. alguén
somehow adv. dalgún modo
someone v. somebody
something pr. algo, un pouco
sometimes adv. algunha vez
son n. son, compás, ritmo
song n. canción, cántiga, cantar
son-in-law n. xenro
sonnet n. soneto
soon adv. pronto, rápido, lixeiro, veloz
sorcerer (m) n. feticeiro, meigo, bruxo
sorceress (f) n. feticeira, meiga, bruxa
sore a. dorido -a, mogoado -a
sorrow p. pesar, mágoa
sorrowful a. pesaroso -a, apenado -a
sorry a. pesaroso -a
sort n. clase, especie
sort v. dividir, separar
soul n. alma, espírito, ánima
soulful a. sentimental
sound a. san, firme, sólido
sound n. son
sound v. sonar
soup n. sopa,
sour a. agre, acedo -a
sour v. agrear(se), acedar(se)

south n. sur, mediodia
southeast n. sueste
southern a. meridional
southwest n. suoeste
souvenir n. recordo, lembranza, memoria
sovereign a. & n. soberano -a
sow (f), n. marrán (pl. marráns)
soya n. soia
space n. espacio
spade n. pa
Spanish a. & n. español -a (pl. españois, españolas)
spanner n. chave (ferramenta)
spare parts n. pl. recambios, accesorios
spark n. chispa, faisca
spark plug n. buxía
spark v. chispear, faiscar
sparkle n. escintileo, brillo, fulgor
sparrow n. gorrión, pardal, pintarroxo, liñaceiro
spatial a. espacial
speak v. falar, expresarse, parrafear
speaker n. orador
speaker of the house n. presidente da casa de representantes
special a. especial
specify v. especificar

specimen n. espécime
spectacles n.pl. lentes, gafas, anteollos
spectator n. espectador -a
specter n. espectro, fantasma, pantasma, vision, aparecido, ánima
speech n. discurso, alocución, oración
speed n. velocidade, rapidez
speedy a. veloz, lixeiro -a, rápido
spell v. deletrear, soletrear
spend v. gastar, consumir
sphere n. esfera, bola, globo
spider n. araña; lámpada
spider web n. tea de araña
spin v. xirar, virar
spine (anatomy) n. espiñazo, columna vertebral
spine n. espiña, pua (de plantas e animais)
spinster n. solteira, solterona
spiral a. espiral
spire n. espira (parte de columna)
spirit n. espíritu, alma, ánima
spit n. saliva, cuspe, chuspe, cuspia
spit v. cuspir, chuspir
spite n. rencor, resentimento
spittle n. saliva, cuspe, chuspe, cuspia
spittoon n. cuspideira
splotch n. mancha

spoil v. estragarse, deteriorarse
sponge n. esponxa
sponsor n. patrocinador -a
sponsor v. patrocinar
spontaneous a. espóntaneo-a
spoon n. culler
sport n. deporte
sportsman n. deportista
spot n. sitio, lugar, parte
spot v. manchar, salpicar
spout n. caño, canavela (dunha fonte)
spray n. orballada, orballo
spray v. orballar
spread n. extensión, propagación
spread v. propagar, difundir
spring v. saltar
Spring (season) n. primavera
spring n. resorte (peza elástica)
sprinkle n. aspersión, rega
sprinkle v. asperxir
sprint v. correr rapidamente
sprout n. xermolo, broche, agromo, gromo, botón
sprout v. xermolar, brotar, abrochar
spur n. espora
spy n. espia, esculeta
spy v. espiar, alucar

square a. cadrado -a
square n. praza
square v. cadrar
squash n. esmagamento, esmagadura
squash p. cabaza, cabazo
squash v. esmagar, machucar, amagallar
squint-eyed a. & n. birollo, vesgo, estrábico, breco
squirrel n. esquío
stadium n. estadio
stage n. escena, escenario (parte do teatro)
stage v. representar, poñer en escena)
stain n. macha, máula
stain v. manchar, ensuciar, lixar
stainless n. inmaculado -a, implecable
stainless steel n. aceiro inoxidable
stair n. chanzo, banzo, paso
staircase n. escaleira
stalk n. talo (dunha planta)
stalk v. axexar, asexar, espreitar, espiar, aseitar
stammer n. tartamudeo, gaguexo, tababexo
stammer v. tatexar
stammerer n. tartamudo, tatexo, tababexo
stamp p. selo
stamp v. selar, estampar
stand n. posición, postura
standard n. normal, corrente, común

standing a. dereito -a, de pes
staple a. principal, esencial, fundamental
staple n. grampa, armela
star n. estrela
starboard n. estribor, banda
starch n. amidón
starch v. amidonar
stare v. fitar, observar, catar
starfish n. estrelamar
start n. comenzo, inicio, principio
start v. empezar, comenzar
starvation n. inanición, fame
state n. estado (territorio político)
state v. afirmar, asegurar, afianzar, asentar
statement n. afirmación, declaración
statesman n. home de estado
station n. estación; epoca, tempo
station v. aparcar, estacionar
stationary a. estacionario -a
statue n. estatua, figura
statuesque a. escultural
status n. estado, condición, índole
statutory a. regulamentario
steady a. firme, fixo
steak n. filete, posta, bisté
steal v. roubar, furtar

steam n. vapor, befo

steamship n. barco a vapor

steel n. aceiro

steelyard n. romana (especie de balanza)

steer n. xuvenco, xato, cuxo, pucho, novelo, becerro

steer v. dirixir, guiar

steersman n. timoneiro (dun barco)

stem n. talo (dunha planta)

stem v. represar

step n. paso

step v. pisar

stepbrother n. medio-irmán

stepdaughter n. fillastra

stepfather n. padrasto

stepmother n. madrasta

stepsister n. media-irmá

stepson n. filastro

sterling p. & a. esterlina

sterling pound n. libra esterlina

stern (ship) n. popa (dun baco)

stern a. severo -a, rixido -a

sternness n. severidade, rigor

stethoscope n. estetoscopio, fonendoscopio

stew n. estufado, guisado

stew v. estufar, guisar

steward n. mordomo

stewardess n. camareira, ama, criada principal, azafata (dun avión)

stick n. pao

stick v. apegar, pegar, adherir

sticking plaster n. esparadrapo

sticky a. apegañoso -a, apegadizo -a

stiff a. rixido -a, teso, irto, inflexible

stiffen v. endurecer (poñer duro)

still a. quieto, quedo, inmóbil

still adv. ainda, inda

still n. alambique, alquitara

still v. aquietar, acougar

stimulation n. estímulo

sting n. aguillón, picadura, picada

sting v. aguilloar, aguillar (picar coa aguillada)

stir n. revolta

stir v. revolver, axitar

stirrup n. estribo, estribeira

stock broker n. corredor de bolsa

stock n. variedade, abundancia

stock v. abastecer, fornecer, prover, equipar

stocking n. media(s)

stomach n. estómago

stone n. pedra; calculo (que se forma nos riles, vexigas, vías urinarias)

stool n. tallo, tallolo, banqueta

stoop p. inclinación

stop n. parada, alto

stop v. parar, deter

storage n. almacenamento, almacenaxe

store n. almacén, tenda

store v. almacenar, acumular

storeroom n. despensa

stork n. cegoña

storm n. tempestade, vendaval

storm v. asaltar, atacar unha praza ou fortaleza

story n. coto, narración

stout a. macizo, sólido

stove n. estufa

stowaway n. polisón

straight a. recto -a, dereito -a

strain v. esforzar(se)

strainer n. coador, coadoiro

strand n. febra, fibra

strange p. estraño -a, alleo -a

stranger n. extranxeiro, alleo, estraño

strangle v. estrangular, esganar, afogar

strap n. correo, cinto

straw n. palla

strawberry bush n. erbedeiro, érbedo, albedro,
   morogueiro

strawberry n. amodoro, morote

stray v. extraviar(se), perder(se)

streak n. raia, liña

streak v. raiar

stream n. arroio, regueiro

stream v. verter, derramar

street n. rua, via

strength n. forza, poder, potencia

strengthen v. fortalecer

stress n. tensión, ansiedade

stress v. recalcar, subliñar, acentuar

stretch v. estirar, estender

stretcher n. angarellas, padiola

strict a. estricto -a, rigoroso -a

strike n. folga

strike n. golpe

striker n. folguista

string n. corda

string n. corda (dos instrumentos musicais)

strip n. tira, fita

strip v. espir(se), desvertir(se)

stripe n. raia

strong a. forte, rexo

structure n. estructura

struggle n. loita, contenda, pelexa, enfrontamento

struggle v. loitar, combater, pelexar

stub n. pava, cabicha (do cigarro)

student n. estudiante

study n. estudio

study v. estudiar

stuff v. material, materia

stumble v. tropezar

stupid a. estúpido -a; parvo, imbécil, menticato, insensagto

style n. estilo

stylish a. estilísta

subdue v. subxugar, oprimir

subject n. suxeito, individuo

submarine n. submarino (navio somerxible)

submit v. someter, dominar, subxugar

substance n. substancia

substitute v. substituir

substitution n. substitución

subtle a. sutil (pl. sutís)

subtract v. substraer; restar

subtraction n. substracción

suburb n. suburbio

succeed v. triunfar, vencer, gañar

success n. éxito

such a. semellante, parecido -a

such as pr. quen

suck n. chupada, chupadela
suck v. chupar, chuchar, mamar
sucking fish n. rémora (peixe)
suckling n. mamó´n, mamalón
suckling pig n. leitón, bácoro, bacoriño, roncho
sudden a. repentino -a, súpeto -a
suffer v. sufrir, padecer
suffice v. satisfacer
sufficient a. suficiente, abondo, bastante
suffix n. sufixo
suffrage n. sufraxio, voto
sugar n. azucre
suggest v. suxerir, insinuar
suggestion n. suxestión (pl. suxestións)
suit n. preito, xuiso
suit p. traxe (vestido exterior)
suitable a. apropiado -a, xusto -a, propio -a
suitor n. pretendente, namorado
sulfur n. xofre
sullen a. fusco, ríspero, áspero, túzaro
sum n. suma, adición
sum v. sumar; agregar, unirse
summary n. sumano
summer n. verao
summit n. cima, cumbre
sun n. sol

Sunday n. domingo

sunder v. fender, abrir, esgazar

sunflower n. xirasol, mirasol

sunrise n. sol nacente

sunset n. sol ponente

superior a. & n. superior -a

superiority n. superioridade

supermarket n. supermercado

supper n. cea

supply n. provisión, abastecemento, fornecemento

supply v. subministrar, abastecer, fornecer, proveer

support n. apoio, sostén

support v. apoiar, pusar

supporter n. partidario, seguidor, simptizante, adicto

suppose v. supoñer, supor

suppress v. suprimir, eliminar

suppression n. supresión (pl. supresións), eliminación

sure a. seguro -a; gardado, protexido

surety n. garantla, seguridade

surf n. ondada

surface n. superficie

surgeon n. cirurxán -a

surgery n. cirurxía

surly a. fusco, ríspero, áspero
surmount v. superar, resolver, vencer
surname n. apelido; alcume
surpass v. superar, resolver, mellorar
surprise n. sorpresa, estrañeza
surrender v. render
surround v. cercar, rodear
surroundings n.pl. medio ambiente
survive v. sobrevivir
survivor n. sobrevivente, supervivente
suspect v. sospeitar
suspend v. suspender
suspense n. incerteza, inseguridade
suspicious a. desconfiado -a, receoso -a
sustain v. soster, sustentar, aguantar
swallow (bird) n. andoriña
swallow n. trago, sorbo
swallow v. tragar
swamp n. pantano
swamp, to. v. inundar
swan n. cisne
swarm n. exambre (conxuncto de abellas)
swear v. xurar
sweat n. suor
sweat v. suar, transpirar
sweep v. varrer, balear

sweet a. & n.doce
sweeten v. adozar, azucarar, dulcificar
sweetness n. dozura; afabilidade, bondade
swell a. moi elegante, estupendo
swell v. inchar, inflar
swift a. veloz, lixeiro -a, rápido -a
swim n. natación
swim v. nadar
swimmer n. nadador -a
swimming pool n. piscina
swindle n. estafa, calote, fraude, engano
swindle v. estafar
swine n. marrán, porco, cocho
swing n. randeeira, bambán
swing v. arrandear(se)
switch n. interruptor, chave (electricidade)
switch off v. apagar, extinguir, desconectar
switch on v. conectar, acender
switch v. cambiar, permutar
swoon n. desmaio
swoon v. desmaiar
sword n. espada (arma)
swordfish n. peixe espada
sycamore tree n. sicómoro (árbore)
syllable n. sílaba
symbol n. símbolo

sympathetic a. compasivo -a
sympathy n. compaixón, compadecemento
symphony n. sinfonía
symptom n. síntoma
syntax n. sintaxe
synthesis n. síntese
syringe n. xiringa
syringe v. xiringear
syrup n. xarope
system n. sistema, procedemento, método

T

table cloth n. mantel (pl. manteis)
table n. mesa (moble)
table tennis n. pimpón
tablespoon n. culler
tablet (pharmaceutical) n. pastilla, comprimido
tablet n. taboiña (taboa pequena)
tack n. chatola, brocha
tack v. cravar con chatolas
tact n. tacto
tactics n.pl. táctica, extratexia
tactile a. táctil

tadpole n. cágado, cabezolo, cagote, cullarapo, cullareto, culleriña, relo

tail n. cola, rabo

tailor n. xastre

tailoring n. xastrería

taint n. mancha; penca

take v. comer, coller

taking n. toma, tomada

talc n. talco

tale n. conto, historia, narración

talk n. conversación

talk v. conversar, charlar, dialogar

talkative a. locuaz, falador, faladoiro -a

tall a. alto -a

tallness n. altura, altor

tame a. manso -a, dócil

tame v. domar, amansar, domesticar

tamper v. interferir

tan a. marrón, castaño -a

tan v. broncearse, tostarse

tangerine n. mandarina (clase de laranxa)

tangle n. enredo, maraña

tangle v. enredar(se)

tank n. cisterna, depósito

tank n. tanque (de guerra)

tanner n. curtidor

tantalize v. atormentar, mortificar
tap (a tree) v. sangrar, resinar (unha árbore)
tap dance n. zapateado
tap n. billa, chave (auga)
tap v. exploitar, aproveitar, voitar, traballar
tape measure n. cinta métrica
tape n. cinta, fita
tape recorder n. cinta magnética para gravar
tape v. gravar en cinta ou un disco
taper a. cónico -a
tapestry n. tapicería
tapeworm n. tenia, bicha solitaria, solitaria
tar n. alcatrán, chapote
tar v. embrear, alcatranar
tardy n. tarde; serán
target n. branco, diana (obxetivo dun disparo)
tariff n. tarifa
tarnish v. deslucir, deslustrar, afear
tart a. acre, ácedo, agre
task n. tarefa, traballo, quefacer
taste n. gusto, sabor
tasteful a. bo gusto
tavern n. taberna, cantina
tax n. imposto, tributo
tea n. té (planta)
teach v. ensinar

teacher n. mestre, profesor
teachings n. ensinanzas
teak, teak wood n. teca
team n. equipo, grupo
team up v. asociar(se), axuntar(se)
teapot n. teteira
tear (anatomy) n. lágrima, bágoa, bagulla
tear n. rachón, rachadura
tear v. bogoar, bagoxar, bagullar, choricar
tearful a. lacrimoso -a
tease n. retranca, sorna, leria, broma
teaspoon n. culleriña
teat n. teta, peito, seo, ubre
technical a. & n. técnico
teething n. dentición
teetotaler a. & n. abstemio -a
telegraph n. telégrafo
telephone n. teléfono
telescope n. telescopio
television n. televisión
tell v. dicir
temerity n. temeridade, imprudencia
temper n. temperamento
temperance n. tempranza, moderación
temperate a. temperado -a, moderado -a
temperature n. temperatura

tempest n. tempestade, borrasca, temporal
temple n. templo
temporary a. temporal
temporize v. temporalizar
tempt v. tentar, inducir, incitar
temptation n. tentación
tempter a. tendador -a
ten a. dez
tenacious a. tenaz, persistente
tenant n. arrendatario -a
tench (fish) n. tenca (peixe)
tend v. coidar, atender
tendency n. tendencia, inclinación
tendentious a. tendecioso -a
tender a. terno -a
tenderness n. ternura, cariño; agarimo
tendon n. tendón
tennis n. tenis
tenor n. tenor (voz)
tense a. tiempo (gramática)
tense n. tenso -a, tirante
tension n. tensión (pl. tensións)
tentacle n. tentáculo
tentative a. tentativo -a
tenth a. décimo -a
tenuous a. tenue, delgado -a, sútil

tepid a. temperado -a, tépido -a
term n. término
terminate v. terminar, acabar
termite n. termita, formiga brava
terrace n. terraza, azotea
terrestrial a. terrestre, terráqueo
terrible a. terrible
terribly adv. terriblemente
territory n. territono
terror n. terror, horror
tertiary a. terciario -a, terceiro -a
test n. proba, ensaio
test tube n. probeta, tubo de ensaio
test v. probar, experimentar
testify v. testemuñar, testificar
testimony n. testemuño
text n. texto
textbook n. libro de texto
textile n. téxtil
than conj. que
thankful n. agradecido -a
thankfulness n. agradecemento, gratitude
thanks n. gracias
thanksgiving n. acción de gracias
that a. ese, esa, eso
thaw n. desxeo

the art. o, lo (m); a, la (f)

theater n. teatro

their pr. seu (m); sua (f)

them pr. os, -los -nos (m); as, -las, as, -las, -nas (f)

theme n. tema, asunto, materia

themselves pr. elas mismas (f); elos mismos (m)

then adv. entón, daquela

theology n. teoloxía

theorem n. teorema

theoretical a. teórico -a

theory n. teoría

therapeutics n pl. terapia

there adv. alá, aló, alí

thereof adv. de iso, de isto

thermometer n. termómetro

thesaurus n. tesoro léxico, diccionario de
sinónimos

these pr. estes (m), estas (f), istos (neutro)

thesis n. tese, opinión, idea, teoría

they pr. eles (m), elas (f)

thick a. espeso -a, denso -a, condensado -a

thicken v. espesar, condensar, concentrar

thicket of brambles n. fraga

thickness n. espesura, densidade

thief (f), **thieves** (pl) n. sing. ladroa, ladrona; pl.
ladroas, ladronas

thief (m), **thieves** (pl) n. sing. ladron; pl. ladróns

thigh n. coxa

thimble n. dedal, alferga

thin a. delgado -a, fraco -a

thing n. cousa

think v. pensar, razoar

thinker n. pensador

third a. terceiro -a

thirst a. sede, secura

thirsty a. sedento -a

thirteen a. treze

thirteenth a. décimo terceiro

thirteenth a. trixésimo

thirty a. trinta

this pr. este, esta, esto/ista

thorback (fish) n. raia espiñosa (peixe)

thorn apple n. estramonio

thorn n. espiña, pua

thorough a. completo -a, cheo -a

thoroughfare n. via pública

those pr. esos, esas

though conj. ainda que, inda que, anque, mesmo que

thought n. pensamento; idea principal

thoughtful a. pensativo -a, cabiloso -a, meditabundo -a

thousand a. mil
thousandth a. milésimo -a
thread n. fio
threat n. ameaza
threaten v. ameazar
three a. tres
threshold n. limear, soleira
thrift n. frugalidade
thrifty a. frugal, parco -a
thrill n. emoción (pl. emocións)
thrill v. emocionar(se), conmover(se)
thrive v. prosperar, mellorar, progresar
throat n. garganta, gorxa
throb v. latexar, palpitar, choutar (o corazón)
thrombosis n. trombose
throne n. trono
throttle n. acelerador
throttle v. acelerar (un vehículo)
through a. continuo -a
throughout adv. de todo
throw n. tiro, tirada
throw v. tirar, guindar, botar
thumb b. pulgar
thump n. porrada, mocada, mocazo
thunder n. trono, tronido
thunderstorm n. tormento de tronos

Thursday n. xoves, quinta feira

thyme n. tomiño

ticket n. billete; boleto, tarxeita

tickle v. formiguear, proer

tickling n. formigueo, pruido

tide n. marea

tidiness n. pulcritude

tidings n. noticia(s)

tidy a. pulcro -a, limpo -a, aseado -a

tidy v. ordenar, colocar (por orde)

tie n. gravata

tie v. amarrar, atar

tiger (m) n. tigre

tight a. apertado -a, estreito -a, angosto -a

tighten v. apertar, presionar

tightwad a. mesquiño -a, mísero -a, miserable

tigress (f) n. trigresa

tile n. baldosa, azulexo

till n. caixa rexistradora

till prep. ata

till v. cultivar, traballar (a terra)

tilt v. inclinar, ladear

timber n. madeira

time n. tempo; estado de atmosfera

timetable n. horario

tin can n. lata, bote

tin n. estaño

tingle v. estremecer

tinker n. remendón

tinkle n. campaiña

tinsel n. ouropel

tint n. tinxidura, tinguidura, tintura

tint v. tinxir

tip (gratuity) n. propina

tip n. punta, cabo, extremo

tiptoe n. nas puntas dos pes

tire n. lamia

tire v. cansar, fatigar(se)

tired a. cansado -a

tiredness n. cansazo, canseira

tireless n. incansable, infatigable

tiresome a. molesto -a, anfadoso -a

tissue n. papel de seda

tissue n. tecido

title n. título

title v. titular

to prep. cara a, para

toad n. sapo; inflamacion da mucosa bucal que afecta nenos mal nutridos

tobacco n. tabaco

toboggan n. zorra

today adv, hoxe

toe n. deda (apéndice dos pes)

together adv. xunto -a , unido -a, reunido -a, próximo -a

toil n. traballo, esforzo

toil v. traballar, esforzarse

toilet n. retrete, latrina

token n. disco

tolerance n. tolerancia

tolerate v. tolerar

toll (bells) n. taxe-las campás

toll n. peaxe

tomato n. tomate

tomb n. tumba, sepultura

tomorrow adv. mañá; o tempo futuro

ton n. tonelada

tonality n. tonalidade

tone n. ton

tongs n.pl. tenaces

tongue n. lingua; idioma

tonnage n. tonelaxe

tonsils n.pl. amígdalas, tonsilas

too adv. tamén

tool n. ferramenta

tooth n. dente

toothache n. dor de moas

toothbrush n. cepillo de dentes

top a. o máis alto
top hat n. chistera
topaz n. topacio
topic n. tópico
topical a. tópico -a
topple v. derribar, derrubar, abater
torch n. facha, facho, fachico, fachuco
torment n. tormento, tortura, suplicio
torment v. atormentar, mortificar, torturar
tornado n. tornado, furacán
torpedo n. torpedo (proxéctil naval)
torrent n. torrente, regato
tortoise n. tartaruga, sapoconcho
torture n. tortura, tormento, suplicio
torture v. torturar, atormentar
toss v. botar, tirar, lanzar
total a. & n. total
total v. sumar
totalitarian a. totalitario -a
totally adv. totalmente
totter v. bambear, oscilar
touch n. toque, contacto
touch v. tocar
touching a. conmovedor
touchy a. susceptible
tough a. duro -a

toughen v. endurecer

toughness n. dureza

tour n. xira, viaxe

tour v. viaxar

tourism n. turismo

tourist n. turista

tourney n. torneo

tow v. remolcar

towards prep. cara a, en dirección a

tower n. torre

town n. pobo, poboación

toy n. xoguete

trace n. pegada, pisada

trace v. trazar

trachea n. traquea

track n. rastro, vestixio, sinal

track v. rastrear, rastrexar

traction n. tracción

tractor n. tractor

trade n. comercio, negocio

trade union n. sindicato

trade v. comerciar

trader n. comerciante

tradition n. tradición (pl. tradicións)

traffic n. tráfico, trasfego, tránsito

traffic v. traficar, transfegar, comerciar

tragedy n. traxedia (peza teatral); desgracia
trail n. pista, rastro
trail v. rastrear, rastrexar
trailer n. remolque
train n. adestramento
train n. tren, ferrocarril
train v. entrenar, adestrar
trainer n. adestrador
trait n. característica
traitor n. traidor, trazoeiro -a
tramp n. vagabundo, errante, vadío
trance n. transo; estádo hipnótico do médium
transfer n. transferencia
transfer v. transferir
transit n. tránsito
translate v. traducir
translation n. traducción
translator n. traductor
transmit v. transmitir, comunicar
transport n. transporte
transport v. caer en éctase; extasiarse; transportar
transporter n. transportador
transubstantiation n. transubtanciación
transverse v. transversar
trap n. trampa, trapela, arento
trap v. atrapar, pillar, capturar, agarrar

trapeze n. trapecio
trash n. lixo, desperdicio
travel n. viaxe
travel v. viaxar
traveler n. viaxeiro -a
tray n. bandexa
treachery n. traizón, deslealdade
treadle n. pedal
treason n. traizón (pl. traizóns)
treasure n. tesouro
treasurer n. tesoureiro
treasury n. tesoureria
treat n. regalo, obsequio
treatise n. tratado, manual
treatment n. tratamento, trato
treaty n. tratado, axuste, convenio
treble n. triple
treble v. triplicar
tree n. árbore
tremble v. tremer, vibrar
trench n. trincheira
trend n. tendencia, inclinación
trespass v. infrixir, violar
trial n. xuizo, preito, proceso
triangle n. triángulo
tribe n. tribo

tribunal n. tribunal (pl. tribunais)
tribune n. tribuna
tribute n. tributo
triceps n. tríceps
trick n. truco
trick v. engañar, confundir
trick, dirty n. trasnada, trasgada, falcatrua
trickle n. chorriño, pinga
trickle v. gotear, gotexar, pingar
tricolor a. tricolor
tricycle n. triciclo
trifle n. bagatela, insignificancia
trifling a. insignificante
trigger n. gatillo, percusor
trill n. rechouchío, chio
trill v. rechouchiar, garullar, chiar
trimester n. trimestre
trinity n. trinidade (A Santísima Trinidade)
tripod n. trífpode
triumph n. triumfo, victoria
triumph v. triunfar, vencer
Trojan a. troiano -a
trolley bus n. trolebus
trolley car n. tranvía
trolley n. trole
trombone n. trombón

troop n. tropa

trophy n. trofeo

tropics n.pl. trópicos

troubadour n. trobador -a

trouble n. apuro, aperto

trouble v. aflixir, apenar

troublesome a. molesto -a, afectado -a

trousers n.pl. pantalons

trout n. reo (peixe)

trowel n. paleta (utensilio do albañel)

truant a. & n. estudiante que falta á escola

truck n. camión

true a. verdadeiro -a

truffle n. trufa

truly adv. verdadeiramente

trumpet n. trompeta

truncheon n. moca, moco, cachaba, baloco

trunk (botany) n. tronco (talo leñoso dunha árbore)

trunk n. baul, arca

trust n. confianza, seguranza, seguridade

trust v. confiar

trusty a. fiel (pl. fieis), leal (pl. leais)

truth n. verdade

truthful a. verdadeiro -a

try v. intentar, tentar

tube n. tubo
tuber n. tubérculo
tubing n. canalizacíon, tubo
Tuesday n. martes, terza feira
tug boat n. remolcador
tug n. tirón
tug v. halar, remolcar
tulip n. tulipán
tumor n. tumor
tuna n. atún (pl. atúns)
tune n. melodía
tune v. afinar, harmonizar
tunic n. túnica
tunnel n. túnel (pl. tuneles)
tunny n. atún (pl. atúns)
turbine n. turbina
tureen n. sopeira
turf n. céspede; panasco
turkey n. pavo -a
turmeric n. cúrcuma
turmoil n. tumulto, balbordo, desorde
turn n. volta, xiro, virada, turno
turn v. voltear, xirar, virar
turnip n. nabo
turnsole n. tornasol, xirasol
turtle n. tartaruga; sapoconcho

turtledove n. rula
tusk n. dente (de elefante)
tweezers n. (pl.) pinzas
twelfth a. duodécimo -a, décimo segundo -a
twentieth a. vixésimo -a
twenty a. vinte
twice adv. dos veces
twig n. ramallo
twilight n. crepúsculo, solpor, lusco-fusco
twin n. xemelgo -a, xemeo -a
twinge n. picada, aguilloada
twinkle v. escintillar, estrelecer
twist n. torsión
twist v. torcer, curvar, virar
two a. dous, duas
type n. tipo
typewriter n. máquina de escribir
typhoon n. tifón, furacán, ciclón
typical a. típico -a, peculiar
typist n. mecanógrafo -a, dactilógrafo -a
typography n. tipografía, prelo, imprenta
tyrannize v. tiranizar
tyranny n. tiranía
tyrant a. & n. tirano -a, déspota, autoritario -a
tzar (m) n. tsar
tzarina (f) n. tsarina

U

ubiquitous a. ubicuo -a
udder n. ubre
ugly a. feo -a, laido -a, desagradable
ulcer n. úlcera, chaga
ulcerous a. ulceroso -a, chagado -a
ultimatum n. ultimato
ultraviolet a. ultravioleta
ululate v. ouvear, oulear
umbrella n. paraugas
umbrella seller or maker n. paraugueiro -a
unable a. incapaz, inútil
unacceptable a. inaceptable, intolerable
unaccountable a. inexplicable
unanimous a. únanime, acorde
unarmed a. inerme, desarmado-a
unavoidable a. inevitable, ineludible
unaware a. inconsciente, mecánico, reflexo
unbaptized a. sen bautizar
unbearable a. insoportable, intolerable
unbeliever n. incrédulo -a
unbending a. inflexible, ríxido -a
unbroken n. intacto -a, enteiro -a
uncanny a. misterioroso -a, enigm a tico -a
uncertain a. incerto -a, dubidoso -a

unclad a. espido -a, despido -a, nu (m), nua (f)

uncle n. tio

unconscious a. inconsciente

uncover v. descubrir, destapar

unction n. unción (pl. uncións)

undamaged a. indemne, ileso -a, incólume,
  intacto -a

undaunted a. impávido -a, afouto -a, audaz,
  ousado -a, valente

undecided a. indeciso -a, irresoluto -a, vacilante

under adv. debaixo, embaixo, abaixo

underclothes n.pl. roupa interior, roupa de baixo

undergo an operation p. operarse

undergo v. sufrir, padecer, experimentar dor
  físico ou moral

underground a. subterráneo -a

underline v. subliñar

undershirt n. camiseta

undersign v. firmar, asinar

understand v. entender, comprender

understanding n. entendemento

undertake v. emprender

underwear V. underclothes

underwood n. matagueira, mato, matogueira

underworld (mythology, religion)n. verno,
  inferno, tártaro

underworld n. canalla, baixos fondos
undesirable a. indesexable
undisputed a. indiscutible
undivided a. indiviso
undo v. desfacer, descompoñer, desbaratar
undue a. indebido
undulate v. ondular
unearthly a. sobrenatural
uneasiness n. inquietude, intranquilidade
uneasy a. inquieto -a, turbado -a
unending a. inacabable, interminable
unequal a. desigual (pl. desiguais)
unfold v. despregar, desobrar
ungodly a. impio -a, irreverente, sacr lego
unguarded a. indefenso -a, desamparado -a
unhappy a. infeliz, desgraciado, desventurado, aciago
unhealthy a. enfermizo -a
unicorn n. unicornio
uniform a. & n. uniforme
uninjured a. ileso, intacto, salvo -a
union n. unión
unique a. único -a
unit n. unidade
unite v. unir, xuntar, asociarse
unity n. unidade

universal a. universal
universe n. universo
university n. universidade
university n. universidade
unkempt a. desaseado -a
unkind a. malintentado -a, malicioso -a, mal
    intencionado -a
unknown a. descoñecido -a
unless conj. a menos que
unlike a. diferente, distinto -a
unload v. descargar
unmannered a. maleducado -a
unmoved a. impasible
unpleasant a. desagradable
unrest n. inquietude, desacougo; desasosego,
    ansiedade, inquietude
unsafe a. inseguro -a
unsalable a. invendible
unseen a. invisible, oculto -a
untidy a. desordenando -a; abandonado -a,
    desleixado -a
until prep. hata
untold a. incontable (que non pode ser contado)
untruth n. falsidade; deslealdade ou hipocrisía
untutored a. indouto, inculto -a
unwell a. indisposto -a

unworthy a. indigno, sen mérito
up adv. arriba, enriba, por riba
upkeep n. manutención, mantemento
uplift n. elevación (pl. elevacións)
upon prep. en, en riba de, sobre, encima de
upper a. superior, mais elevado -a
uproar n. alboroto, barullo, boureo
uproot v. desarraigar, desenraizar
upset v. disgustar, magoar
upside-down a. ó revés, ó contrario, ás avesas
upstairs adv. piso, planta superior
upstream adv. rio arriba
up-to-date a. ó dia
upward a. ascendente
uranium n. uranio (metal)
Uranus n. uranio (planeta)
urban (polite) a. urbano cortés, educado -a
urban a. urbano (cidade)
urchin n. pillabán -ana, gallopín, pillo -a
urge v. urxir, apremar, compeler
urgency n. urxencia
urgent a. urxente
urinal n. bacia, bañado, penico, ouriñal
urinary a. urinario -a
urine n. ouriños, mexo
urn n. urna

urology n. uroloxía
us pr. nos
usage n. uso, emprego
use n. uso, emprego
use v. usar, empregar, utilizar
useful a. útil
useless a. inútil, inepto
user a. & n. usuario -a
usher n. porteiro -a
usher v. introducir
usurp v. usurpar
usury n. usura
uterus n. útero
utility n. utilidade
utilize v. utilizar, empregar
utmost a. extremo -a, extremado -a, m ximo -a
utter a. completo -a, absoluto -a
utter v. pronunciar, producir e emitir sons
utterance n. pronunciamento, declaración

V

vacant a. vacante, libre, desocoupado -a
vacation n. vacación (pl. vacacións)
vaccinate v. vacinar(se)

vaccine n. vacina
vacillate v. vacilar, abalar, abanear
vacillation n. vacilación
vacuity n. vacuidade
vacuum n. baleiro, oco
vagabond a. vagabundo -a, errante, vadío
vagary n. capricho, antollo
vague a. vago -a, impreciso -a, indeterminado -a
vagueness n. vaguidade; cualidade de vago, imprecisión
vain a. van, frivolo -a
vainly adv. en van, enbalde
valiant a. valente
valid a. válido -a, lexítimo -a
validity n. validez
valise n. maleta
valley n. val (pl. vales)
valor n. valor, coraxe
valuable a. valioso -a, precioso -a
value n. valor, prezo
value v. valorar, apreciar, estimar
valve n. válvula
vamp n. vampiresa
vampire n. vampiro (ser imaxinario); especie de morcego
van n. camioneta

vane n. paleta, aleta (dunha hélice)

vanguard n. vangardia, diantera

vanilla n. vainilla

vanish v. desaparecer, esvaer(se)

vanity n. vanidade

vanquish v. vencer, derrotar

vanquisher n. vencedor, gañador, triunfador

vantage n. vantaxe, avantaxe

vapor n. vapor, bafo

vaporous a. vaporoso -a

variable a. variable, cambiable

variance n. disidencia, desacordo, diverxencia

variation n. variación

variety n. variedade, diversidade

variola n. vexigas, variola

various a. varios -as, diversos -as

varnish n. verniz (pl. vernices)

varnish v. vernizar

vary v. variar, alterar

vase n. floreiro, vaso

vaseline n. vaselina

vassal n. vasalo -a, servo -a

vast a. vasto -a, amplio -a, largacío -a

vastness n. vasteza

Vatican a. & n. Vaticano

vault n. bóveda, sepultura, tumba, sepulcro

veal n. vitela
vegetable a & n. vexetal (pl. vexetais)
vegetarian a. & n. vexetariano -a
vegetate v. vexetar
vegetation n. vexetación
vehemence n. vehemencia
vehicle n. vehículo
veil n. veo
vein n. vea (vaso sanguíneo)
velocity n. velocidade, rapidez
velvet n. veludo, felpa
velvety a. aveludado -a
venerate v. venerar, adorar
veneration n. veneración (pl. veneracións),
  adoración
vengeance n. vinganza, desquite
vengeful a. vingativo -a
venom n. veleno, pezoña
vent n. buraco, burato, furaco
vent v. purgar, desafogar
ventilate v. ventilar, airear
ventilator n. ventilador
ventricle n. ventrículo
ventriloquist a. & n. ventrílocuo -a
venture n. aventura, empresa, éxito dubidoso
venture v. aventurar, arriscar

venturer n. aventureiro
veracious a. verídico, verdadeiro
veracity n. veracidade, verdade
veranda n. terraza
verb n. verbo
verbal a. oral, verbal (pl. verbais)
verbatim n. textual, literal
verbosity n. verba; labia, leria
verdancy n. verdor, verdura
verdict n. veredicto, dictame, fallo, sentencia
verdure n. verdor, frondosidade, louzanía
verge n. borde, borda, beira
verification n. verificación, comprobación
verify v. verificar, probar
veritable a. verdadeiro -a
verity n. verdade
vermicelli n. fideo
vermin n. bichos
vermouth n. vermú
versatile a. versátil
verse n. verso (lina dun poema)
versed a. versado -a, competente, entendido -a,
    instruido -a
versify v. versificar, rimar, facer versos
version n. versión (pl. versións), interpretación
versus prep. contra

vertebrate a. & n. vertebrado -a
vertex n. vértice, cume, cúspide
vertical a. vertical (pl. verticais)
vertiginous a. vertixinoso -a
very adv. moito
vesper n. véspera (día que antecede a outro)
vespers n.pl. vésperas, hora de oficio divino
vessel (nautical) n. nave, barco, embarcación
vessel n. vaso, vasilla
vest n. chaleco
vestry n. sancristía, sacristía
vetch n. veza
veteran a. & n. veterano -a
veterinary a. & n. veterinario -a, albeite
vex v. molestar, amolar, enfastiar
vexation n. fastío, molestia
viaduct n. viaducto
vial n. frasco pequeno
viand n. vianda, alimento,
vibrate v. vibrar, tremer, tremeler
vibration n. vibración, oscilación
vicar n. vigairo, párroco, crego, abade, rector
vice n. defecto, falta, vicio, vezo
vicereine n. vicerraíña
viceroy n. vicerrei

vicinity n. veciñanza, arrededores, cercanía, proximidade

vicious a. vicioso -a

vicissitude n. vicisitude, avatar, eventualidade

victim n. víctima

victor n. vencedor, triunfador, gañador

victorious a. victorioso -a

victory n. victoria, triunfo

victual n. vitualla, viveres, provisións

view n. vista, mirada, ollada

view v. ver, mirar, contemplar, ollar

vigil n. vixilia, vela

vigilance n. vixilancia

vignette n. viñeta

vigor n. vigor, enerxia, forza

vile a. vil, vilán, malvado -a

vilify v. villipendiar, desprezar, aldrexar, humillar

villa (country house) n. vila (casa do campo)

villa n. vila, lugar, pobación

village n. aldea, vilar, lugarexo (aldea pequena)

vindicate v. vindicar, vingar

vine n. viño

vinegar n. vinagre

vineyard n. viña

vintage n. viño maduro, viño vello

vintner n. viñateiro

violate v. violar, profanar, abusar sexualmente

violence n. violencia

violent a. violento -a

violet a. & n. viola, violeta

violin n. violín (pl. violíns)

violinist n. violinista

violoncello n. violoncelo

viper n. víbora

virgin n. virxe, doncella; na relixión católica, a nai de Xesús Cristo

virile a. viril (pl. virís)

virtue n. virtude

virtuoso n. virtuoso, hábil (con dotes especiais para algo)

viscera n. víscera

viscount n. vizconde

viscountess n. vizcondesa

vise n. parafuso de banco

visibility n. visibilidade

visible a. visible

vísion n. visión (pl. visións)

visit n. visita

visit v. visitar

visitor n. visitante

visor n. viseira

visual a. visual (pl. visuais)

vital a. vital (pl. vitais)

vitality n. vitalidade

vitamin n. vitamina

vitiate v. vixiar

vitreous a. vitreo -a

vitrify v. vitrificar(se)

vocabulary n. léxico, glosario, vocabulario

vocal a. vocal (pl. vocais)

vocation n. vocación (pl. vocacións)

vocative a. vocativo -a

vogue n. moda

voice n. voz (pl. voces)

void a. nub -a, anulado -a, revocado -a

volcano n. volcán (pl. volcáns)

volition n. vontade, volicíón

volley n. descarga (de artillería)

voltage n. voltaxe

voluble a. voluble

volume n. volume

voluntary a. voluntario -a

volunteer n. voluntario -a

voluptuous a. voluptuoso -a, sexual, pracenteiro -a

voracious a. voraz (pl. voraces)

vortex n. vórtice, remuiño, turbillón

votary a. & n. devoto -a

vote n. voto, sufraxio

vote v. votar
voter n. votante
votive a. votivo -a (misa votiva)
vouch v. afirmar, asegurar, afianzar
voucher n. bono, vale
vow n. voto, promesa
vow v. prometer, xurar
vowel n. vocal
voyage n. viaxe
voyager n. viaxeiro -a
vulgarity n. vulgaridade, vulgarismo
vulture n. voitre (ave rapaz)

W

wad n. feixe (de papel moeda)
wade v. ;vadear, atravesar, pasar
wag n. meneo, abaladura
wag v. menear, mover, abanear, bambear
wage n. salario, paga, xornal
wager n. aposta
wager v. apostar
wagon n. vagon
wail n. lamento, queixume, queixa, laio
wail v. lamentarse, queixarse, doerse, laiarse

waist n. cintura, talle

wait n. espera

wait v. esperar, agardar

waiter n. (m.) mozo, criado

waitress n. (f.) moza, criada

waive v. prescindir de

wake n. velorio

wake v. espertar

walk n. camiñada, andada

walk v. camiñar, andar, pasear

walker n. camiñante, andador, andarego; peatón

wall n. muro, parede

wallet n. carteira

walnut n. noz

walrus n. morsa, vaca mariña

waltz n. valse

wan a. macilento -a, triste, esmorcido -a

wand n. vara/varita; variña máxica

wander v. vagar, vaguear, folgar

wanderer n. vagabundo -a, errante, vadio

wane n. minguante (dise da lúa cando está desvelando)

wane v. minguar, diminuir

want n. falta, carencia, escaseza

want v. querer, desexar

wanton a. impúdico -a

war n. guerra, contenda
war v. guerrear, batallar, loitar, pelexar, combater
warble n. rechoichio, chio, canto dos paxaros
warble v. rechouchiar, gurular, chiar
ward (hospital room) n. sala (de hospital, asilo, etc.)
ward (political) n. distrito eléctoral
ward n. tutela, protección, coidado dunha persona memor de idade
ward v. gardar, protexer, defender
warden n. director de prisión
warden n. gardian, vixiante, garda
wardrobe n. gardarpa, vestiario, roupeiro
ware n. louza, vaixela
warehouse n. almacén depósito
warlike a. guerreiro, bélico, marcial
warm a. quente
warming pan n. quentador
warmth n. calor, ardor
warn v. advertir, avisar
warning n. aviso, advertencia
warrant v. autorizar
warrant, n. autorización, poder
warranty n. garantia
warren n. colleira, tobo, tobeira, covo (de coellos)
warrior n. guerreiro

warship n. barco, buque ou navio de guerra

wart n. verruga, espulla, espunlla

wary a. cauto -a, cauteloso -a, precavido -a,
  prudente

wash v. lavar

washer n. arandela, anel, disco

washing machine n. lavadora

wasp n. avespa, avéspora, nespra

waste n. desperdicio, lixo

waste v. desperdiciar

wasteful a. pródigo, gastador, malgastador,
  desbaldidor

wastefulness n. despilfarro

watch n. vixilancia

watch v. vixiar, observar, coidar

watchful a. vixiante, vixilante, observador

watchmaker n. reloxeiro -a

watchman n. sereno, vixilante, nocturno

water n. auga

water v. regar

waterfall n. catarata, abanqueiro, salto

waterfront n. peirao

watering can n. regador

watermelon n. sandia

waterproof n. impermeable

watery a. acuoso -a, augacento -a

watt n. vatio
wave n. ola (marítima); onda (de radio)
wave v. axiar, ondear, ondular
waver v. titubear, vacilar, alabar
wax n. cera
wax v. encerar
way n. camiño
Way to Santiago, the p. Camiño de Santiago
wayside n. a beira de camiño
wayward a. caprichoso -a
we pr. nós
weak a. débil, feble
weaken v. debilitar, esmorecer, decever
weakly adv. debilmente
weakness n. debilidade, febleza, frouxedade, esmorcemento
weal n. negrón, mazadura, hematoma
wealth n. riqueza, abundancia, opulencia
wealthy a. rico -a, adiñeirado -a
wean v. desteitar, desleitar
weapon n. arma
wear out v. usarse, gastarse
wear v. usar
weariness n. fatiga, canzanzo, canseira
weary a. fatigado -a, cansado -a
weasel n. donicela, doñina, garridiña

weather n. tempo (estado da atmosfera)

weather vane n. catavento, viraventos

weave (textile) v. tecer

weave v. serpear, cobreguear

weaver n. tecedor -a, tecelán, tecedeiro

web n. tecido

wed v. casar, deposar

wedding n. voda, casamento, matrimonio, desposorio, enlace, nuncias

wedge n. cuña, calzo (peza de madeira)

wedlock n. matrimonio

Wednesday n. mércores, corta-feira

weed n. maleza, mato, xoio, mala herba

week n. semana

weekday n. dia da semana

weekend n. fin da semana

weep v. chorar

weeping willow n. salgueiro chorón

weft n. trama (de tecidos)

weigh v. pesar

weight n. peso

weird a. estraño -a

welcome n. benvido, benvindo

weld v. soldar

welding n. soldadura

welfare n. benestar

well adv. ben
west n. oeste, occidente, ponente
western a. occidental
wet a. húmedo -a
wet v. mollar
wetness n. humidade
whale n. balea
whaler n. baleeiro
wharf n. (sing.) **wharves** (pl.) porte, peirao, cargadeiro
what pr. que
whatever pr. calquera
wheat n. trigo
wheel n. roda
wheel v. rodar, xirar
wheelbarrow n. carreta
wheelwright n. carretero, conductor de carros; carreiro (constructor de carros)
wheezing n. resollo
whelp n. cachorro, cadelo, cria de can
when adv. cando
where adv. onde
whereas conj. mentres que, entrementres que
wherever adv. onde queira, en calquera parte
whet (sharpening) v. afiar, aguzar
whet v. activar, excitar, estimular

whetstone n. afiador
which pr. cul
whichever a. calquera
whiff n. sopro
while adv. mentres
whim n. capricho, antollo
whimsical a. caprichoso -a, arbitrario -a
whine n. xemido, laxo, salouco, salaio
whine v. xemir, laiar, saloucar, salaiar
whip n. látego
whip v. azoutar
whirl n. remuiño
whirl n. xiro, volta
whirl v. voltear, xirar, virar
whirlpool n. turbillón, vórtice
whisk n. vasoirina; brocha
whisker n. patilla, pelo de barba
whiskey n. whisky
whisper n. murmurio
whisper v. murmurar
whistle n. pito, silbido
whistle v. pitar
white a. branco -a, albar, albo -a
whiten v. branquear, albear, calear, encalar
whiteness n. brancura, brancor, albura
whither adv. onde

who pr. quen
whoever pr. quenquera que
whole a. enteiro -a, completo -a, integro -a
wholesale n. por xunto
wholesome a. san (m), sá (f), saudable
whose pr. do cal, da cal, dos
why conj. porqué
wick n. mecha, pabio
wicked a. malvado -a, perverso -a, canalla
wickedness n. maldade, crueldade
wicker n. vime, vimia
wicket n. poxigo, postigo
wide a. ancho -a, amplo -a, folgado -a
widen v. ampliar, aumentar, agrandar
widespread a. moi difundido
widow n. viúva
widower n. viuvo
widowhood n. viuvez
width n. ancho, largo
wield v. manexar, empuñar, exercer, posuir
wife n. muller, dona, esposa
wig n. perruca, postizo
wild a. salvaxe
wilderness n. deserto, ermo, soidade
wiles n.pl. trampas, tretas, trucos
will n. vontade; testamento; última vondade

willful a. voluntarioso -a, testán -ana
willing a. disposto -a, listo -a, disponible
willow n. salgueiro, salgueira
win v. gañar, ganar
wind n. vento, corrente de aire
wind the clock p. deille corda o reloxo
wind up v. dar corda
windmill n. muíño
window n. ventá, fiestra, xanela
wine n. viño
wing (of a roof) n. sobrepena (borde do tellado)
wing (military) n. ala (do exército)
wing (of a building) n. ala (do edificio)
wing (of a hat) n. aba (do sombreiro)
wing n. á
wink v. chiscar, choscar de ollo, chuscar, asenar
winner n. ganador, gañador
winning n. ganancia, gaño
winnow v. aventar, airear (o trigo)
winsome a. atraente, atractivo -a
winter n inverno
wipe v. limpiar
wire (telegraphy) n. telegrama
wire n. arame
wire v. aramar
wire v. telegrafar (mandar telegramas)

wireless n. sen fío, sen fíos (telefonía ou micrófono sen fío)

wisdom n. sabedoría, sapenza, saber, sapiencia, erudición

wise a. & n. sabio, douto

wish n. desexo, devezo, degoro, agoada

wish v. desexar, querer

wistful a. melancólico -a, meditabundo -a, pensativo -a

wit n. ensenño, agudeza

witch n. bruxa, maiga, feticeira, maga

with prep. con

withdraw v. retirar, retraer

withdrawal n. retirada

wither v. murchar, muchar

withhold v. reter

within prep. dentro

without prep. sen

withstand v. resister, loitar, contra, aguantar

witness n. testemuño -a

witness v. testificar, tertamuñar

witty a. gracioso -a, chistoso -a, cómico -a

wizard n. mago, meigo, bruxo, feiticeiro, nigromante

woe n. pena, dor, coita, tristura

wolf n. lobo

wolf's bane n. acónito (planta medicinal)
wolly a. laúdo, peludo, que ten la
woman n. muller, esposa, dona
womb n. matriz, útero
wonder n. marabilla, prodigio, portento
wonder v. marabillar, asombrar
wonderful a. marabilloso -a, portentoso -a
woo v. cortexar, face las beiras, face-la corte,
    pretender, namorar
wood n. madeira
woodchuck n. marmota
woodcock n. chopaperdiz
woodpecker n. paxaro carpinteiro, pito
woodsman n. leñador
wool n. la
woolen a. lanar
word n. palabra, verba, termo, vocá´bulo
work n. traballo
work v. traballar
workable a. laborable, práctico, factible
worker n. traballador, obreiro
workshop n. taller, obradoiro
world n. mundo, universo
worldwide a. mundial
worm n. verme, helminto
worry n. preocupación

worry v. preocupar(se)

worse adv. peor

worship n. culto, adoración, veneración

worship v. adorar, reverenciar, render culto a
    Deus ou ás divinidades

worst a. o mais malo

worth n. valor, prezo, valía

worthless a. non ten valor

worthwhile a. vale, ter valor

worthy a. digno -a, merecedor -a, merecente,
    digno de gabanza

wound n. ferida, lesión

wound v. ferir, magoar, mancar, lesionar

wrap n. manto, capa

wrap v. arroupar, abrigar(se)

wrath n. ira, furia, coleria, rabia

wreath n. grillanda, grinalda

wreck v. naufragarse, afundirse, ir a pique

wrench (tool) n. chave (ferramenta), chave
    inglesa

wrench n. torcedura, sacudida violenta

wrench v. arrincar, arrancar

wrest v. arrebatar, arrancar

wrestle v. forcexar, pelexar

wrestler n. loitador

wretch a. & n. desgraciado -a, infeliz

wriggle v. menear, bambear
wring v. torcer, retorcer
wrinkle n. engurra, enruga
wrinkle v. enrrugar, engurrar
wrist n. pulso
wristwatch n. reloxo de pulseira
write v. escribir
writer n. escritor
writing n. escrito

X

xenon n. xenón
xerophthalmia n. xeroftalmia
Xmas (abbreviation) n. Nadal
xylography n. xilografia, xilogravado
xylophone n. xilófono

Y

yacht n. iate
yak n. iac (ruminante bóvido)
yam n. ñame
yank n. tirón

yank v. tirar
Yankee a. & n. ianqui
yap v. ladrar
yard (measurement) n. iarda
yard n. patio, curral
yarn n. fiada, fio groso
yawl n. iola (embarcación lixeira)
yawn n. bocezo
yawn v. bocezar, boquexar, boquear
year n. ano
yearling n. becerro, xato, cuxo, terneiro, xevenca
yearn v. anhelar, afogar, ofegar, abafar
yeast n. levadura, fermento
yell n. berro, grito, brado, brúo
yell v. berrar, gritar, barregar
yellow a. amarelo, marelo
yellowish a. amarelado -a
yelp v. ganir, ouvear, oulear
yelping v. ganido, ouveo, ouleo
yesterday n. onte
yet adv. ainda, inda
yew n. teixo (árbore)
yield n rendemento, proveito, beneficio, utilidade
yield v. producir, dar, render
yogurt n. iogurt
yoke n. xugo, canga

yoke v. xunguir
yolk n. xema (de ovo)
yonder adv. aló
yore adv antaño, noutrora
you pr. ti, vostede
young n xove, novo, mozo
your pr. teu, túa; voso -a; seu, súa
youth n. xuventude, mocidade
youthful a. xuvenil
yucca n. iuca

Z

zany a. louco -a, desmesurado -a
zeal n. celo, fervor, entusiasmo
zealot n. fanático
zebra n. cebra
zebu n cebú
zenith n. cénit, apoxeo, cume
zephyr n. céfiro
zero n. cero
zest n. entusiasmo, gusto
zigzag n. zigzag
zigzag v. zigzaguear
zinc n. cinc, zinc

zither n. cítara, citola
zodiac n. zodíaco
zombie n. zombi
zone n. zona, area
zoo n. parque zoolóxico
zoological a. zoolóxico -a
zoology n. zooloxía
zoom n. zunido
zoom v. zumbar, zoar

Other titles of interest from Hippocrene Books...

DICTIONARIES AND LANGUAGE GUIDES

Children's Illustrated Spanish Dictionary
94 pages • 8 x 11 • 500 words with full color illustrations
• 0-7818-0733-6 • W • $14.95hc • (206)

**Spanish-English/English-Spanish Concise Dictionary
(Latin American)**
310 pages • 4 x 6 • 8,000 entries • 0-7818-0261-X • W
• $11.95pb • (258)

**Spanish-English/English-Spanish Compact Dictionary
(Latin American)**
310 pages • 3 x 4 • 8,000 entries • 0-7818-0497-3 • W
• $8.95pb • (549)

**Spanish-English/English-Spanish Dictionary and
Phrasebook (Latin America)**
220 pages • 3½ x 7 • 2,000 entries • 0-7818-0773-5 • W
• $11.95pb • (261)

Dictionary of 1,000 Spanish Proverbs: Bilingual
131 pages • 5 x 8 • 0-7818-0412-4 • W • $11.95pb • (254)

Spanish Grammar
211 pages • 5 x 8 • 0-87052-893-9 • W • $12.95pb • (273)

Spanish Verbs: Ser and Estar
220 pages • 5 x 8 • 0-7818-0024-2 • W • $8.95pb • (292)

Mastering Spanish
338 pages • 5 x 8 • 0-87052-059-8 • USA • $11.95pb • (527)
2 Cassettes: ca. 2 hours • 0-87052-067-9 • USA
• $12.95pb • (528)

Mastering Advanced Spanish
326 pages • 5 x 8 • 0-7818-0081-1 • W • $14.95pb • (413)
2 Cassettes: ca. 2 hours • 0-7818-0089-7 • W
• $12.95pb • (426)

Spanish Proverbs, Idioms and Slang
350 pages • 6 x 9 • 0-7818-0675-5 • W • $14.95pb • (760)

Language and Travel Guide to Mexico
224 pages • 5 x 8 • 0-87052-622-7 • W • $14.95pb • (503)

**Basque-English/English-Basque Dictionary
and Phrasebook**
240 pages • 3 x 7 • 1,500 entries • 0-7818-0622-4 • W
• $11.95pb • (751)

Catalan-English/English-Catalan Concise Dictionary
224 pages • 4 x 6 • 9,000 entries • 0-7818-0099-4 • NA
• $8.95pb • (451)

Portuguese Handy Dictionary
120 pages • 5 x 7 • 3,000 entries • 0-87052-053-9
• W • $8.95pb • (324)

Portuguese-English/English-Portuguese Dictionary
426 pages • 4 x 7 • 30,000 entries • 0-87052-980-3 • W
• $19.95pb • (477)